AIMING HIGHER

25 STORIES OF
HOW COMPANIES PROSPER
BY COMBINING
SOUND MANAGEMENT
AND SOCIAL VISION

DAVID BOLLIER
for The Business Enterprise Trust

amacom
American Management Association

New York • Atlanta • Boston • Chicago • Kansas City • San Francisco • Washington, D.C.
Brussels • Mexico City • Tokyo • Toronto

This publication is designed to provide accurate and authoritative
information in regard to the subject matter covered. It is sold with the
understanding that the publisher is not engaged in rendering legal,
accounting, or other professional service. If legal advice or other expert
assistance is required, the services of a competent professional person
should be sought.

Library of Congress Cataloging-in-Publication Data

Bollier, David.
     Aiming higher : 25 stories of how companies prosper by combining
sound management and social vision / David Bollier ; foreword by
Norman Lear.
        p.   cm.
     Includes index.
     ISBN 0-8144-0319-0
     1. Social responsibility of business—United States—Case studies.
     2. Management—Moral and ethical aspects—United States—Case
studies.   I. Title.
     HD60.5.U5B65   1997
     658.4'08—dc20   96-21828
                                                              CIP

Printing number

10   9   8   7   6   5   4   3   2   1

CONTENTS

FOREWORD

by Norman Lear

Norman Lear is the founder of The Business Enterprise Trust and the chairman and chief executive officer of Act III Communications. Mr. Lear began his career as a television comedy writer during the 1950s, and became the creative force behind All in the Family, Maude, *and* The Jeffersons, *among many other programs in the 1970s. As a founder of Tandem Productions, T.A.T. Communications, and Act III, Mr. Lear has been involved in theatrical production, broadcast television, cable television, home video, and movie theaters. He is also founder of People for the American Way.*

Nearly ten years ago I embarked upon an odyssey with James E. Burke, the much-admired former chairman and CEO of Johnson & Johnson. Unexpectedly we learned that we shared a deep concern about the influence of business on American society.

Not so long ago, the church, the family, schools, and civil authority were the preeminent institutions of our culture. They were respected sources of moral authority. They transmitted the wisdom of one generation to the next.

Now, for many complex economic and social reasons, these institutions have become less influential. And whether it likes it or not, American business has stepped into the breach. Business leaders have become role models. Their decisions set a moral benchmark for the nation. Their activities dominate the headlines, and our culture absorbs, as if by osmosis, the language, perceptions, and values of business.

As the old ancestral order wanes, we are presented with an unprecedented challenge. In a culture that yearns for hope and constructive change—yet seems overwhelmed by cynicism, fear, and resentment—we urgently need new leadership. A new generation of business managers must explore how cherished democratic and social values can be combined with the economic and business imperatives of our time.

For this we need to hear more about businesspeople at their best. There are, in fact, scores of socially concerned businesses in this country, in every imaginable industry. Yet for many reasons our society does not do enough to recognize such management, explore its distinctive practices, or honor its achievements. A great wellspring of social renewal is thus squandered.

This is not a matter of hoisting up cardboard idols. We need to seek out and tell the stories of resourceful men and women who are tackling serious social challenges through their businesses—while helping them thrive. The evidence seems clear that those businesses which actively serve their many constituencies in creative, morally thoughtful ways also, over the long run, serve their shareholders best. Companies do, in fact, do well by doing good.

Unfortunately this venerable tradition has never been more besieged—by fierce global competition, by Wall Street's fixation on short-term results, by a jaded press, among other forces.

How, then, to give moral support and cultural validation to a vital tradition in American business?

The answer was the founding, in 1989, of The Business Enterprise Trust, an independent nonprofit organization led by prominent leaders of American business, labor, academia, and the media. We drew upon the advice of such people as Warren E. Buffett, chairman and chief executive officer of Berkshire Hathaway Inc.; Katharine Graham, chairman of the executive committee of The Washington Post Company; Ambassador Sol Linowitz; and Henry B. Schacht, the longtime chairman of Cummins Engine Company and now chairman and chief executive officer of Lucent Technologies, AT&T's spinoff of its communications and technology divisions. With the support of many others as well, we began an intensive effort to identify and honor acts of courage, integrity, and social vision in business.

Each year the Trust honors five awardees who have shown bold, creative leadership in combining sound management and social conscience. The Trust has assembled twenty-five such stories of socially minded innovation in business. *Aiming Higher* brings these stories together for the first time. It is the power of stories that makes these accounts so compelling, and that yields a deeper appreciation of what people can truly achieve in business.

Psychologist Robert Coles pioneered the use of literature to teach business students about the complex personal and professional dilemmas that they would face in the "real world." In like manner these stories help us to focus on the challenges of our times. It is one reason that more than 500 business schools, universities, and corporate training programs now use The Business Enterprise Trust's stories in their curricula: They illuminate the complicated, gritty challenges being faced, and overcome, by public-spirited executives.

The stories of *Aiming Higher* feature individuals, work teams, and entire companies who have pioneered new programs in the normal course of daily management. Their achievements do not involve philanthropy or voluntarism, as vital as these are to our society, but rather core management challenges. And they do not necessarily conform to established norms; they *break* established norms and defy our expectations. They surprise.

I have discovered through my own career in television, and through the twenty-five stories of this book, that some of the ingredients most critical to business success are utterly intangible. The loyalty of employees, the integrity and social vision of CEOs, the collaborative spirit of a management team, the mysterious "creative juices" that generate breakthrough products and top-flight services: These constitute a vast "hidden economy" of moral and spiritual dimensions that are profoundly influential in business management.

It is an insight worth remembering as today's business managers simultaneously grapple with marketplace demands and societal needs. Combining this double vision into one is imperative. As business professor Yale Brozen and his colleagues once wrote: "A society is in a serious state of decadence when its members come to depend primarily on either the market or paternalism or any combination of the two for generating and sustaining an adequate ethic." This book is about those exemplary business managers who look within themselves as they struggle to generate a more constructive business ethic.

Seeking to aim higher, they have that rare enthusiasm and drive to give their very best. It is like a magnetic charge that invisibly attracts people who want to experience the same energy and pride in achievement.

Companies imbued with this spirit cannot help but become fierce competitors of great social conscience. If this seems a paradox, let us make the most of it. The twenty-five companies and managers of *Aiming Higher* most certainly have.

INTRODUCTION

by David Bollier

If the stories of this book sometimes seem strikingly original yet strangely familiar, it is because the language for talking about them as a group has not really evolved. The stories must speak for themselves in the meantime for what they are: singular episodes in which creative, socially committed business managers have enhanced their long-term profitability by instilling the best of their humanity into the nitty-gritty operations of their organizations.

The conjoining of profits and social ideals is a disquieting proposition for some people. It forces an intermingling of objectives generally kept separate. There is "business" and there are "good works," and never the twain shall meet.

So *how* can sound management and venturesome social initiatives actually converge and bear fruit?

The answers are illustrated by the stories in this book. The businesspeople profiled here do not just demonstrate the compatibility of business success and socially motivated action, they prove the constructive *synergies* of such a convergence.

Instead of seeing social problems as utterly extraneous to business or as burdens to be grudgingly borne, the businesspeople of *Aiming Higher* see social engagement as an affirmative business opportunity. These twenty-five stories show that socially oriented business innovation can contribute significantly to an enterprise's success. The spectrum of profitable business behaviors is far broader than many of us dare to imagine.

We see this in the California banker who pioneered a lucra-

1

tive new market for home mortgage lending in a region from which most banks had fled, South Central Los Angeles. We see this in a real estate developer who had the audacity to imagine that the derelict waterfronts of Boston and Baltimore could be made lively sites of recreation, conviviality, and economic development. The results were Faneuil Hall and Harborplace.

The Missouri engine remanufacturer that shares all its financial data with its workers is strengthening, not weakening, the company. Management recognizes that empowered, educated employees can yield astonishing cost savings if their intelligence and enthusiasm are nurtured. So, too, with the Philadelphia restaurateur who has inaugurated community outreach projects and a lively lecture series. She is not just building civic spirit; she is making her business one of the most distinctive, popular eating spots in the city.

What distinguishes the stories of this book is the questing spirit of the enterprises they exemplify. It may be useful to call this capacity the "moral imagination." It needs a name if only to help us grasp its reality, because in conventional economics, these are fuzzy intangibles without standing. In business, after all, if a certain intangible cannot be measured, and if no one's willing to pay for it . . . *what good is it?* Certain human capacities are considered too subtle, and their payoffs too long-term or diffuse, for them to be accorded the business respect they deserve.

Yet the most farsighted businesspeople know otherwise. When Robert Haas of Levi Strauss & Co. was asked in 1995 why his company has shown such aggressive social leadership, he replied, "It's too costly, too risky, and too inefficient not to anticipate what your customers need. Not to protect your brand reputation. Not to involve your employees in solving your problems. By sticking with conventional wisdom and conventional practice—and not daring to take the lead in social practices as well as business practices—you're dooming yourself to extinction."

Even the most transforming innovations start small and provisionally, often with a single individual. Managers rarely have road maps to help them reach their self-invented destinations. They have only intuitions and ideas and personal values to propel them forward. The rest is improvisation—and faith.

In explaining their impressive careers, such business leaders as J. Irwin Miller, James Rouse, Walter Haas, Jr., and Frank Stanton have credited the role of the human spirit and the power of the moral imagination: how they energize, how they enhance creative collaboration, how they inspire trust, how they fulfill our need to connect with each other, how they help a company *make money* over the long term.

If the moral imagination helps a business thrive, the economic imperatives of a business provide a vital discipline. "Profit is the thing that hauls dreams into focus," said James Rouse, once described as "a man with the zeal of a missionary and the hard, calculating head of a banker." The foremost challenge of our time may be to find a more fruitful reconciliation between our social ideals and market discipline. But the tension must be regarded constructively and creatively, not as illegitimate from the start.

Viewing these tensions through stories helps make this clear. One begins to realize that social performance indices or numbers cannot really capture the achievements of the moral imagination in the marketplace. Guardians of the politically correct, too, will miss the point if they regard these stories primarily as policy parables.

These stories are more fundamentally about a personal *disposition* in the conduct of business. Going beyond legal requirements and marketplace norms, these men and women are determined to bring their personal values and professional lives into closer alignment. They are aiming higher.

SECTION ONE

BLENDING PRODUCT INNOVATION WITH SOCIAL CONCERN

Introduction by James E. Burke

James E. Burke is the former chairman of the board and chief executive officer of Johnson & Johnson, the world's most diversified health care company. Under his leadership, Johnson & Johnson's worldwide sales grew from $2.5 billion to $9 billion over a twelve-year period. Mr. Burke currently serves as chairman of the Partnership for a Drug-Free America and as chairman of The Business Enterprise Trust.

There is a philosophy of doing business that goes well beyond the selling of goods or services. It calls for serving the public interest as well as that of the customer. More often than not, these goals are markedly similar. It is a growing trend in American business, and it deserves far greater recognition. That is what The Business Enterprise Trust is all about—bringing much-deserved recognition to those companies that look beyond the profit motive.

The behavior I have in mind is not just the showcasing of a company's social concern through cause-oriented marketing, for example, or philanthropy and community service—important as all these are. Values-driven business is different in that it can directly improve one's business. Section One of this book examines several companies that have integrated their highest social ideals into the business transaction—and in so doing made themselves more successful enterprises.

What is most notable about this style of business is the incredible goodwill and customer loyalty it engenders. When Vermont National Bank inaugurated a new kind of bank account that enables depositors to channel all their money into worthy local enterprises, it was flooded with $34 million in new deposits during the program's first year. When entrepreneur Gun Denhart, president of the popular Hanna Andersson children's clothing firm, decided to give customers a 20 percent purchase credit for the return of its used clothing, which was then donated to needy children, the company earned great admiration from its customers, and more business to boot.

So, too, when Prudential Insurance Company pioneered the first major "accelerated death benefits" rider for life insurance policies. By allowing terminally ill policyholders to obtain their life insurance benefits while living, thus enabling them to live out their final days in dignity, Prudential reaped an extraordinary windfall in customer appreciation while simultaneously opening up new sales opportunities.

The wisdom of serving the public good was driven home to me when I was chairman of Johnson & Johnson and we were faced with the Tylenol tragedy. Overnight one of our Tylenol products went from being a thriving business to becoming a murder weapon that killed seven people. To this day we do not know who poisoned the Tylenol capsules. But our response was to put the customer first—to serve the public interest—regardless of the cost. The critical difference was the social and ethical commitment we shared with our customers.

We are too accustomed to conceiving of marketplace exchanges as a strict quid pro quo between buyer and seller, as short-term transactions, not long-term relationships. As a result, we too often fail to see the impressive results that can be achieved when buyer and seller honor their best impulses. The companies described here are cases in point: They have shown that aggressive social concern and higher profitability need not be at loggerheads. With creativity and commitment, they can be made entirely complementary. Indeed, businesses have far more opportunities to do good—for themselves and their communities—than is commonly appreciated.

Seizing any of these opportunities, however, requires a management that is innovative, visionary, and willing to stretch itself in new ways. It should not be surprising that the companies which succeed in integrating their social ideals with their business objectives are among the best in the business. Like the pentathlon athlete who has developed the coordination and stamina for a variety of sports, the socially engaged business is a hardier, more versatile organization. It has voluntarily submitted itself to a more diverse set of bracing challenges—and in so doing made itself a more robust competitor.

These stories deserve close scrutiny and wider emulation. They contain important seeds of rejuvenation for businesses that may not have suspected the rewards—financial, social, and personal—of conscience-driven management.

1

Vermont National Bank's Socially Responsible Banking Fund

THE RICH REWARDS OF COMMUNITY LENDING

For years Patricia Pedreira, an art therapist, helped emotionally troubled children learn to draw and at-risk teenagers to reconstruct their lives through art classes held in a run-down brick mill. It was an exceedingly valuable service for the people of North Bennington, Vermont, an economically distressed village with few social services.

Then Pedreira's landlord went bankrupt in 1994. It looked as though the Vermont Arts Exchange, the struggling nonprofit that Pedreira directs, would have no place to go, since there was no other rental space in the area. Pedreira recalls, "Nobody could see a way that we could acquire the mill and pay the money back." Meanwhile a housing developer was attempting to acquire the mill and turn it into luxury condominiums.

That was before David Berge, director of the Socially Responsible Banking (SRB) Fund of Vermont National Bank (VNB), arrived on the scene. By proposing a customized loan package that combined state economic development funds, tax abatements, and a matching grant—additional sources of equity that Berge urged Pedreira to pursue—Berge was able to offer a $77,000 mortgage that posed no unusual financial risks to her or the bank.

With the enthusiastic backing of townspeople, Pedreira unexpectedly acquired the building at auction, becoming the developer of 25,000 square feet for social services, vocational training, artisans, microenterprises, and community events. A vibrant local resource was saved, and the State of Vermont acquired a new model of community economic development that it hopes can be replicated in other rural towns.

AN INGENIOUS NEW MODEL OF COMMUNITY LENDING

The dramatic rescue of the Vermont Arts Exchange is just one of dozens of remarkable stories spawned by the Socially Responsible Banking Fund, a special loan program created by Vermont National Bank in 1989. Through the fund, VNB, the state's second largest bank, with about $994 million in assets (September 30, 1995) and thirty-one branches, has harnessed the power of private capital to finance socially valuable, fiscally sound enterprises without incurring additional risk. Indeed, from the start Vermont National Bank viewed the program as a great business opportunity: a way to boost deposits, nurture customer loyalty, and expand the bank's market share while actively helping Vermont communities.

The concept is simple. VNB depositors can assign any of their conventional bank accounts, including checking and savings, to the SRB Fund, while still receiving the same interest and FDIC insurance coverage. The monies earmarked for the SRB Fund are then lent to companies and nonprofits that "make positive contributions to the environment, their communities and their employees."

Special priority is given to lending in five key areas: affordable housing, organic and sustainable farming, small business, education, and the environment. The idea is to extend credit where it has not necessarily been available so that it can bolster the "social capital" of the community.

In just six years the Socially Responsible Banking Fund has attracted $85 million in deposits, about 75 percent of which is "new money" not previously deposited at the bank. Depositors—mostly individuals, not institutions—have been eager to place their money with a bank that shows a genuine commitment to its communities. Besides boosting the bank's deposits, the SRB Fund has given Vermont National Bank a stellar public image and a market differentiation that no amount of marketing could buy.

In an era of growing bank centralization and computer-driven lending formulas, it seems improbable that such a prosaic concept, community banking, could succeed, let alone become a significant profit center. After all, many industry leaders have long criticized the federal Community Reinvestment Act. For VNB, however, aggressive lending to unconventional borrowers for the express purpose of advancing specific social goals has been a remarkably effective competitive strategy.

How could such a brazenly contrarian idea actually work?

THE CREATION OF THE SRB FUND

In a state known for its progressive values, at a bank with a reputation for community concern, the idea of an SRB Fund was hardly preposterous. Still, the seeds did not begin to sprout until 1988, when catalysts from both inside and outside the bank converged.

First, the head of Vermont National Bank's trust department, Jack Davidson, noticed that increasing numbers of his clients were concerned about the social implications of their investments. Although VNB already offered "screened investments" to its trust customers (avoiding stock holdings in companies that made tobacco products, produced nuclear weapons, and polluted the environment, among other criteria), Davidson wondered if depositors of more modest means might welcome similar choices.

A special study by management trainee Elizabeth Kent Glenshaw suggested that there was an attractive market waiting to be tapped. According to the Social Investment Forum, a trade group, socially screened investment portfolios, including mutual funds, were managing more than $450 billion in 1988—up from $40 billion only five years earlier. Meanwhile, the celebrated South Shore Bank of Chicago, as well as some community development banks and credit unions, had shown that it was feasible to use deposits to finance the rehabilitation of distressed urban neighborhoods.

If the potential was there, VNB lenders worried that a special fund might force significant changes in the bank's overall lending style. The key question was whether social investing goals could be integrated with "conventional banking"—and how.

At about this time, a group of Brattleboro citizens was thinking about creating or buying a bank to make loans for socially responsible purposes. It quickly discovered that the challenges of raising capital and meeting regulatory requirements were too formidable. So the group turned to J. D. "Rick" Hashagen, Jr., the new president of Vermont National Bank, to suggest that his bank create such a program.

Hashagen was immediately receptive to the idea. "I had just taken over as president of the bank," he recalls, "and I was looking for something to differentiate us from the other banks. We had just restructured the management of the bank, so I think we decided, let's try some new things." At the time, VNB was the second-largest bank in the state, with $700 million in assets and twenty-six branches.

VNB management liked the idea of an SRB Fund because it resonated with its own long-standing commitment to community lending. "We are a community bank," said Hashagen. "We are only as strong as our communities are. If we can funnel this money into things that will strengthen our community, we think it will make us stronger in the long run."

In a time of increasing industry consolidation and regionalization, VNB, an independent bank in a secondary market, also saw the SRB Fund as a way to carve out its own market niches and build a more distinctive public identity. The fund could help it expand deposits without having to engage in a potentially expensive interest-rate war. It could also attract institutional investors such as pension funds and college endowments, which often have restrictions on their investments.

Led primarily by Hashagen and executive vice presidents Robert Soucy and Bruce Fenn, Vermont National Bank decided that one of its first challenges would be how to define "socially responsible" lending. For this, the bank convened an advisory committee of people often considered adversaries in banking circles: community reinvestment activists, low-income housing advocates, environmentalists, and social investment managers. The panel recommended the five lending categories and helped craft a set of guidelines enumerating priorities for each area.

THE STUNNING PUBLIC RESPONSE

Having refined the concept of the fund, VNB announced the new program in January 1989. Anyone with a minimum deposit of $500 (a requirement later eliminated) could assign to the SRB Fund any of their accounts: passbook savings, checking, money market, individual retirement accounts, certificates of deposit.

The fund immediately attracted a series of major profiles by national news media: *60 Minutes, ABC News,* the *CBS Evening News,* the Associated Press, the *Boston Globe,* and others. In one typical story, *The New York Times* announced, "Bank Puts Your Money Where Your Heart Is," and even informed readers how to open an SRB Fund account at VNB.

Depositor response was swift and stunning. After only four months, more than $7 million had been deposited in the SRB Fund—a sum that swelled to nearly $34 million by the end of the first year. By the end of 1994 the fund had $87 million in deposits, mostly from in-state depositors, but also from people in forty-two states and twelve foreign countries. All this was achieved with only modest in-state advertising and virtually no national marketing.

"We didn't realize the untapped resources that were out there that were really interested in this," recalls Bruce Fenn. "The word of mouth among people interested in the movement for social responsibility is just phenomenal. I mean, our borrowers and depositors sell this fund for us."

INTEGRATING THE FUND INTO THE BANK'S CULTURE

If obtaining new deposits was easy, making the SRB Fund work internally took concerted effort. The first coordinator of the

fund, Glenshaw, spent most of her time establishing internal systems to integrate the fund with daily bank operations. Tellers
and account representatives at nearly three dozen branch offices
were trained how to explain the fund to depositors; employee
training programs and job evaluations were altered; twenty-
seven officials with commercial lending authority were trained
in the special ways of SRB Fund lending.

Despite the bank's astonishing success in attracting new deposits, it soon discovered that lending the money out was a far
more formidable task than originally imagined. One year after
the fund's launch, less than half of the $7 million in SRB deposits
had been lent out. This was a serious problem, VNB officials
realized, because it could potentially jeopardize the entire
fund—and the profits it would generate. To preserve the integrity of the fund, VNB executives felt they could not seek out new
deposits unless they could indeed lend those monies to community-oriented borrowers.

At about this time, in mid-1990, Glenshaw chose to leave
VNB to pursue new career opportunities in Boston. She left behind a strong concept, a basic infrastructure of systems, and
about $35 million in deposits. But the most difficult challenge
remained: inventing new ways to make sound loans to unconventional enterprises with avowed social missions.

REINVENTING THE LENDING PROCESS

There were few people better equipped to tackle this singular
challenge than David Berge, who joined VNB in June 1990 as
vice president and director of the SRB Fund. Although borrowers are sometimes startled by Berge's relative youth and casual
style, they uniformly cite his creativity in crafting some of the
most unusually structured, financially solid loans being made in
contemporary banking.

Berge acquired these rare skills as a senior loan officer with
the Institute for Community Economics, a nonprofit group that
provides technical advice and modest assets to help finance affordable housing, land trusts and cooperative businesses. Now,
improbably, a major mainstream bank wanted the then-twenty-

nine-year-old Berge to apply his rare talents to the button-down world of commercial banking. His challenge: to reconceptualize the entire loan-making process for the SRB Fund.

Berge already knew that one of the chief impediments to community-oriented lending is overcoming many unwarranted prejudices. A nonprofit with stable cash flow, for example, could easily be more creditworthy than a wealthy person who is financially overextended. From dozens of deals, Berge knew that it is eminently feasible to make strong, profitable loans to unconventional borrowers—*if* the lender takes the time and energy to understand their real needs and shows flexibility in developing loan packages.

In revamping SRB lending, therefore, Berge took pains to develop a more personal, conversational loan application and review process. Loan officers must have "space" to talk about the idiosyncracies of a given enterprise and the authority to come up with creative lending solutions, Berge insists. A 1993 article about the SRB Fund published by The Federal Home Loan Bank of Boston explains why this counterintuitive, humanized approach makes great business sense:

> Lowering the risk of a loan through flexible underwriting and flexible loan terms may, in the traditional sense, lower the profitability of the loan if, as a result, the bank experiences a lower profit margin. However, if the flexibility that is offered [to the borrower] increases the feasibility of the project and, by extension, the certainty that the loan will perform well, the profitability of the project may actually improve when one considers the likelihood of the profit margin—albeit smaller—actually being earned.

It is a subtle but profound point. The banker who truly understands the internal finances of a given borrower, and establishes a sustained relationship of openness and trust with that individual or enterprise can affirmatively enhance the business success of the borrower. "Instead of being the last to know that something's going wrong," Berge explained, "we're one of the first. There's enough trust between us and the borrower, and enough time to work things out, if we need to."

Assembling a high-quality portfolio of SRB loans, however, requires that VNB lenders spend an unusual amount of time studying a borrower's financial needs and special problems. But this extra time and attention builds a stronger relationship with borrowers as well as less risky loans. It also gives the bank greater insight into the market. "Our research and development is customer contact," says Soucy. "That's all we have in banking. If you lose that investment of face-to-face research, you've lost a lot."

Yet instilling a more creative lending mind-set among "some of our old-time, old-line commercial lenders," says Soucy, "has been the hardest thing about getting this fund started." Some loan officers balked at making loans to borrowers whose needs and finances did not fit into established lending formulas. Meeting the needs of these applicants often seemed too complicated and financially risky.

Besides instituting special training programs, Berge and other VNB managers take pains to show loan officers how seemingly risky loans can be creatively modified to make them sound. In annual job performance reviews, too, lenders are evaluated for their effectiveness in making SRB Fund loans. Senior management's overarching goal is to change the internal culture of the bank so that difficult loans and flexible loan packages are not denigrated but, rather, respected as a source of professional creativity and personal satisfaction. The majority of SRB Fund loans now originate in the bank's thirty-one branches, while Berge manages the fund's operations and oversees its loan portfolio.

COLLABORATING WITH BORROWERS TO MAKE LOANS WORK

VNB has found that this more engaged lending style engenders incredible goodwill among borrowers. An organic farmer in Tunbridge, Vermont, seeking long-term financing was grateful for Berge's insightful review of his business:

> He basically realized we were going to be in trouble before we did. Even though our planned expansion would increase

cash flow, we didn't really know what our additional marginal costs would be as volumes increased. David gave us incredible business advice. We're becoming more seasoned now.

In the case of nonprofits, Berge often suggests supplemental sources of equity or grants, which, combined with a VNB loan, can make a deal work. "David Berge is a mix-and-match specialist," explains David Dangler, executive director of Rutland West Neighborhood Housing Services, a nonprofit group that helps low-income people buy and rehabilitate homes. Berge often packages money from various sources—a community land trust, the Vermont Community Loan Fund, the U.S. Department of Housing and Urban Development, and other sources—in order to minimize VNB's exposure to risk. Yet it is VNB's tenacity and creativity that allows the deals to be assembled in the first place and ultimately consummated.

USING INTERMEDIARIES TO INCREASE LOAN VOLUME

Much of the SRB Fund's lending is facilitated by the bank's ongoing relationships with intermediaries such as Dangler's housing group. Rutland West Neighborhood Housing, for example, helps potential low-income home buyers manage their credit and credit history so that they can become "bankable" loan applicants. Then it "brokers" the risk by bringing in additional sources of equity and debt. "We, the intermediary, take the lion's share of the risk by taking the junior lien position on distressed, discounted properties so that the bank can make the loan," Dangler says.

By strengthening the quality of loan applicants and increasing the market for private-sector housing, Rutland West has come to enjoy the kind of preferential interest rates that customarily go to prime business borrowers. Rutland West has, in turn, used this spread to recover more of its own costs and extend more loans to low-income home buyers. It currently has a $1,250,000 line of credit from VNB.

VNB is cultivating a similar relationship with the Northeast

Organic Farming Association (NOFA), which actively promotes the environmental and health benefits of organic agriculture. Conventional banks often perceive such borrowers as risky because they have little credit history and sell to an unconventional, fledgling market. By helping the association's 500 members become more astute businesspeople while extending the credit they need, the SRB Fund is helping develop sustainable agriculture as a major Vermont industry.

To reach microbusinesses in a similar manner, VNB has developed a "peer lending" package administered by a nonprofit to a group of small business operators in Burlington. A microbusiness applicant applies to the group for a loan rather than to the bank. This saves the bank the great time and effort it would otherwise have to expend to lend small sums such as $5,000. Yet it can provide vital support to the micro-operator who may have no other access to capital. For its part, the microbusiness peer group has every incentive to make sound loans because its reputation and future credit are at stake.

Perhaps the most surprising twist is how the SRB Fund has transformed the traditional adversaries of many banks—community activists, affordable housing advocates, environmentalists—into VNB's most energetic marketers. Members of the advisory panel are constantly referring new borrowers to the fund and extolling its work through their own networks.

FINANCIAL RIGOR AND SOCIAL COMMITMENT

Eager as it is to help socially committed businesses, VNB is no easy mark for "cheap" loans, however. "Just because you're starting a new business that will provide huge environmental benefits doesn't mean the business is financially viable," cautions Berge. "On the other hand, you could have great cash flow, and if you can afford a 'prime plus two' loan [prime interest rate plus two points], that's what you'll pay." The SRB Fund deliberately gives preferential treatment to the "neediest" applicants. "We are always reaching for the loans that are harder to do," says Berge.

Berge is equally adamant in refusing to lend to enterprises

that instead need to raise equity capital. "When all is said and done, if you don't have the cash flow to cover your debt service," says Berge, "then the money [you need] is equity. We are a cash-flow lender. High risks, high returns, are what defines venture capital."

Although VNB executives are eager to expand the SRB Fund, they also want to make sure that marketing zeal does not outpace the fund's ability to make solid, socially worthwhile loans. When less than 50 percent of the fund was loaned out, for example, VNB refused to do any marketing until lending volume had increased. There have been only two marketing campaigns for the fund—in 1992 and 1994; in both instances, SRB funds were 90 to 100 percent loaned out and the bank felt it had the capacity to make suitable loans. The goal, says Berge, is to be 75 to 80 percent loaned out, leaving sufficient operating liquidity.

A Different Kind of "Relationship Banking"

There are some sound reasons why the SRB Fund can work even in the competitive interstate banking environment of the 1990s. First, the people of Vermont have a highly developed sense of community and state pride. This is not surprising in a state whose seventh-largest city, Brattleboro, has only 12,000 people. Vermont culture prizes localism, and its people generally prefer to show loyalty to state and local businesses.

If Vermont customers are perhaps more predisposed to embrace an SRB Fund, it is also true that Vermont National Bank recognized a profound nationwide trend among banking customers. "The average depositor is a lot more sophisticated today than five or ten years ago," says Berge.

> Every time someone picks up a newspaper they read a story about a savings and loan scandal or international banking problem. People understand that their money doesn't sit in a vault or a drawer. The average depositor now comes in and asks, "What's being done with my money?" The SRB Fund is an answer to that question.

The answers come in the form of stories—stories about the environmental education center that got a loan from the SRB Fund; about the land trust that saved a precious stretch of Lewis Creek land from development; about the energy recycling business that recovers methane gas from the bottom of the Brattleboro landfill. Through a quarterly newsletter sent to more than 10,000 customers, Vermont National Bank tells dozens of such stories. This not only inspires people to reflect on how their money is helping Vermont; it has built an enormous reservoir of goodwill among its customers.

Borrowers, too, treasure their relationships with the SRB Fund, as reflected in the minuscule default rate. "The loan portfolio has a yield that is probably a bit less than the rest of the portfolio," admits VNB president Hashagen. "But surprisingly enough to many outsiders, the loan quality is better. We have fewer defaults on these loans." Of more than $50 million of outstanding principal and more than 1,000 loans, the delinquency rate as of September 30, 1995, was zero percent.

Executive vice president Soucy attributes this performance to the upfront collaboration with loan applicants as well as to "peer pressure" among borrowers. Organic farmers, microbusinesses, and nonprofits realize that their individual loan performances can affect the reputations of all SRB Fund borrowers. A default becomes an event with community repercussions, not an impersonal, morally neutral matter for bankruptcy courts to resolve. Explains Soucy:

> The more you create those personal links between families and friends who borrow money, and those who deposit money, the more you create the feeling of obligation—the feeling of "I'd better be in touch with the bank right away if I can't pay." It becomes a "we thing"—not a case of "I'd better keep this from the bank."

If VNB's brand of relationship banking is an unusually effective form of lending, it is also more difficult to replicate. It takes time to cultivate networks of loyal depositors and borrowers; it requires a wholesale commitment from senior management down to loan officers and tellers; and it requires support by the bank's entire work culture. Dozens of banks have approached VNB over the years, eager to learn the secrets of attracting tens of millions of dollars in new deposits. But when they learn of the formidable changes that the SRB Fund entails—from educating loan officers to revamping the lending process, and more—most banks lose interest.

Vermont National Bank's community lending is so routinely aggressive that a Boston community reinvestment activist, Mary O'Hara, marveled that the bank was "doing so much of what counts [toward the legal requirements of the Community Reinvestment Act] and not realizing it." O'Hara hailed the SRB Fund as "an unparalleled CRA tool" whose great strength is "its delivery of service and products through the existing bank structure . . . a truly integrated community reinvestment program."

THE BUSINESS REWARDS OF THE SRB FUND

What surprises many outsiders is that Vermont National Bank's innovations have not diminished the bank's profits or competitive strength. Quite the contrary. "At a time when total deposits in the State of Vermont shrunk by $115 million (the four-year period between June 30, 1990, and June 30, 1994)," says Berge, "the SRB Fund actually grew by more than $25 million, to a total of $64 million. And in the past eighteen months, the Fund has grown another $23 million, to a total of $87 million."

Equally remarkable, the growth of the SRB Fund from 1991 to mid-1995 slightly exceeded the growth of the entire bank's deposits ($33.1 million in new SRB deposits versus $32 million in total deposit growth) even though the SRB Fund represents only about 9 percent of the bank's deposits and repurchase agreements. "When we look at our market share," says VNB President Hashagen, "we have grown nine of the past ten years. I can't measure it, but part of that, I know, is because we have the SRB Fund."

Following its 1994 acquisition of United Savings Bank in Western Massachusetts, VNB's parent company, Vermont Financial Services Corp., hopes to replicate the SRB Fund in six new bank branches. Already several other banks around the country are experimenting with similar models.

VNB officials reject the notion that the SRB Fund has anything to do with political correctness or soft-headed business judgment. "It's not a liberal issue, it's not a conservative issue," says Robert Soucy. "It's the way banking *should* be done in the local communities, throughout the country. It's what banking is all about."

2

Gun Denhart and Hanna Andersson

RECYCLING CLOTHES WHILE BUILDING CUSTOMER LOYALTY

Ever since her childhood days in Sweden, Gun Denhart has hated waste. She remembers sitting in Simrishamn, a small fishing town in southern Sweden, watching the fishermen dock their daily catches in wooden boats that had obviously been mended and repaired for more than one fisherman's lifetime.

"As I watched their caretaking ways," Gun recalled, "I began to think about what makes Sweden so attractive to me—the instinctive habit of using everything until it's completely used up."

It was this obsession with frugality, along with offering the best quality possible, that would help make Denhart a thriving entrepreneur in the children's clothing business.

In the 1980s, at a time when choices and quality in mail order children's clothing were limited, Denhart introduced to the American market a stunning collection of highly durable, all-cotton clothing. Through innovative marketing and a social concern, she devised a program that communicated to customers the high quality of her product while encouraging repeat business and helping provide clothes to children in need.

She called the program *Hannadowns*, and it led Denhart, her husband, Tom, and her employees to become increasingly aware of—and committed to—the needy people of their community.

They discovered how to creatively align the financial requirements of the company, their employees' desire to find greater
meaning through work, and assistance to children in need.

A BABY INSPIRES A BUSINESS

When thirteen-year-old Gun Brime accompanied her father on a
business trip to the United States in 1959, she never imagined
she would later return to run a successful American company
herself. Born and educated in Lund, Sweden, Gun left for Paris
in 1973 with the Swedish equivalent of an M.B.A. in business
economics.

In Paris, Gun met Tom Denhart, an American working there
as a television commercial producer. Two years later, the couple
married and moved to Connecticut. Tom became a producer for
Ogilvy & Mather, the Manhattan advertising firm, and Gun the
financial manager of the U.S. branch of a foreign language
school. With two fast-track careers and a lovely home in Greenwich, the couple seemed to have it all. But in reality, the Denharts yearned to escape the hectic, fast-paced life of the New
York City area.

In 1980 the Denharts' son, Christian, was born. Gun was
disappointed by the scarcity and costliness of high-quality, cotton baby clothes. "You always want the best for your baby,"
Gun explains, "and we just couldn't find the kind of children's
clothes that I was used to kids having in Sweden." The cotton/
polyester blends that filled the stores didn't last past a few wash-
ings.

The Denharts had an inkling that they had stumbled onto
a market niche. The second generation of the baby boom was
maturing, and consumers were increasingly demanding natural
fabrics. A business based on colorful, well-made, all-cotton children's clothing seemed a promising idea.

During a trip to Sweden the couple began to seriously consider starting an entrepreneurial venture. "We bought a large
box of clothes, came home, passed them out among people we
knew and people we didn't know," recalls Tom. "We said that
we were thinking about this business and said, 'Take these

clothes, they're yours. Use them, wash them, and then we'll call you in a few weeks to see what you think of them.' " The response was overwhelmingly positive.

Gradually, two inclinations began to converge. Increasingly frustrated with their frenetic commuting lifestyle, the Denharts had been toying with the idea of moving across the country to a smaller, less frenetic locale like Portland, Oregon. Given the enthusiastic feedback on their Swedish garments, they were also eager to start up a children's mail order clothing business.

So why not do both? "We decided to start the business if we sold our house," admits Tom. "That's a crazy reason, but we said we'd put the house on the market and if it sells, we do it. And if it doesn't, we'll wait and we'll think. It sold in a day and a half."

GETTING STARTED IN BUSINESS

Abandoning their Greenwich home for the hills outlying Portland, the Denharts were delighted to find twice the house for half the price. With the remaining $250,000 proceeds, they stocked up on inventory and set about producing their first catalog.

"We decided to name the company after my grandmother, Hanna Andersson," explains Gun. "Swedish, but easy for the American ear." Gun's grandmother, who believed very strongly in the Swedish philosophy that equated waste with sin, would have approved of the durable frocks and play clothes sold under her name. Clothing, and everything else, she believed, should be made of a quality allowing it to be used over and over again.

The first Hanna Andersson catalogs—75,000 in all—were mailed in February 1984. Says Gun:

> Just to show the kind of quality the clothes were made out of, we cut out little one-inch by one-inch pieces of fabric and glued them into each catalog. We cut them by hand—75,000 pieces. . . . I remember looking over at Tom and he looked at me and we both had the same thought—what are we doing here?!

At that point, Gun and Tom Denhart were running Hanna
Andersson by themselves, with only occasional help from their
baby-sitter. They started with just a telephone and an index card
file. Within six months, they had sold $53,000 worth of vibrant,
loose-fitting, Swedish-style children's play clothes.

For the first two years, the Denharts ran Hanna Andersson
out of their home. Having grown to twenty employees, they had
a front yard and driveway full of cars and a house full of desks
and inventory. Gun admits that they were ill-prepared for the
uncontrolled growth of the first year. She remembers polling
every customer on the phone, constantly doing market research.

Their naïveté did not last long. Their complementary talents
quickly produced tremendous growth. Tom was the creative
mastermind, and she, the financial and managerial wizard.
Within ten years Hanna Andersson became a well-known,
highly respected mail order firm, employing over 200 people
and sending out ten million catalogs annually.

The Denharts' venture was blessed with impeccable timing.
Not only were baby boomers creating a baby boomlet and clamoring for natural fabrics, the 1980s also proved to be a period of
tremendous growth for mail order marketing. According to the
Direct Marketing Association, the American population grew by
14.3 percent between 1983 and 1990, but the number of American adults who shopped by mail or phone increased a whopping
71.8 percent.

Despite the industry's phenomenal growth, the majority of
new mail order businesses fail. "There is so much competition,
the only successful catalogs are those with a distinct personality," says mail order consultant Katie Muldoon. She describes
Hanna Andersson as being very warm and involved. "You know
this woman cares. You can identify with a real person behind
the catalog."

If that personality shines through so clearly, it is because it
genuinely pervades the day-to-day operations of Hanna Andersson. The company's mission statement, crafted early in its history, reflected the Denharts' desire to "supply high quality
children's clothing at the best possible price and to provide superior, informed customer service." It would strive "to maxi-

mize benefits not only for ourselves and our families, but the customer who makes it all possible, and the community at large which supports us."

And the clothes truly are the stars. Customers are unusually effusive about the quality: "Today I received my first Hanna," wrote one New York mother. "Now *this* is a piece of clothing. I have yet to see the workmanship, quality of cloth, and softness in any other manufacturer. . . . I look forward to being a customer for years to come."

Gun happily admits, "We hear over and over again people saying, 'Oh, I didn't have any idea that there was quality like this.' You buy these clothes and you can use them and use them and use them." But it isn't just the quality that customers have fallen for; it is also the style. Reporter Stephan Wilkins once described the colors as "so bright they vibrate."

The other key to Hanna's success is the exceptional level of service. Phone representatives are instructed to do everything in their power to see that customers' questions are answered correctly. Every article in the current catalog is tacked to huge bulletin boards in the phone room, so when a customer has questions about sizes, colors, or fabrics, the employee can simply hop up and measure, look, or touch to get an answer. Moreover, customer service representatives are predominantly working mothers who particularly relate to their customers' concerns, creating a special affinity that many other mail order businesses lack.

The business rapidly outgrew the Denhart house. After two moves, the company in 1987 found its permanent home—a five-story, 80,000-square-foot warehouse facility. The building, the old Ballow & Wright bicycle supply company, qualifies for the National Register of Historic Places and has been refurbished under Tom's direction into a beautiful office facility. Nearly all business activities, including management, product development, catalog design and layout, marketing, customer service, and order entry are performed in the facility. The clothing is manufactured by exclusive vendors in Scandinavia, Asia, and the United States, then shipped to customers from the company's Kentucky distribution center.

THE INVENTION OF *HANNADOWNS*

A year after the company began, on a flight to Sweden in 1985, Gun and Tom fell into a conversation about waste with a dear friend, Asa Rundkvist. The essence of the discussion, Tom recalls, is that "northern Europeans buy something that is good quality, and then they wear it and they use it and they use it and then they pass it on—until it is just worn out. It is a tremendously satisfying feeling." Americans, by contrast, do not generally live by this ethic.

The Denharts and Rundkvist wondered how they might popularize this ethic through their business. They wanted new ways to communicate the company's primary marketing message—that Hanna Andersson clothes will last a very long time, and for more than one child. Discussion drifted to the relatively high amount of waste tolerated in the United States as opposed to Sweden and how nice it would be to do something about that waste. Finally, the conversation turned to the startling number of women and children in the States who were needy—people who would never have the chance to wear clothes of Hanna Andersson quality.

How to stress quality . . . reduce waste . . . and help the needy? As the conversation proceeded, it generated a surprisingly simple idea that could simultaneously address all three concerns: the *Hannadowns* program.

Hanna Andersson would encourage its customers to return their "Hannas" once their children had outgrown them, in exchange for a 20 percent credit on the original purchase price, which could then be used toward future purchases. The company would in turn donate the returned clothes to needy women and children.

Hannadowns was introduced in the company's very next catalog. Early customer response was modest, but it quickly picked up. Gun attributes the tentative beginning to the concept's newness. *Hannadowns* was an unfamiliar idea to parents, but once they "got it," say company representatives, they loved it.

Gun Denhart has been thrilled with the program, calling it a "win-win-win situation."

> It's good for Hanna as a company because it is a way, marketing-wise, to show our customers that these are great products and can be used for more than one baby. It makes the customer feel good because they have all these clothes in their closets and the kids have outgrown them. They don't know what to do with them and they feel good that they will be used again by someone who really needs them. Employees love it, and finally, but not least, it is just wonderful for the kids who get the clothes because, normally, they wouldn't have this kind of quality clothing.

Through the years, the program has become increasingly important in stimulating repeat business, a critical element for success in the competitive direct mail business. A description of the program is always prominent in the catalog, both on the first page, which includes a written message from "Hanna," and on the order form. Gun frequently mentions the program during public appearances, and when customer calls are placed on hold, the outgoing message is often a pitch for *Hannadowns*.

THOUSANDS OF CLOTHES FOR CHILDREN IN NEED

As Hanna Andersson has grown, so has the *Hannadowns* program. Customers currently return approximately 10,000 items each month for *Hannadowns* credits. Since its inception, the program has collected and donated nearly 500,000 items to several hundred organizations and given customer credits totaling $2.2 million.

The returned Hannas are given primarily to organizations within the Portland area, but in some cases they have been sent as far away as Russia. Often, Hanna employees will make suggestions when they hear of a charity in need or a church collecting donations. When disaster strikes—Hurricane Hugo, for example—*Hannadowns* have been sent.

Early in the program, Hanna Andersson developed a particularly strong attachment to a local Portland organization, Raphael House, a social service agency that provides emergency shelter and transitional housing for women and children leaving situations of domestic violence.

Mitchell Jacover, director of Raphael House, remembers meeting Gun Denhart when the company was just beginning: "I explained the work that I was doing as director of Raphael House. Immediately she was very interested and responsive, asking if there was something that she could do to help." The organization soon became the most regular recipient of *Hannadowns* donations.

GOODWILL MAKES FOR GOOD BUSINESS

The immediate beneficiaries of the *Hannadowns* program are thrilled. Jacover explains:

> When we get a box of *Hannadowns* and bring them to the shelter, the only articles that never quite make it all the way downstairs to be put away are the *Hannadowns*. . . . You come back maybe an hour later to find twenty to twenty-five children walking around in Hanna outfits. It's a very sweet moment in the course of a very difficult time in their lives.

Jeannine Jenkins, the original coordinator of the program, recalls that one shelter always gives out Hanna clothes at special times like birthdays because "even though they have had wear, they are always the brightest and best quality they have in their clothes closet." Tom Denhart recalls meeting a small child who, after receiving some *Hannadowns* clothing, murmured, "I didn't know anybody cared that much about me."

"It broke my heart," Tom says.

"The *Hannadowns* program makes employees feel really good about working here," says Gretchen Peterson, vice president of human relations. "People overwhelmingly say, 'It just makes me feel wonderful to know I've been a part of this.' "

Although Gun Denhart was initially wary of translating the goodwill gained through the *Hannadowns* program into numbers, a recent company study proves that the program has helped Hanna Andersson prosper. Research shows that *Hannadowns* participants are the company's best customers, making repeat purchases at a rate 50 percent higher than the average customer and spending three times more money, cumulatively, than the average customer.

The *Hannadowns* program reinforces customer awareness of the durability of Hanna Andersson clothes. "Thanks for having such high-quality, all-cotton clothing that lasts through one to two years of my child's life and on to last through another child's. What a great program!" says one letter that accompanied a customer's *Hannadowns* return. Says another: "I just wanted to say thank you for impressing me as a company with a heart."

As important as emphasizing product durability, *Hannadowns* demonstrates to the public that Hanna Andersson is a caring company. "Increasingly, consumers are looking for socially responsible qualities in the businesses from which they make purchases," notes Lisa Holm, director of the Direct Marketing Association's Shop-At-Home Information Center in 1993. "There are other mail order companies using their medium to communicate to their customers about major concerns like the environment, literacy, and missing children, but *Hannadowns* represents the only ongoing, customer-involved program."

Stimulated in part by customers' enthusiastic response to the *Hannadowns* program and the ethic it represents, Hanna Andersson has grown quickly. In 1994, ten years after the first catalog was sent out, annual sales reached $45 million.

THE DISTINCTIVE HANNA CULTURE

It is tempting to regard the *Hannadowns* program as an ingenious but discrete marketing idea and little more. But in fact, the program's influence on the company and its work culture has been far-reaching. In a concrete way the *Hannadowns* program exemplifies a certain spirit of doing business. And this spirit, by being given a prominent showcase, has invigorated the company's community outreach and philanthropy as well as its values-driven employee policies and even its long-term business decisions.

From the start, Gun and Tom Denhart wanted their employees to be as happy and productive at work as they were at home.

That is one reason that child care reimbursement is sacrosanct. From the third year of the company's existence it has paid one-half of all employees' child care expenses. "I have two boys myself," explains Gun sympathetically. "And I know so well that if your child is not taken care of . . . then you can't do a good job."

For the same reason, the company allows flexible work schedules. Employees may request to work anywhere from twenty to forty hours per week, and great efforts are made to accommodate employees who want to be with their families during certain times of the day.

These two benefits led *Working Mother* magazine in 1991 to name Hanna Andersson as one of the eighty-five best companies for working parents in the United States, along with industrial powerhouses such as Procter & Gamble and Johnson & Johnson and smaller businesses like Ben & Jerry's Homemade, Inc.

Hanna Andersson also subsidizes employee fitness classes and a gourmet cafeteria, sponsors a formal wellness program, and offers tuition reimbursement to employees. The company's wage scales are competitive for the Portland area, but a profit-sharing plan can bring a significant pay boost.

In very specific ways, the *Hannadowns* program helped the Denharts and their employees grow closer and more committed to their community. As Tom puts it, "The *Hannadowns* idea has introduced us to all these broader ramifications [of families in crisis], and really educated us to the crying need for help with regard to battered women and children."

What began as a donation of children's clothing has grown into much more. Hanna Andersson has made significant financial contributions to Raphael House, sponsored programs, designed and donated a playroom, and even hired a number of women who have been residents of the shelter. Gun calls the shelter "a great employment agency!" The company also earmarks 5 percent of its pretax profits for charitable organizations, including a matching donations program for employees.

As Hanna Andersson grew and its reputation spread, it was inundated with requests for help from worthy organizations. To simplify its efforts, Gun and Tom formalized a community outreach/philanthropy program in 1993.

An employee-run committee and senior management select

three "target organizations" each year to receive cash donations, clothing, and employee time. Employees are encouraged to become personally involved with the organizations, and are allowed up to eight hours each year to volunteer on company time.

As an employer with a keen social conscience, striving to do better for its employees and community while competing in the marketplace, Hanna Andersson has become an employer of choice in the Portland area. It no longer needs to advertise when recruiting for positions, and it has a distinct advantage over conventional businesses in competing for qualified employees.

TROUBLE IN PARADISE

The plethora of social service efforts brought Hanna Andersson praise and recognition but, Gun admits, distracted the company from its most critical task—maintaining a profitable organization. As she explained in a 1994 *Inc.* article, "We became so introspective that we lost sight of what was happening outside the company."

By the early 1990s, increased competition and a slowed economy signaled trouble. Consumers, even Hanna Andersson's more upscale customers, began shopping for bargains as lower markups began to outweigh prestige. Moreover, costs on everything, from postage to health insurance, were rising.

A commitment to employing only ethical vendors forced the company to source material and manufacturing at higher prices than their competitors faced. The result: The double-digit growth to which they had become accustomed disappeared and profits began to shrink. Average earnings in the industry were between 6 and 10 percent, but, by 1993, Hanna's earnings had fallen below 5 percent. Most alarming, Gun and Tom had been so busy running things day to day that they had put no strategic plan in place for the future.

It was clear that dramatic change was required. Interestingly, Gun decided that she preferred not to be the one to implement that change. Instead, she promoted from within a new president to run all of Hanna Andersson's operations. While the new president worried about cutting costs and keeping the company viable, Gun instead began to concentrate on the overall strategic decision making.

The new president, Mary Roberts, faced a difficult task in controlling spiraling costs. She began by limiting some of the generous benefits provided to employees. For the first time, employees were forced to contribute to the cost of their health insurance. Parking, for years a perquisite, became the financial responsibility of employees. While Hanna Andersson's child care benefits remain intact, a cap was added limiting the total contribution the company will make. And the most unsettling change of all: In April 1993, the company announced it would lay off 10 percent of its work force.

HANNA ANDERSSON'S NEXT STAGE

By 1996, many of the employees had been called back to work. While the culture at Hanna Andersson may never completely return to what it once was, Gun explains that the changes were necessary—for survival and growth. She insists that the company is not abandoning its values, only putting them on a more solid footing. "We're not compromising the way we do things," she insists. "It's still a place where people want to be."

Some detractors are quick to blame the company's social aspirations for its competitive problems. And critics may be correct to the extent that the Denharts were not sufficiently alert to changing market conditions, particularly the rise of new competition.

But the issue is far more complicated than this analysis suggests. It was precisely the high-quality, no-waste, caring ethic that had attracted so many customers to Hanna Andersson in the first place and encouraged their repeat business. Its frenetic growth, unfortunately, had allowed the Denharts to neglect the delicate balance between financial and social goals. Once the baby boomlet waned and growth began to flatten out, the company has had to develop a more rigorous, integrated approach.

Revenues have grown slowly, and reached about $50 million in 1995. Although the company has not restored income to previous levels, Gun predicts that continued cost containment and a more focused mailing strategy will bring profits back to a competitive level by 1996. The *Hannadowns* program remains the same, however, and continues to be popular with customers, who earned about $800,000 in credits in 1995 alone.

The company is also putting a new emphasis on value to woo price-sensitive consumers and plans future expansion internationally. Hanna has begun mailing catalogs to Japan and has opened a new Japanese telephone service center. In addition, a traditional retail-store format is being tested in White Plains, New York.

The competitive challenges faced by Hanna Andersson only strengthen the Denharts' resolve to expand their company's special ethic. Quoting Thornton Wilder, Gun Denhart firmly believes that "money is like manure. If you let it pile up, it just smells. But if you spread it around, you can encourage things to grow."

3

Prudential Insurance's Living Needs Benefits

DEATH BENEFITS FOR THE LIVING

Cornell Hills of Fairfax, Virginia, shudders to think what might have happened if he had not been watching football on television in early October 1991. During a break in the action, an unusual commercial flashed across the screen. A man who needed a heart transplant, said the announcer, could now obtain funds from his life insurance policy *while he was still living.*

"At first, I wasn't sure what the ad was all about," says Hills. "But then I saw it during another football game. And my wife saw it." The new insurance provision, it turned out, was being offered by The Prudential Insurance Company of America to new and existing policyholders of permanent life insurance.

This was of more than passing concern because Hills's thirty-year-old wife, Karen, diagnosed with a lymphoma of the central nervous system, was scheduled to have a bone marrow transplant later that month. By happenstance, she had a Prudential life insurance policy for $50,000.

The Hillses immediately called up the local Prudential agent and discovered that Karen would indeed be eligible for the benefit. Within the month, they obtained $48,000—96 percent of her benefit—which they used to pay for child care and travel and lodging expenses while Karen Hills received medical treatment at a distant medical center.

Fortunately, the operation was a success. Says Cornell Hills, "The insurance benefit took the financial pressure off us during the medical care, and allowed us to concentrate on that. It also allowed us to keep our house. Without some sort of help, something was going to give."

What made Prudential's innovation so noteworthy was its upfront cost to policyholders—nothing. Prudential, the nation's largest insurance company, had retroactively applied the benefit to about 3.5 million existing permanent life insurance policies.

Establishing the option involved significant actuarial and legal challenges, including a radical new approach to the product design of life insurance and a two-year campaign to secure the approval of regulators in all fifty states. But Prudential's product enhancement provided a much wider range of benefits at much lower cost than the few existing, more modest riders did and established a new industry norm for serving an acute social need through life insurance.

RON BARBARO LEARNS ABOUT AIDS

Living Needs Benefits got its start when Ron Barbaro, president of Prudential in Canada, one of the few insurance agents ever to take the helm of a major insurance company, agreed to attend a fund-raiser in March 1988 for Casey House, a newly built AIDS hospice in Toronto. "I really didn't know much about AIDS," says Barbaro, "except that you keep a distance. You would send some money, but you really did not want to get too close."

A born raconteur and affable iconoclast, Barbaro had always lived by his instincts and quick rapport with people. It served him well in sales, as he became the youngest salesman, at age 22, ever to qualify for the insurance industry's prestigious Million Dollar Round Table. He soon became branch manager for North American Life Assurance Company, Toronto, a position he held from 1960 to 1970, and then co-founded the highly successful Win-Bar Insurance Brokers. Prudential asked Barbaro to become president of its Canadian operations in 1986; he became president of Newark-based Prudential Insurance in 1990.

As he toured Casey House, Barbaro confronted for the first time the awful reality of destitute, frail men waiting for death.

One patient told Barbaro that before he died, he desperately wanted to see his parents, who lived in Europe. But because neither he nor they had enough money to pay for the travel expenses, he would die alone, penniless. He added that he had a $20,000 life insurance policy but that it would pay off only *after* he died.

"Is there anything I can do?" Barbaro asked weakly, knowing it was a "throwaway line." "Yes," the man replied bitterly, looking him squarely in the face. "Help us die with dignity."

Recalling the gut-wrenching shock of the encounter, Barbaro reels back in his chair. "There was nothing to be done for the man, who in fact died a few weeks later. As I drove back to the office that day," Barbaro says, "I was convinced that there had to be some way to ease the financial stress of dying."

CONFRONTING PREJUDICES WITHIN THE INSURANCE INDUSTRY

Barbaro immediately called in an actuary, a lawyer, a doctor, and a claims administrator and related his experience at Casey House. He asked them if there was any way that terminally ill policyholders could receive advance benefits from their life insurance policies. These people are under a terrible strain, he told his staff. "They're facing their own imminent deaths while trying to cope with the financial problems the illness has caused. It seems so inhumane, especially when you consider that many of them have life insurance policies that pay out when it's too late."

By any conventional standard, Barbaro's determination to find a solution seemed unnecessary. Policyholders had always been able to obtain loans for the present cash value (or "surrender value") of their life insurance policies. Why was a new product design needed for policies that seemed eminently sturdy and serviceable?

Glenn J. Daniels, then assistant general counsel for Prudential in Canada, recalls the group's skeptical reaction: "We presented one hundred reasons why we should not embark on an advance of death proceeds payment program." Since an accelerated benefit was not in the insurance contract, why would the company *want* to pay a benefit before death? In any case, the company's actuaries had never calculated the mortality statistics needed for such an option or determined a pricing scheme. Nor had they studied which diseases ought to be included and how eligibility should be defined.

There were other questions: What special sensitivities would company officials need to learn in approaching terminally ill policyholders? And how would their confidentiality be protected?

In particular, Barbaro's ad hoc group worried about the tax consequences of accelerated benefits. Normally, death benefits are not taxed. Would the Canadian government tax these benefits, to the detriment of policyholders or their families? And would beneficiaries be left destitute if the insured used up all his or her benefits before death? A more self-interested concern was whether this idea could actually hurt Prudential by casting the company as the favored insurer for the terminally ill, thereby eliciting a flood of unacceptable new applicants.

For Barbaro and the team, these questions were mostly a matter of ethical concern and business calculation, not legality. No Canadian laws or regulations prohibited the very idea of living benefits. "The biggest problem," Barbaro says, "was attitude. For one hundred years this was the way it was. We couldn't get past that attitude that it's impossible."

TAKING THE RISK FOR A WORTHY IDEA

Barbaro eventually decided that the only way to explore the feasibility of the idea was to give it a try. Working with Prudential's medical director in the summer of 1988, Barbaro identified six or seven terminally ill people who might want to take advantage of Prudential's unusual offer.

The experiment proceeded for seven months on a quiet live-and-learn basis. Barbaro was so nervous that he had the medical director personally deliver the checks to policyholders. "I was scared stiff," Barbaro said. "I did not know whether we were doing the right thing. It is such a sensitive thing. You're dealing with the final stages of someone's life. It's not something you advertise. We just wanted to learn how we could make it better."

Then one Monday morning in February 1989, the lid blew off the project. A reporter from the *Toronto Globe and Mail* called up and asked, "Is it true that Prudential is giving out death benefits before people die?"

Fortunately, the resulting story was sympathetic. Within days, word of the Prudential venture hit the wire services, a popular Canadian radio show, and the Knight-Ridder syndicate in the United States. While many industry peers were skeptical or noncommittal, the general public's reaction was overwhelmingly positive. Personal finances expert Sylvia Porter praised the Prudential rider as an overdue change in the concept of life insurance that could revolutionize the industry. Inquiries poured in from England, Australia, Tobago, and the United States.

Some AIDS advocacy groups were *not* impressed. Ellen West, an attorney with AIDS Action Committee of Massachusetts, called living benefits "a nice gesture for the news," but complained that "it does not help improve access to life insurance, which is the real problem." AIDS activists in the United States have strongly criticized insurers for refusing to provide insurance to individuals who test positive for the HIV virus, for excluding coverage for experimental AIDS treatments, and for placing caps on AIDS-related insurance claims.

To date, U.S. courts have generally sided with insurers, who argue that the insurance policies sought by AIDS activists would be financially devastating to the industry and contrary to the philosophical premise of insurance, which is that people facing similar risks should pay similar premiums for similar protection.

Notwithstanding these disputes, some AIDS activists applauded Prudential's move. Leonard Graff, legal director of National Gay Rights Advocates in San Francisco, told a reporter, "I think it's a very generous and caring thing for them to do. We have been looking for a long time to see some leadership from the insurance industry [in the AIDS crisis], and I think this is very creative and a tremendous step forward."

Soon Prudential in Canada was offering living benefits to any policyholder certified as having a disease, illness, or condition that was medically classified as "terminal" within twelve months. Financial need of the insured or his dependents was not a consideration, and no restrictions were put on how the money could be used.

Although still in an experimental phase at that time, in early 1989, Prudential's approach to living benefits was clearly a hit—and not so crazy after all. It just needed a real-life demonstration—and some accidental publicity—to prove its appeal.

MEANWHILE IN THE UNITED STATES . . .

In the late 1980s Prudential's top actuary, Bob Hill, realized that the market for life insurance was changing in some significant ways. Life insurance executives had fretted for years that sales were slipping as the baby boomer generation grew older. According to the Life Insurance Marketing and Research Association, spending on life insurance had slipped from 22 percent of all financial security spending to 13 percent. During the same period, health insurance spending rose from 27 percent to 32 percent, and spending for retirement funding increased from 41 percent to 47 percent.

The changing demographics were forcing a shift in life insurance products, according to John E. Fisher, chairman of the American Council of Life Insurance:

> Increasingly, seniors have become more concerned with maintaining their quality of life than with leaving an estate for their heirs. This has caused a product revolution within the industry that has emphasized short-term cash value and de-emphasized the significance of long-term death benefits.

These changes were already being exploited by an unusual new breed of companies known as "viatical settlement firms." (*Viaticum* is an ancient Roman term for a provision or allowance given to travelers for transportation and supplies.) These entrepreneurs were offering to pay terminally ill people 50 to 75 cents on the dollar for their life insurance policies. For people medically certified as likely to die within two or three years, for example, these companies might pay $50,000 to $70,000 for a $100,000 policy, in return for being named the policy beneficiary.

By 1994 there were about sixty independent viatical companies nationwide, which together were estimated to have bought out more than $30 million in life insurance policies.

Because viaticals are not selling an insurance product, they are not subject to insurance regulation; they are considered lenders, relying upon someone's life insurance as collateral in the same way banks or creditors do. In 1995, however, a federal judge ruled that one major viatical settlement firm was actually in the business of selling securities, thus requiring SEC registration. At least nine state legislatures have sought to regulate viaticals.

UNSEEMLY SPECULATION IN HUMAN LIFE?

The life insurance industry was understandably disturbed at the emergence of this line of business. It was not just the blunt manner of some of these entrepreneurs, such as BGR International, which stands for "Beat the Grim Reaper." Insurers argue that the viatical firms are in the business of exploiting desperate people, as reflected in their unconscionably low payments—50 to 75 cents on the dollar—for life insurance policies.

Robert Waldron, a spokesman for the American Council of Life Insurance, told a reporter that it was "a bad concept. You are giving a third party an interest in your early death. It makes the hair on the back of my neck rise."

Joseph M. Belth, a respected industry watchdog, explained that viatical settlement companies are ethically questionable because they have no "insurable interest" in the insured. An insurable interest, says Belth, citing *Law and the Life Insurance Contract* by Janice E. Greider et al., is "a relationship between two persons which justifies one having a reasonable expectation of advantage or benefit from the continued life of the other."

Viatical companies do not have such a relationship to the insured; they profit from the insured's death—the earlier, the better. Belth praised Prudential's innovation as one "that needs to be emulated."

Some foreign insurers were already wading into this area. Crusader Insurance in South Africa attempted to graft several "dread disease" provisions onto life insurance in 1983. Within five years an estimated 70 percent of South Africa's life insurance policies included similar riders. The idea of living benefits spread to the United Kingdom by 1985, where it also became popular.

The idea got another boost in 1987 when Professor John E. Stinton spelled out the business advantages of accelerated benefits in *Best's Review*, an industry trade journal. Stinton proposed that life insurers advance a significant portion of a death benefit so that the insured could obtain otherwise unobtainable organ transplants.

"What I concluded," Stinton recalled in 1992, "was that survival rates were so impressive and increasing, that if a company paid out 50 percent of a death benefit as soon as the insured was certified as a transplant candidate, the company would make more money by retaining the other half of the policy [and earning investment income] rather than by paying out 100 percent when the insured died within sixty days or so." It was a startling analysis that opened up new vistas of innovation for life insurers.

THE COMPLEX DESIGN OF A NEW INSURANCE PRODUCT

As Prudential's Bob Hill contemplated the major changes in consumer spending for life insurance, the increasing public concern over health care, and the rise of the viatical industry fueled chiefly by the AIDS epidemic, he wondered how Prudential might respond. Could it redesign its policies to make them more useful and flexible?

In mid-1987, with the sanction of Prudential President Joseph Melone, Hill formed a small task force of actuaries and lawyers to explore the issues. Suddenly, in February 1989, Ron Barbaro's experiment blazed into the news, and a flood of public acclaim and legislative interest materialized.

The task force soon learned that Barbaro was already grappling with some of its concerns in an improvisational way, and in a very different legal and regulatory environment. Still, the Barbaro experiment brought a flood of calls from journalists, legislators, and regulators, recalls Rick Meade, a vice president and assistant general counsel involved with the task force. "They were saying, 'What is this all about? Are you going to do it in the U.S.? What are the issues?' "

The first order of business was to design a more versatile, refined product that could satisfy the more demanding legal and regulatory environment in the United States. Whereas Barbaro could legally improvise the experiment in Canada, Prudential in the United States would first have to satisfy fifty separate state insurance commissions.

Actuarial data had to be gathered and analyzed. Specific legal definitions of coverage needed to be drafted. Prudential analysts also had to assess the cost impact on the company, the tax implications for policyholders, and the serious ethical implications of shifting life insurance benefits from the beneficiary to the insured.

The prospects for regulatory approval and market acceptance had to be realistically assessed. Also, Prudential, as a mutual company that must treat all its policyholders equitably, had to find some way to offer a living benefits option that would apply to all policyholders.

The other key threshold issue that had to be confronted was the financing structure for accelerated benefits. How was the money to be advanced, consistent with the existing life insurance contract, without *losing* money for Prudential? Since any money paid out before death would represent a loss of anticipated premium and investment income for Prudential, what fair and reasonable discount rate should be applied to living benefits? And how should that formula be constructed?

Unlike the early entrants into living benefits, Prudential did not want its option to be an add-on to existing policies, requiring a new premium. "What we wanted," says Rick Meade, "was to create a benefit that would be self-funded so that it could be made available without charge immediately to a large number of our existing policyholders." For Prudential, the benefits of the rider would be derived from goodwill among existing customers and perhaps the stimulation of new sales.

Initially, the task force concentrated on the idea of providing a loan to policyholders, with the policy as collateral. But this idea ran smack into a major impediment: state laws that generally limit the loan value of a life insurance policy to the cash surrender value, which is usually much less than the full death benefit. The unassailable rationale behind these laws is that no loan should exceed the equity of the insurance policy. Yet, as Prudential actuary Jim Connor explains, "We *knew* that the real value of the policy of a terminally ill person was greater than the cash surrender value, because the person was going to die soon."

The task force broke through this conceptual barrier by considering the accelerated benefit a "settlement option," not a loan. The benefit would be financed from the death benefit itself, using a formula that took into account lost investment income, administrative costs, and, in the case of nursing home confinement, expected longevity. In the case of most terminal illnesses, the discounted payout would be about 95 to 97 percent, minus a $150 processing fee.

When the task force examined whether beneficiaries would be left penniless if a dying person "wasted" his death benefits on an expensive last fling, it determined that living benefits would not depart from current beneficiary rights. "We've had to make cash surrender values available to the owner of a policy at any time," says Meade. "Or a policyholder could take out the maximum loan value at any time. Either one of those acts could have the same repercussions for beneficiaries as accelerated death benefits." (In actuality, few, if any, policyholders have used their living benefits frivolously.)

Prudential also wanted to ensure that policyholders would not be involuntarily forced by public assistance programs or creditors to use their living benefits. To pin down this issue, Prudential secured formal declarations from the Department of Health and Human Services and the Social Security Administration that access to living benefits would not affect a person's eligibility for Medicaid, food stamps, or welfare. (A person who actually received the benefit, however, could be deemed ineligible for means-based programs.)

As for creditors seeking access to someone's death benefit,

Prudential refuses to pay claims in such cases. Meade concedes that the courts have not rendered a judgment on this position. That is one reason why Prudential made living benefits an option, not a standard feature, in its policies.

By April 1989 the task force had successfully answered all of the actuarial, legal, and ethical issues surrounding the living benefits package. To be eligible, existing policyholders would have to hold at least $25,000 of insurance coverage; new policyholders would need $50,000 of coverage. The rider would be offered retroactively, for free, to the three million policyholders of Prudential permanent life insurance at the time. It would contain no restrictions on how the accelerated benefit could be spent.

The task force believed it had designed a sound, responsive insurance rider. Difficult as it had been, it was only a first step. Now came an equally difficult challenge: convincing insurance regulators in all fifty states.

NAVIGATING THE REGULATORY MAZE

Fortunately, in its internal deliberations, Prudential had anticipated most of the potential objections. But perhaps the most compelling argument for a living benefits option was its potential to help people immediately, as demonstrated by its real-life implementation in Canada.

In November 1989, Florida became the first state to approve Prudential's product, followed soon thereafter by New Jersey. By late January 1990, six states had given their approval and Prudential announced the program to the public. The lengthy process of shepherding Living Needs Benefits through the regulatory labyrinth of the remaining forty-four states began.

The six actuaries and attorneys of the task force divvied up the states and, in ones and twos, met with regulatory officials to explain the innovation and answer specific objections. Slowly, Prudential won approvals in state after state throughout 1990 and 1991. Living benefits finally became a legal option for life insurance policyholders in all fifty states when New York State approved it in May 1992.

Ron Anderson of Tallahassee, Florida, a fifty-four-year-old man afflicted with terminal cancer, became the first U.S. recipient of Prudential's Living Needs Benefit on February 19, 1990. Anderson obtained $44,800, $1,200 less than the full death benefit. "We paid off a second and third mortgage, the car, and assorted bills," says Jan Anderson, Ron's wife. "It relieved Ron's mind so much." Anderson died seven weeks later.

By November 1995, Prudential had paid more than $73 million in living benefits to 941 policyholders, for an average claim of $77,673. Some 43 percent of these claims were filed by people with cancer, another 22 percent by people with AIDS, 15 percent by people needing nursing home care, and 4 percent by people awaiting vital organ transplants.

THE MULTIPLIER EFFECT OF A GOOD IDEA

As expected, Prudential reaped a harvest of favorable publicity as one state after another considered, then approved, the new option. For an industry that has received more than its share of negative publicity, says Glenn Daniels of Prudential in Canada, living benefits has been "a real plus."

Overall, Prudential's life insurance sales for the first half of 1990 were up 25 percent, a rise that the company attributed in significant part to the new living benefits rider and to a new survivorship life insurance policy. This increase was important for the company as a whole because 27 percent of Prudential's revenues at this time stemmed from life insurance.

A 1990 market survey conducted by Prudential found that its Living Needs Benefit has had a substantial positive impact on sales, in part because it has given Prudential's 25,000 insurance agents a new opportunity to contact clients. "They all want to add the rider," Fred Bush, a Prudential sales manager in North Versailles, Pennsylvania, told *Life Association News* in February 1991. "That leads to the agent reviewing the client's total insurance portfolio. The result is that we are writing a lot of new business." Approximately 90 percent of Prudential's eligible new policyholders have opted for the rider.

By late 1995, at least 215 companies were offering some version of living benefits, according to the American Council of Life Insurance. The ACLI estimated in 1994 that at least 18.1 million Americans were covered by some sort of accelerated death benefit. Industrywide, the biggest growth has come in group policies; fifty-eight companies now offer the rider in a total of sixty-five group insurance products, according to the ACLI. Sales are expected to grow further as a result of a provision in the 1995 federal budget that makes accelerated death benefits tax-free for terminally ill policyholders.

Several years after visiting the Toronto AIDS hospice, Barbaro, who left Prudential in 1993, was astounded at what had resulted. The response reinforced his belief that humane impulses, no matter how small, should be honored for their own sake. One can never know where they will lead.

He recalls the time he was running along the beach when he spotted a shiny penny in the sand:

> I took two strides past the penny and came to a stop. "Who am I to be too proud to pick up one cent?" I asked myself. As I was bending over for the penny I saw two silver coins next to it. I said to myself, "There's an important lesson here."

SECTION TWO

BUSINESSES THAT THRIVE IN THE INNER CITY

Introduction by Karen N. Horn

Karen Horn is chairman of Bank One, Cleveland. Previously, as president of the Federal Reserve Bank of Cleveland, Mrs. Horn earned praise for her handling of Ohio's savings and loan crisis. She is also chairman of the board of trustees of Case Western Reserve University. Mrs. Horn holds a Ph.D. in economics from The Johns Hopkins University.

It is not widely appreciated that the inner cities of America represent a huge, largely untapped market that can profitably sustain a wide variety of businesses. To be sure, there are many reasons why businesses often avoid troubled urban locations. Chief among these are crime, drug abuse, higher construction costs, a less educated labor pool, greater regulatory burdens, and restricted access to debt and equity.

Yet it is equally true, as Harvard Business School Professor Michael E. Porter points out in a landmark 1995 article in the *Harvard Business Review*, that the inner city has many distinct competitive advantages. These include, says Porter, strategic location, local market demand, integration with regional clusters of business specialties, and human resources.

One key to doing business in the inner city is a fresh, more accurate assessment of how to operate profitably there. Unfounded prejudices must be overcome; government and community-based organizations must reassess their roles in revitalizing the inner city; and businesses themselves must develop a tenacity and resourceful-

ness in meeting the special challenges posed by urban neighborhoods.

The four businesses profiled in Section Two have done just that.
Their stories suggest some of the special capacities, tactics, and attitudes that are needed to thrive in distressed urban environments.

A first indispensable need: Newcomers to the inner city must
truly understand the cultural attitudes and habits of the people who
live there. Entrepreneur Lou Krouse, for example, was able to make
his electronic bill-paying system work only because he understood
the special financial habits and cash-flow problems facing many
inner-city households. Similarly, American Savings Bank of Irvine,
California, was able to prosper in the inner city only because it recognized that residents there tend to have work patterns and credit
profiles that differ from those of suburban customers. This insight
enabled the bank to reinvent its mortgage lending program and
thereby tap a market that few businesspeople imagined could be
profitable.

In like manner, the Finast supermarket chain realized that it
needed to understand the inner city as a niche market with highly
specific consumer preferences, not as a generic market similar to
suburban counterparts. By offering a more tailored mix of foods—a
wide variety of greens, fish, and other foods popular in African-
American neighborhoods—Finast was able to boost its revenues
and, by implementing other management innovations as well, develop a profitable inner-city presence.

Because the inner city has distinct consumer characteristics, the
companies that succeed there must develop new sets of managerial
muscles. They must learn to be more flexible and creative. They
must be willing to overcome subtle prejudices about what their employees can and cannot achieve, and what their customers will and
will not buy. They must be willing to improvise and have the patience to experiment with innovative solutions.

Once American Savings Bank realized that many inner-city residents are quite creditworthy despite their different credit card usage,
participation in the cash economy, and greater reliance on part-time
jobs, the bank created a new, less restrictive set of underwriting criteria. That initiative opened the door to a lucrative new loan market.
Bus company entrepreneur Rachel Hubka realized that there was a
large, untapped labor pool in the troubled North Lawndale section

of Chicago. But that group needed special training, personal support, and an immersion in a rigorous work culture. Hubka's program helped develop a highly professional and loyal base of employees.

One common denominator in many successful inner-city businesses is their close collaboration with community leaders and organizations as a core business strategy. Although establishing working partnerships with the community can consume great time and legwork, the relationships that result can be remarkably powerful business resources. When Finast sought to reduce pilferage by customers and improve the work habits of cashiers, local church leaders were very willing to put out the word and lend support. Because American Savings developed partnerships with various community nonprofits and schools, it became widely respected in the community—and the first place that home mortgage customers would go for a loan.

There is an unfortunate tendency, when contemplating solutions to the serious woes of the inner city, to make a specious division between altruistic social-service models and hard-nosed business models. This assumed dichotomy is not necessarily useful. The four businesses profiled here show that successful inner-city businesses must creatively combine *both* sensibilities into a new synthesis. The rewards: the opening of new and profitable markets for American business and much-needed economic development for America's urban centers.

4

Mario J. Antoci and American Savings Bank

CULTIVATING THE AMERICAN DREAM

For years Abzalon and Rosa Uribe lived in a rented apartment with their two small children. Then Abzalon went to a bank branch in his neighborhood, met with a loan agent, and worked out a mortgage agreement. Four weeks later the Uribes moved into their first home.

A routine tale of an American family? Hardly, because in the Uribes' neighborhood, home ownership has long seemed an impossible goal. The Uribes live in East Los Angeles, an economically distressed community that few major financial institutions even attempt to serve. Most consider the area too risky, the residents too poor and unreliable, and the housing stock too dilapidated.

Like many area residents, Rosa and Abzalon are Mexican immigrants and deeply distrustful of banks. They built up savings, but kept the money at home. When the Uribes first talked about buying a home, their friends told them they would never be able to qualify for a loan. When Abzalon did approach one bank for a mortgage, he was told flatly that he couldn't qualify.

Abzalon decided to try a different lender, American Savings Bank, which had a large, modern branch located in the heart of East Los Angeles. At American, loan officer Tom Ramirez met with the Uribes, verified their savings, and helped establish their credit. The result was a loan that left both parties feeling good. Abzalon is thrilled with his new home, and with the bank that made it possible. "At American," he explains, "I felt like they wanted to give me the loan. . . . They treated me like a customer, not just a number."

Over the past six years, American Savings Bank has made home ownership a reality for thousands of nontraditional borrowers. Under Chairman and CEO Mario J. Antoci, American has become a national leader in serving low-income and minority communities. The bank's creative efforts to understand and serve these customers has opened much-needed credit to some of California's most underserved communities. What's more, to the surprise of industry observers, these efforts have carved out a strong and profitable niche for the bank, forming the cornerstone of a remarkable business turnaround.

HOW "REDLINING" AFFECTS INNER-CITY NEIGHBORHOODS

The older neighborhoods of Los Angeles, and particularly South Central Los Angeles, are really rather genteel parts of the city, at least historically. Financial reporter Elliott Blair Smith of the *Orange County Register* describes the community:

> You have midwestern-style houses, you have large, grassy lawns. But beginning more than thirty years ago, you had an out-migration of the white, urban middle class. And what was left was very little. Today you can go for miles without coming across a major supermarket. You can go for miles without finding movie theaters. And you can go for miles without finding a bank or a savings and loan. . . . There was just not a mechanism to lend into these areas.

As often happens with communities in transition, this lack of credit accelerated the neighborhoods' decline into absentee ownership. "[Today] 61 percent of the residents who live in the city don't own their own homes," says Los Angeles housing advocate Lori Gay, "and 99 percent of those 61 percent are in low- to moderate-income neighborhoods." The residents of these areas, lacking a long-term stake in their neighborhoods, began to lose the sense of pride and habit of investment that create the fabric of a community. The result: a steady deterioration of the housing stock and commercial base. Yet the desire to purchase a home, to have a stake, to build real communities remains strong. What has been lacking is the opportunity.

Some of this can be attributed to the practice of "redlining," the systematic denial of service to a particular region or neighborhood by a financial institution. Some mortgage lenders, in particular, are accused of drawing a "red line" around low-income and minority neighborhoods, refusing to lend inside this line. This blatant discrimination was outlawed by the Fair Housing Act of 1968; Congress sought to strengthen fair lending practices in 1977 by enacting the Community Reinvestment Act (CRA). As a condition of their federal insurance, the CRA requires banks and thrifts to lend in all areas where they take deposits. This statute, combined with other broad antidiscrimination measures, was meant to legislate redlining out of existence.

Nonetheless widespread discrepancies in lending persist. A comprehensive Federal Reserve Board study in 1992 found that of 6.3 million mortgage applications submitted nationwide during 1990, 34 percent of applications by African-Americans were rejected. The rejection rate for Whites was just 14 percent. This vast discrepancy holds true even when differences in income level are taken into account. For instance, among loan applicants who earned $35,000 to $50,000 a year and who sought home loans of $55,000 to $80,000, African-Americans faced a 26 percent rejection rate, compared with only 9 percent for Whites.

Lenders have responded that the rejection rate alone is a poor indicator of discrimination. Efforts to recruit minority applicants can inadvertently raise minority rejection rates by encouraging applications from unqualified borrowers or those with poor credit histories. This is true to a degree. But a 1994 *Wall Street Journal* study found that lenders recruited proportionately fewer loan applications from minority communities within their lending areas than they did overall, leaving prospective borrowers in those areas to rely on smaller, more expensive loan sources.

THE TROUBLES OF AMERICAN SAVINGS BANK

Despite the glaring need for equitable mortgage lending, American Savings Bank was an unlikely candidate to accept the challenge. After acquiring American in 1983, financier Charles W. Knapp transformed it into a freewheeling institution that exemplified all the risks of deregulation. The bank aggressively pushed high-risk, high-interest loans, and top executives enjoyed lavish compensation and perks. In less than two years the bank had become the second largest S&L in the country, with $30 billion in assets, but it was also reeling from large operating deficits and an ever-growing pool of nonperforming loans.

Less than two years after acquiring the thrift, Knapp resigned under growing scrutiny from federal regulators, and a new management team struggled unsuccessfully to return the institution to a firm footing. Eventually, after the Federal Savings & Loan Insurance Corporation intervened, Texas billionaire Robert M. Bass and a group of private investors acquired the bank. In late 1988 the troubled assets were spun off into New West Federal Savings & Loan, while the performing assets, branch system, and other holdings were assigned to a new entity, American Savings Bank, which was given an invaluable two-year federal guarantee against losses.

ENTER MARIO J. ANTOCI

To rebuild the bank, Bass recruited Mario Antoci, president and chief operating officer of Home Savings of America, California's largest and most stable savings and loan. At the time, industry analyst Jonathan Gray called Antoci's appointment "a signal of the company's commitment to quit smoking and start running three miles a day."

Antoci, a Los Angeles native, grew up in a blue-collar family on the east side of Los Angeles, one of the city's "melting pot" neighborhoods. Although his family sent him to a private Jesuit high school in a well-to-do west side neighborhood, Antoci was uncomfortable with the homogeneous, affluent student body and he chose to return to a predominantly Latino high school. There, he developed a deep respect for cultural diversity and a belief that disparate groups could, and should, live comfortably together. "I have lived all my life in a diverse community," Antoci explains. "I went to school with diverse groups of kids. . . . Everybody plays together, lives together."

Antoci first learned the banking business in the 1960s at Southern California Savings and Loan, as a protégé of CEO Ken Childs. When it became clear that leadership of the family-owned bank would remain within the family, Antoci left to become treasurer at Home Savings. He spent the next twenty years focused on mortgage lending and retail deposits, a conservative philosophy that kept the bank on solid footing while its more adventurous competitors faltered.

When Robert Bass approached him about leading American Savings Bank, Antoci was intrigued by the unusual prospect of working with a virtual tabula rasa—a bank stripped of its non-performing assets, waiting for an entirely new management and new management structure, yet with the resources and branch system of a major institution. He realized, also, that dramatic leadership would be needed to restore American's strength and reputation.

This was made vividly clear the first day that Antoci reported for work at American Savings. The Greenlining Coalition, a community activist group based in northern California, was picketing an Oakland branch of the bank, charging that less than 3 percent of American's loans went to African-American and Latino communities [prior to 1989]. The group also complained that the bank did not have any division devoted to community outreach, and that previous community reinvestment efforts, in the words of spokesman Robert Gamboa, represented "public relations gimmicks . . . rather than systematic changes."

Many banks do regard community reinvestment primarily as a regulatory issue. They strive only to meet the minimal standards of the Community Reinvestment Act (CRA), and no higher, regarding such efforts as a social responsibility or public service but hardly as a basic business concern. But Antoci envisioned something more. He believed that low-income and minority lending could become an integral—and profitable—part of American Savings Bank's core business strategy. Antoci therefore refused to make any commitments to the Greenlining Coalition; he was determined that American, on its own initiative, would not merely achieve the goals in question but surpass them.

Reorganizing American's management structure, Antoci created a new division of Community Outreach and Urban Development, with four new vice presidents assigned to oversee different geographic regions. The division would not focus primarily on philanthropic activities, public relations, and community relations, as most similar bank divisions do. Rather, its mandate would be to make the bank a more effective lender to California's low-income communities.

Antoci selected John Nunn, senior vice president for retail banking, to lead the new department. Nunn not only had a thorough knowledge of the bank and the communities it served; he also had the credibility, as an African-American, to establish the necessary rapport with minority neighborhood leaders and borrowers. Nunn initially resisted the new assignment, fearing he would be relegated to a backwater of the bank's operations. But Antoci won Nunn over with his vision of an aggressive, income-generating division seriously committed to underserved communities.

One of the first challenges facing Nunn and his vice presidents was to show their sincerity about serious community outreach. Joetta Brown, a twenty-year veteran of American Savings who grew up in South Central Los Angeles, took to the front lines of this task. As Outreach Coordinator for Los Angeles, Brown began to help affordable housing organizations, literacy groups, mentor programs for schoolchildren, and the Rebuild L.A. recovery effort following the 1992 riots. Through an annual "paint-a-thon," American Savings provided paint to volunteers who painted the houses of low-income senior citizens. The bank also developed working relationships with civic organizations such as the Los Angeles Urban League, the National Association for the Advancement of Colored People and the Southern Christian Leadership Conference.

Such persistent and highly visible involvement has been rewarded. "We are trusted. We are recognized. We are applauded," says Brown. "I don't have to say anything about

American Savings when I go to conventions or conferences or community meetings. The community, in its introduction of me or of American Savings, says what we have done."

BUILDING THE INFRASTRUCTURE OF SERVICE

Nunn and Antoci soon concluded that their low-income lending initiative would never fully succeed without a physical presence within those communities. "In the Hispanic area," Antoci says, "the closest branch that we had was Arcadia. It was silly. That is a very affluent area miles and miles away. . . . Unless you get your feet wet and get into the area, you are not going to get business from the area." Based on the bank's success in penetrating low-income and minority markets in northern California, Antoci decided to open two new inner-city branches: one in largely Latino East Los Angeles and one in largely African-American South Central L.A. It was the first time in ten years that a financial institution had sought to open a new branch in inner-city Los Angeles.

Initially, recalls Joetta Brown, local residents "thought that this was just one more story where another large corporation would come in and put up just anything. A few people would work in it, but it would not provide the same kind of services that [they] would in Beverly Hills." But when the branch opened in 1990, American hosted a gala celebration in the parking lot that featured an impressive roster of top city officials, including the mayor flying in by helicopter. "Everyone from that point in time felt that this was just the beginning of something big," says Brown.

In staffing the new branches, American strove to reflect the makeup of the surrounding communities. This was especially important in East Los Angeles, where many residents speak only Spanish. "This business can be very intimidating to people who speak and understand English," says Nunn. "Now, if you *don't* understand English, and you don't understand all the loan terms and things like that, can you imagine what it must be like? Totally intimidating." All employees at American's East Los Angeles branch are bilingual in Spanish and English. American also began to actively recruit seasoned minority lending professionals.

Antoci and Nunn also let it be known throughout the company that discrimination, no matter how subtle, would not be tolerated. Antoci was energized in part by a hidden-camera video produced by a local television news program. It showed how various Los Angeles businesses treated two men, one White and one African-American. Even though the two men had very similar clothing, backgrounds, and economic status, the White man was eagerly offered assistance; the African-American man was often rebuffed, discouraged, or simply ignored. "When we watched this tape," Nunn recalls, "Mario was just outraged." A special in-house training video was produced and shown to all employees to make the bank's policies clear.

But for Antoci it was not enough to be nondiscriminatory. He wanted to proactively seek out low-income loan applicants. One particularly successful tool was a series of home-buying seminars, conducted in various languages. "Many of the seminar participants don't feel that they can possibly obtain a home loan," says Nunn. "Maybe their parents have never had a home. Maybe their grandparents have never had a home. So there isn't this tradition of home ownership at work. But through counseling sessions and through our seminars, sometimes these people will say, 'You know, I think I can do that.' "

This sort of credit counseling, as well as the special mortgage lending process at inner-city branches, required specialized training. Loan officers had to learn to accommodate their customers' sometimes unyielding work schedules, for example, by staying at the office in the evening or on weekends. They had to become familiar with government affordable housing programs that offer financial assistance to low-income borrowers.

Antoci also realized that the bank's compensation structure would have to be modified. It takes more time and energy for loan officers to give greater personalized attention to smaller-than-usual loan amounts. Indeed, this is precisely why many loan officers nationwide are not eager to serve lower-income clients. Antoci responded by offering enhanced compensation to loan officers who serviced low-income loans.

HOW HOUSEHOLD FINANCES DIFFER IN THE INNER CITY

Once this infrastructure was in place, a new approach to underwriting was needed to make the new process work. The criteria lenders typically use to evaluate the creditworthiness of loan applicants tend to reflect middle- and upper-income norms. An estimated 60 percent of all residents in lower-income communities, for example, have no bank accounts, let alone credit cards. Many distrust financial institutions and are reluctant to pay the fees that are commonly assessed on low-balance accounts. Cash income is common, and many people hold multiple part-time jobs to support their families. The source of a family's savings may be poorly documented, especially if the people are recent immigrants. Any of these factors can doom a loan application in the traditional process.

American Savings Bank recognized these pervasive problems and set out to reinvent its underwriting criteria. Banks traditionally do not count cash income as part of an applicant's qualifying income because it is not considered steady or verifiable. In low-income neighborhoods, however, cash can represent a substantial—and reliable—portion of total income. "People work at swap meets, they work at the flea market, and they work as domestic servants," Nunn says. "If we were to ignore that in terms of qualifying someone for a loan, we'd be ignoring their ability to repay."

American's solution was to accept cash income as part of a couple's qualifying income, provided that at least one of them did receive a federal W-2 wage report. Similar underwriting changes were made to recognize multiple part-time jobs and other work patterns common in low-income communities.

A next step was the relaxation of credit history requirements. In Latino communities, credit cards are not at all common. Antoci explains how the bank dealt with this:

> We had to figure out if there was another way that we could determine if these people paid their bills. One way was to start looking to see if they paid their rent on time. If they were being charged for utilities, were they paying those on time? So, there are other ways to determine that these people are responsible. That's all you need to know.

In African-American communities, the credit situation was somewhat different. African-Americans were more likely to have credit cards, but they may have fallen behind on payments. American found, however, that a record of delinquency on credit card bills did not necessarily translate into delinquency on a mortgage. This result is affirmed by housing advocate Gay: "Low- to moderate-income people, I often say, pay three people on a monthly basis—their grocer, their minister, and whatever [mortgage] lender they are working with, because they are going to keep that home." In cases where applicants had a stable rent payment history, American decided to overlook late credit card payments, a move that opened up a large pool of minority applicants who otherwise qualified.

THE DRAMATIC COMMUNITY IMPACT

American's comprehensive efforts to revamp its lending process have had dramatic results. In its first year of operation, its East Los Angeles branch made more than 1,500 home loans totaling $220 million, exceeding the bank's target by 65 percent. By 1992, 40 percent of the bank's loans were obtained by African-American, Latino, and Asian borrowers. Tom Ramirez, who does all of his lending in the $100,000 range, has become the most productive loan agent in the entire bank. By 1994, Ramirez had made $650 million worth of home loans in East Los Angeles. "Under traditional underwriting practices," he says, "three out of every four families [I have lent to] would not be living in the homes that they're living in today."

After the first full year of the bank's reinvestment initiative, 1990, American had rejected only 9 percent of applications from African-Americans and 7 percent from Whites, for a ratio of just 1.3. (The ratios fell even lower in 1991 and 1992.) By contrast, the overall loan rejection rate in California in 1990 was 23 percent for African-Americans versus 13 percent for Whites—a 1.7 ratio—according to a 1992 Federal Reserve Bank study.

This record is particularly impressive in view of American's aggressive recruitment of minority applicants, which could inflate minority rejection rates by encouraging marginally qualified minorities to apply for loans. It is striking that American Savings Bank has achieved *both* high minority loan volume and low rejection ratios. It is not surprising that the 1994 *Wall Street Journal* study of the 100 largest mortgage lenders in the country judged American Savings Bank the number one equitable lender in America.

Community activists are vocal in their praise of American Savings Bank. Ana Alvarez-Boyd of Consumer Action, a non-profit group that monitors the banking industry on behalf of Latino consumers, says "no other program stands up to American Savings. . . . They look at a borrower's merits in the old-fashioned sense." Lori Gay of Los Angeles Neighborhood Housing Services says, "When you talk to Mario Antoci, you realize he is as committed as some of us in the community are to changing the communities and revitalizing them." Even the Greenlining Coalition, which had picketed American in 1989, now lauds the bank as a national model of community reinvestment. Says Greenlining Coalition spokesman Robert Gnaizda: "Their chairman is willing to take chances, because he doesn't think they are chances. . . . We've been very impressed with the bank's commitment."

WHY LENDING FOR LOW-INCOME HOUSING WORKS

American's achievements in low-income and minority lending attest to Antoci's acute insight into the economic realities of lower-income and minority neighborhoods. Such neighborhoods, it turns out, are relatively more stable during economic downturns. Ironically, one source of this stability is the tendency of workers to change jobs frequently, a work pattern traditionally seen as a source of *in*stability. The explanation: When low-income borrowers lose their jobs, American found, they tended to be more flexible in searching for work and to find new jobs more quickly. "They were willing to accept jobs that allowed them to make enough money to make that mortgage payment," Antoci says, "whereas it is pretty hard to tell an electrical engineer that 'maybe you ought to change your career at this time because there are no jobs for electrical engineers.' "

Antoci also realized that residents in inner-city areas are absolutely committed to their homes, even in times of economic distress. Many lower-income borrowers will rent out rooms, if necessary, to help meet mortgage payments. Many put in hours of their own labor to improve their homes' appearance and value. "A lot of the properties that we lend on are fixer-uppers," says Ramirez. "Property that may have been abandoned for some reason or another. And now they are beautiful homes."

Equally counterintuitive is American's discovery that home values in low-income areas are more stable in times of economic upheaval than they are in more upscale neighborhoods. During the California recession of the early 1990s property values in affluent areas such as Beverly Hills and West Los Angeles dropped as much as 40 to 50 percent, whereas property values in the low-income areas, like South Central Los Angeles or Oakland, in some cases actually appreciated. In addition, foreclosures in affluent neighborhoods can involve far greater losses for a bank than foreclosures in the inner city, where property values are lower. On those rare occasions of foreclosure in low-income neighborhoods, American found that the house in question can generally be sold more quickly than houses in more affluent areas, because potential buyers in the latter areas "sit on the fence waiting for better times," as Antoci puts it.

ROBUST PROFITS FROM HIGHER LOAN PERFORMANCE

To the surprise of industry observers who considered the inner city an unreliable and unprofitable market, American's loans in low-income areas have been among the best in its portfolio. Indeed, during the early 1990s the bank's low-income loans had delinquency rates between one-fourth and one-third of the rate in affluent areas. Since American's East Los Angeles branch opened in 1990, it has been the single most profitable lending branch in the entire bank, and the South Central branch is not far behind. Partially on the strength of its inner-city portfolio, American Saving Bank now ranks among the nation's healthiest and most stable thrifts, with 1993 profits of $114 million on $17.3

billion in assets. American has received top "investment grade" ratings by national rating services.

The bank's financial success in low-income areas contributed to Fannie Mae's ground-breaking 1993 decision to securitize $1.4 billion of low-income and inner-city loans from American's portfolio. This represented a departure for the important secondary loan market, which maintains a conservative approach and has typically avoided affordable housing portfolios.

Antoci's insight was to see beyond the common prejudices to understand an underserved market. As he explains:

> We refer to home ownership as the American dream. But Americans are a diverse group of people. . . . Once you realize that, you ask yourself the question of why shouldn't we be able to lend to these people? What is it that stops us? We see that the differences are silly. . . . So, if you don't worry about that, if you start thinking "let's find a way," then you realize that this could be good business. And it *should* be good business.

5

Finast Supermarkets

THE ULTIMATE
NEIGHBORHOOD MARKET

To drive through the Glenville section of Cleveland is to encounter some distressingly familiar scenes of urban America. After the fiery race riots of 1968, most of the retailers remaining are tiny grocery and liquor stores. Commercial thoroughfares are marred by boarded-up storefronts. Residential streets present an uneven patchwork of well-kept family dwellings and dilapidated houses.

The visitor to Glenville is astonished, then, to turn a corner and come upon a huge, gleaming "superstore." Inside, the supermarket is clean and spacious, with huge stacks of mustard greens and kale looming over the aisles, and row after row of giant frozen-food cases. There is an in-store bakery, which accepts custom orders, a drugstore and pharmacy, a flower shop, a video rental outfit, and a branch bank open twenty-four hours a day, seven days a week.

John Shields, the Ohio division president of Finast until 1993, a $132-million supermarket chain, bursts with pride in showing visitors the store:

> There's nothing more exciting to me than to take my Shaker Heights suburban friends to the stores we have in urban Cleveland. The fact of the matter is, when they go down there, they're stunned. They say, "My gosh, this is a nicer store than we have in our neighborhood."

Finast has been one of the few farsighted, resourceful super-market chains to reap new profits by tapping the long-neglected inner-city market. Over the past generation most major retail businesses, including supermarket chains, followed their "best" customers to suburbia. For the twenty million Americans who still reside in the inner city, the "White flight" of business has meant frequent trips to the suburbs to find a satisfactory selection of foodstuffs at affordable prices. It is a lose-lose situation for inner-city residents: Pay an additional $400 to $1,000 in transportation costs each year, as estimated by one study, or pay exorbitant prices for substandard produce at shabby mom-and-pop stores in the local neighborhood.

It is not surprising that most food retailers have abandoned America's metropolises. Urban supermarkets often require substantially higher operating expenses and produce lower net profits than their suburban counterparts do. Land is expensive in urban areas, inflating rents and discouraging new construction, upgrades, and expansions. Vandalism and shoplifting add to operating, insurance, and security costs. The poverty of many inner-city dwellers translates into less purchasing power and lower sales volumes. And since residents tend to have less education and work experience, the labor pool generally needs more intensive training and has a higher turnover rate.

If most supermarket chains see only problems in the inner city, Finast, a visionary subsidiary of Dutch retailing giant Royal Ahold N.V., saw grand possibilities. As suburban markets became saturated, Finast recognized urban centers as a huge underserved market waiting to be tapped. What was needed, it realized, was the imagination and commitment to reinvent food retailing so it could be made profitable there.

Beginning in 1988, Finast opened six state-of-the-art grocery stores in inner-city Cleveland by building new stores entirely and upgrading smaller ones. Its strategy did not just require new capital, but a new set of management attitudes and skills: flexibility, creativity, a long-term perspective, and patience.

Its bold investment, however, now yields $132 million in annual sales while providing an invaluable service and a much-needed economic boost for inner-city neighborhoods. And Finast has taught itself new practices—in store operations, niche-market merchandising, marketing, and more—which also have direct applications in its suburban markets.

FINAST'S HISTORICAL COMMITMENT TO CLEVELAND

The Finast chain is actually the reincarnation of the former Pick-N-Pay grocery stores, longtime landmarks of Cleveland. These stores were bought by Julius Kravitz and his group of investor-managers in 1972. Six years later, Kravitz, whose supermarket career in Cleveland dated back to the 1920s, merged Pick-N-Pay with the larger First National Stores of New England and New York. The resulting public company was First National Super-markets, Inc., or Finast. Kravitz chaired the enterprise of fifty-seven Pick-N-Pays and 235 Finasts until his death in 1979, with Richard Bogomolny serving as president and chief executive officer until 1993.

Despite their industry's retreat from the cities, Kravitz and Bogomolny wanted to stay in Cleveland even though Finast's board of directors was skeptical about the future of urban food retailing. The board, explains Bogomolny, believed that "if you tried to finance projects in those areas, lenders would consider them to be very high risk and either want a very high rate of return or wouldn't fund the project, or some combination of both."

In fact, Finast's continued presence in the city sometimes appeared financially untenable. It was forced to shut down or sell off two-thirds of its stores on the East Coast in the early 1980s, as well as some in Cleveland. Nevertheless, Bogomolny always hoped that Finast could find an opportunity to return to these areas.

Kravitz and Bogomolny suspected that the small size of their stores was at least part of the problem. The rising stars of the retailing industry were giant superstores that carried tens of thousands of products. As profit margins grew thinner, it became more important to have a high volume of sales and "ware-house pricing," as well as a diverse inventory so higher-margin items could offset less profitable ones. Notwithstanding their urban locations, it seemed clear that the Finast/Pick-N-Pay stores would have to go the same route as Wal-Mart and other superstores. In the short term, however, Finast's wary board and lack of investment capital made any such moves impossible.

A critical catalyst for change arrived in 1983 in the person of John Shields, a bluff, confident man then running Jewel supermarkets in the heart of Chicago. Bogomolny lured Shields to Finast, naming him Ohio division president and placing him in charge of the Cleveland-area stores.

One day, to acquaint himself with the political and economic realities of Cleveland, Shields took a bus tour of the city with other business and government leaders. While passing a dilapidated Finast store on Clark Street at 25th, Shields remembers that the city council member for the ward, Helen Smith, urged him to renovate the unsightly store. As an inducement, Smith helped secure a $50,000 interest-free loan from community development funds.

While fairly modest, the sum was enough to spur Shields to launch what would become a significant expansion of Cleveland's inner-city supermarkets. The councilwoman's suggestion was "a great idea," remembers Shields, "and for a very simple reason: it is an underserved market. There's an outstanding business reason to want to do this." The community development loan demonstrated the city's support for Finast's plans and, more critically, convinced Finast's board that it was worth trying to revive its urban operations.

Ironically, the skeptical board, which had resisted inner-city expansion for so long, was soon replaced by an entirely new board of directors. After rival supermarket chains had mounted two unsuccessful hostile takeover attempts in 1984, Bogomolny and other managers orchestrated their own $100-million leveraged buyout of their firm, finalized the following year. Finast became a privately held company again, and Finast managers were now in complete control. They were still eager to expand, but now they had no investment capital.

This cash crunch meant that Finast could implement its expansion plans only in small, incremental steps. In 1986, sixteen Cleveland Pick-N-Pay stores were enlarged and given the Finast name. The twenty-nine other Pick-N-Pays would remain small but would strive to customize their products to meet the preferences of their urban, ethnic clientele.

DISCOVERING THE SECRETS OF
ETHNIC MERCHANDISING

To succeed in its new strategic plans, Finast knew that it had to develop some new operational capacities. One of the most critical new talents would be more responsive merchandising.

When Finast took over a closed Sears store in Westown, a section of Cleveland with a large population of Puerto Ricans, it transformed it into a superstore featuring the same food items all its other superstores carried, including gourmet mushrooms, thirty types of fresh fish, a custom bakery, and a full wine shop. To Finast's surprise, the store did not turn the same profit.

Determined to succeed, Finast decided to make a concerted effort to ascertain the buying tastes of the ethnically diverse Westown clientele. This action was unusual. Historically, most supermarket chains have kept one standard inventory list and then stocked the same products at all their stores, a convenient practice that has worked well enough in the relatively homogeneous suburbs.

After conducting a thorough survey, however, Finast realized that it needed to offer food items that have little appeal in the suburbs but great popularity among certain urban, ethnic customers: fresh yucca, plantain, twenty-pound bags of rice, for instance. Within a year, sales soared above $750,000 per week and the store became profitable, according to *Supermarket News*. The key was ethnic merchandising.

Finast now conducts research at the store level every time it builds a new supermarket. "It's wrong to take a look at the inner city and think of it as just one homogenous situation," Bogomolny explains. "It really isn't. I mean, the eastern part of Cleveland is mostly Black. The western side, west of the Cuyahoga River, has a high Hispanic and southern White population."

Even these ethnic categories are too broad, says Bogomolny, because "Hispanic" can be Puerto Rican, Mexican, or Cuban— and each submarket may have its own distinct buying preferences. "The only way to find out," says Bogomolny, "is to really get in there and study what these various markets really are."

Finast's approach combines three methods: computer analysis of all receipts to determine which products are selling and which are not; individual questionnaires and interviews with customers to determine product preferences; and the hiring of store managers who are familiar with the tastes of particular minority groups.

By developing a more disciplined process for evaluating Finast's product mix, Finast has developed more effective ways to meet actual customer demand in both urban *and* suburban stores. The lessons learned in the inner city have invigorated the company's overall operational intelligence.

THE CAPITAL CRUNCH IN MOVING FORWARD

Despite the early signs of success, Finast's expansion plans stalled shortly after the Westown store's opening in 1987, again for financial reasons. "We came to the realization that the only way to get the company on its feet was to recapitalize it," says Bogomolny. "As brazen as it sounds, we decided to try to buy someone else."

Bogomolny met with a top executive from Ahold, an $18-billion international retailing and wholesaling conglomerate based in Holland, to consider the joint purchase of a third company. Several weeks later, Ahold proposed a new idea entirely— the acquisition of First National by Ahold.

The deal was consummated in 1988 on a four-year, earn-out basis. The chief conditions: Present management would stay in place and Ahold would provide more than $100 million for growth and development over four years. At last Finast had the deep pockets to move beyond experimentation and make inner-city retailing a major business venture.

Over the next eight years Finast spent an estimated $40 million, or about one-third of its Ohio division's capital budget, to renovate existing Cleveland stores or build entirely new ones. The cost of replacing an aging Pick-N-Pay store with a new superstore was between $6 and $7 million. Besides the Westown superstore, the company added four new superstores in inner-city Cleveland, a sixth that is not technically a superstore but still quite large, and two regular supermarkets. Finast closed its last Pick-N-Pays in 1995.

Despite the conventional wisdom of his industry, John Shields was convinced that he could capitalize on a brilliant insight: that urban markets could yield higher profit margins, even with exactly the same prices as suburban stores, because inner-city customers tend to buy more fresh, perishable items that traditionally have higher margins. "Surprisingly," says Shields, "exactly the same prices—higher margins. Higher margins cover higher costs."

For example, African-American and Chicano/Latino customers tend to buy more pork, chicken, fresh fish, smoked meats, grains, rice, prepared foods, and fruits and vegetables than White, suburban customers do. All these items customarily yield higher profit margins. By opening a superstore, moreover, Finast could sell even higher volumes of higher-margin products because as much as 35 percent of superstore sales volume comes from nonfood items such as flowers, health and beauty aids, even books and clothing.

On the other hand, because the size of the average transaction in inner-city supermarkets is lower than that in suburban stores, Finast calculated that achieving comparable profitability would require a traffic volume of 30,000 customers per week instead of the 22,000 customers of a typical suburban supermarket.

THE BIRTH OF THE GARRETT SQUARE SUPERSTORE

To understand the special management commitment and innovations needed to make these superstores operate profitably, it helps to look more closely at one such facility, the Garrett Square Finast superstore in the Glenville area of Cleveland.

Like many urban neighborhoods, Glenville is a low-income area with a predominantly African-American population. For years the unemployment rate in the area has hovered at about twice the national average; up to 40 percent of the population received food stamps, WIC coupons (Women, Infants and Children), AFDC (Aid to Families with Dependent Children), or other government subsidies to buy necessities.

Despite these dismal demographics, Finast's market research plainly indicated that a store was needed and could do brisk business. Less than 30 percent of the population of Glenville owned automobiles, yet the nearest full-service supermarket was eight miles away. Nearby corner grocery stores, meanwhile, were charging the highest food prices in the entire city of Cleveland. Seeing opportunity where others saw only despair, Finast decided to move forward.

Finding a large enough site was the first challenge. While the site of a former bus depot in the middle of Glenville offered 12.5 acres, the city council chair wanted half the land for a new housing development. After consenting to the split, Finast was able to lease the land from its African-American owners. This enabled Finast to channel its equity capital to inventory, not land, while giving Glenville a sense of community ownership.

Before it could proceed, Finast convinced the city to clean up the huge oil puddles left by the bus depot, build new sidewalks, and improve city services in the area. As an "anchor tenant" who would stimulate economic development, Finast also received a city tax abatement and a $1.7-million interest-free construction loan through the Urban Development Action Grant program.

COMMUNITY SUPPORT AS A VITAL BUSINESS RESOURCE

Finast realized that its planned superstore would not succeed if it did not have strong, active support from all segments of the Glenville community. Lynn Harris, the manager of the Garrett Square store, explains: "So many times people here feel like, when they're finished with it in the suburbs—couldn't sell it in the suburbs—they bring it right here to the urban stores and we're just getting garbage."

Developing close ties with the community would be critical, says Bogomolny, to ensure the high customer traffic needed to generate sufficient profits:

Now the only way you can do that is if both you and the neighborhood form some sort of community of interest, where they understand that you need the business to be profitable and continue to operate, but you understand that you have to serve that community very well.

To cultivate this working partnership, Finast hired Henry Edwards, an African-American, as regional vice president of operations-east. (He is now executive vice president of human resources.) Finast managers actively courted church leaders and civic activists and even walked around the neighborhood talking to residents.

It was not just a sales challenge; Finast needed to learn more about community attitudes and needs. "Many of the women and the families in Glenville are determined to improve their lot in life," says William Holsworth, Finast's current Ohio president and CEO. "They found in Finast a way to: one, put some jobs in the community; two, take pride in the fact that their community has a first-class supermarket; and three, find a store that would be responsive to their needs and be a good community citizen."

One way to develop closer bonds of trust was to hire neighborhood residents for the 250 to 300 jobs that needed to be filled in the new superstore, using referrals from local churches and citizens' groups when possible. Although many of the jobs do not pay much more than the minimum wage, Finast also offered a number of higher-paying posts. The company has been conscientious about hiring store managers who understand the ethnic tastes of the local clientele and, in the case of the Garrett Square store, hiring about 80 percent of the employees from the community.

TUXEDOS AND GOWNS AT THE GRAND OPENING

Supermarket openings are usually mundane affairs, but this one, in November 1990, was a milestone in the life of the Glenville community. People arrived at the gala community celebration in tuxedos and formal gowns, ate fancy cakes, and heard ceremonial remarks by Finast executives.

"It was phenomenal," recalls Ernie Burnley, co-manager of the store at the time. "I mean, customers were coming from everywhere. The community was ecstatic." The minister of one church reported that his parishoners were strangely apprehensive, worried that "this would not last—that Finast would come here and find that this is not a good idea."

Finast did, in fact, face some difficult challenges in the first years. Management discovered, for example, that checkout speed was lagging at the Garrett Square Finast because checkers had to serve more customers purchasing fewer items—and those customers generally paid with a cumbersome combination of cash, checks, and food stamps. To boost skills, Finast used special simulation training and also emphasized work attendance records, on the theory that practice makes perfect. Speed increased from sixteen to twenty-two items per minute, rivaling the speed maintained at smoother-flowing suburban checkout lanes.

When some cashiers were caught giving away groceries to their friends, Finast set up video surveillance cameras and asked local church leaders to tell their congregations that the store could not survive such pilferage.

The training costs for a new employee at the Garrett Square store were the same as in suburban stores—between $200 and $300. But Finast's urban stores tend to have an employee turnover rate of between 35 and 40 percent, as against the 20 to 25 percent rate in suburban areas. Workers' compensation claims are also higher. While these higher labor costs probably cannot be entirely eliminated, Shields concedes, they do not negate Finast's "higher-margins-cover-higher-costs" strategy.

NEW CHALLENGES FOR STORE OPERATIONS

Finast met other novel operational challenges with creativity. Traditionally, supermarkets use newspaper supplements as their main form of advertising. But since many Glenville residents do not subscribe to newspapers, Finast relied almost exclusively on mail-delivered circulars.

A more perplexing dilemma was security: How much or

how little should be provided? Finast did not want to make the store seem like an uninviting fortress. But it also did not want potential customers to feel unsafe shopping there. After consulting with community leaders, Finast built an unobtrusive iron fence around the parking lot and hired a security guard in a patrol car. Two or three additional guards patrol inside the store, a force that is sometimes supplemented.

The extra measures cost an average of $12,000 per month, but they are worth it, says manager Lynn Harris: "As word of mouth got around that it's safe, we started to get more and more people who used to go to the suburban stores coming here." According to Shields, urban supermarkets spend, on average, about $2 per square foot of floor space for security measures, while suburban supermarkets might spend only 10 to 50 cents.

An unexpected problem arose when some customers arrived at the checkout stands with more items than they could afford, requiring that the food be set aside and returned to the shelves later. This amounted to a considerable extra labor expense, since as many as thirty carts of surplus food had to be re-shelved each day, a job that often took ten hours. To ease this problem, Finast installed solar-powered calculators on its shopping carts. As customers walk the aisles, they can calculate their bill and avoid putting too many items into their carts. This simple maneuver has saved Finast hundreds of additional work hours per month.

Another unexpected problem was the huge fluctuations in sales volume over the course of a given month, largely because many Glenville customers live from paycheck to paycheck or receive food stamps or welfare checks. When these checks arrive at the same time each month, sales volume soars as much as 40 percent over what it is in other parts of the month. (In the suburbs the peak-to-valley fluctuations rarely exceed 7 percent.) To deal with these surges, Finast routinely brings in extra employees from other locations at these peak times. It also hires extra staff to process food stamps and other federal scrip.

Overall, urban stores appear to be about 1 to 1.5 percent more expensive to operate than suburban stores, according to Henry Edwards. In the "low-margin" supermarket industry, that small difference may represent all the profits. But Finast finds that its focus on greater sales volume and higher sales of high-margin items is working.

Equally critical is sheer persistence. CEO Holsworth emphasizes: "You need to make efforts to understand the uniqueness of the communities, and then you need to stay with it and work very hard and be deliberate and tenacious and say, 'We're going to do this and make it work.' " One special challenge that Finast "needs to get better at," admits Holsworth, is minority management development.

Henry Edwards adds: "We don't claim that we know it all relative to the urban market. We're still learning. But we have been successful because we have been willing to pay the price to learn what those [lessons] are."

Glenville residents are grateful. "Finast has been adventurous and aggressive enough to come in here," says the Reverend Ben Gohlstin. "Many of our pastors have, from their pulpits, made the parishioners aware that Finast gives them a viable alternative to stores that may serve them rotten or outdated produce and that do not have the community at heart."

Many local people regard the Garrett Square Finast as an oasis in Glenville. Shoppers frequently come dressed up in their finest clothes, and socialize in the aisles. Many people come every day, making the store a de facto community center.

Finast's presence in Glenville has instigated, either directly or indirectly, a broader revitalization of the Glenville neighborhood—a new housing development, a Rite-Aid pharmacy, and other small retail stores. The impact is not just economic. Says Cleveland Mayor Michael White: "I think when you look at an enterprise like the Finast operation, it's not only a physical investment, but it's supercharged the whole community."

FINAST'S INNER-CITY INITIATIVE PAYS OFF

In 1996, Finast's eight Cleveland stores were profitable as a group, accounting for about 17 percent of Finast's total sales in forty-five Ohio locations. "The good news about the supermarkets that we opened," says Holsworth, "is they're probably the best year-to-year performers that we have, because they were new in the community. . . . Now they're starting to contribute more and more."

Finast is not the only supermarket chain operating in U.S. inner cities. *The New York Times* counted fifty-eight separate efforts in twenty-five cities in June 1993, and a number of major supermarket chains are expanding in Boston, Chicago, New Orleans, Miami, Atlanta, and other big cities. These efforts may get a push soon from the Local Initiatives Support Corp., a group that plans to channel $24 million from corporate sources to develop a dozen supermarkets in inner-city locations nationwide.

A 1995 report by Public Voice for Food and Health Policy, a consumer advocacy group, found that there continues to be a serious "urban grocery store gap." The singular exception, according to the report, is Cleveland. It is the only major American metropolitan area in which there are more supermarkets in poorer neighborhoods than in richer areas. A leading expert on inner-city food retailing, Donald Marion of the University of Massachusetts at Amherst, salutes Finast for its early and deep commitment. Unlike other forays into the urban center, Finast's move was "not experimentation, but large-scale," says Marion. "Finast made a gutsy move. It was rather courageous. The inner city is still a risky place to be."

Cleveland Mayor White, for one, is appreciative:

> Finast understood, first of all, that it was a good business decision, and that they could make money, which is fine with me. And secondly that a good business decision was also the right thing for the community. So you have the best of both worlds. I think that what they have done is really a model for other corporations who are wondering whether or not they should be investing in the inner cities of America.

6

Rachel Hubka and Rachel's Bus Company

THE LITTLE SCHOOL BUS COMPANY THAT COULD

The street is residential, and to all outward appearances abandoned. Sidewalks are cracked, lawns overgrown, windows
boarded, brickwork crumbling. Block after block reveals a neighborhood that has fallen so deeply into neglect that it seems to
have given up hope.

Yet on one street, a brand-new school bus is pulling into a
busy garage, greeted by the clamor of a bustling business. Dozens of buses are lined up to be washed, while others are being
backed into the repair bay for maintenance. In the main office,
phones ring, microphones crackle, and employees prepare for a
frenetic business day.

In a neighborhood where most legitimate business consists
of fast-food franchises and a few struggling storefronts, Rachel's
Bus Company is an oasis. Rachel's boasts $4.5 million in annual
revenues, twenty-three full-time staff, and 140 part-time bus
drivers. Its modern, sparkling fleet of yellow buses is an incon-
gruous element on the bleak, empty streets. Yet the logic of this
enterprise, and its location, comes sharply into focus when you
meet the company's founder and namesake.

A SELF-RELIANT WOMAN CREATES HER OWN OPPORTUNITIES

Rachel Hubka, at first glance, defies one's expectations of what
an owner of a gritty business in inner-city Chicago will be. A

native of Mablevale, Arkansas, Hubka grew up on a farm as the youngest daughter in a family of thirteen children. Her father was a Nazarene evangelist who built churches, her mother a schoolteacher. The family raised cattle and vegetables, producing most of their own food, and instilled a powerful belief in self-reliance.

"I learned from my parents early on," says Hubka, "especially from my mother, who wouldn't let me say I couldn't do anything. She'd say that was ridiculous. 'You can, and this is how you can do it.' "

After graduating from high school, Hubka spent a year at Arkansas State Teachers College, then moved to Chicago to look for a job. True to her mother's convictions, she quickly began to create her own opportunities, holding her first supervisory position at age 18. Initially hired as a typist for a Muscular Dystrophy Association fund drive, within a month she was mapping the entire campaign for the city of Chicago and directing a pool of twenty-five typists.

Hubka married, started a family, and eventually divorced. For many years her work options were dictated by the demands of raising three young children, yet she continued to make the most of each position she held. Hubka took a part-time job as a clerk at a dry-cleaning establishment because it was close to her home; soon she was the store's manager. She became a telephone solicitor for a driving school, and again ended up managing the entire office.

When Rachel Hubka joined Stewart Bus Company as a dispatcher in 1978, she won the office supervisor job within three weeks. In eighteen months she became its general manager. For the next eight years, Hubka supervised almost every facet of the company's operations. She was responsible for complex routing systems, hiring and training drivers, and developing safety programs. By the mid-1980s, she had become an expert in the specialized field of school bus company operations, and Stewart Bus Company had grown from a fleet of sixty buses at the time of her arrival to more than 400 in 1987.

Then the owners of Stewart Bus Company decided to get out of the business of operating school buses. Their fleet became available for lease to a new company, and Hubka began to contemplate striking out on her own. Throughout her rise at Stewart, Hubka had launched a variety of innovative programs that had helped to fuel the company's success. She had begun a formal training program for new drivers, and hired an instructor to teach defensive driving skills. She had helped devise a new routing system, which was ultimately adopted by the entire Chicago school system. She had instituted the practice of assigning a "lead driver" to work full-time at each school, another practice embraced by the school system. She had envisioned even more experimental ways to run a bus company, which her employers had not felt comfortable implementing. She was determined to put them to the test.

Even more important, Rachel Hubka had always held entrepreneurial dreams. "I had wanted to be in a business of my own since I was about seventeen years old," Hubka recalls. "I had never really wanted to work for anyone else." The school bus business was a business she knew well, and when the opportunity presented itself, she was determined to seize it. But knowing the school bus business meant that she knew the extraordinary challenges she would face.

THE COMPLEX BUSINESS OF SCHOOL TRANSPORTATION

School transportation is a highly competitive, multi billion-dollar industry in the United States, serving twenty-three million children annually. In Chicago alone, fifty providers vie for contracts with the public school system. On top of this intense competition, school bus companies must cope with myriad difficulties unique to the business of transporting children.

School bus driving was once largely the province of homemakers who appreciated the part-time, odd hours that allowed them time for their homemaking and child-rearing responsibilities during the day. Gradually, though, with social and economic shifts in the nation's work force, that labor pool evaporated. More part-time opportunities became available in the service and retail sectors, and more women with children began to seek full-time work.

For school bus companies, the result was the disappearance

of a steady source of reliable drivers. Male blue-collar workers displaced by factory closings picked up the slack for a time, but they often proved transitory substitutes, always looking for better, full-time positions.

This shrinking labor pool was also subject to new regulatory pressures. National, state, and local governments began to require special training and certification for the drivers who would be responsible for the safety of so many children. One formidable obstacle was the requirement that school bus drivers hold Class A commercial licenses, which also qualifies them for more lucrative, full-time trucking jobs. Further screening requirements followed. To become a school bus driver in the State of Illinois today, an applicant must pass three exams, have an absolutely clean criminal record, and go through fingerprinting and frequent drug screening—all for a part-time job.

Operators themselves also face strict requirements. School bus safety is closely tracked and regulated, and insurance costs can be astronomical. The upshot of all these pressures is ever-rising overhead, tightening margins, and a constant battle to recruit qualified drivers. This was the market Hubka chose to enter—and she had ideas on how to make it work.

LAYING THE GROUNDWORK FOR AN INNER-CITY BUSINESS

Because she had a track record with a major carrier, Hubka was able to build a solid foundation. Contacts within the school system knew her capabilities and respected her, and Stewart's owners had introduced her to their banks and insurers. Even leveraging this experience and reputation, though, she found financing a major hurdle. "At the time I started," Hubka recalls, "there was very little interest in dealing with women in businesses that were just trying to get started." To obtain bank financing, she had to take a lien on her own home. "It took everything but my firstborn," she says.

With financing obtained, Hubka's next hurdle was to find an appropriate location for the new "Rachel's Bus Company." She needed an immense garage, modest office space, and fuel pumps—all in a location with easy access to city expressways. She also faced the perpetual challenge of recruiting and retaining drivers.

Hubka decided to address all these needs simultaneously by targeting one of Chicago's most depressed neighborhoods, North Lawndale. In this neglected area, she saw an untapped labor pool of potential bus drivers. She also believed that Rachel's Bus Company had a chance to help people whom other employers had forgotten.

Hubka chose North Lawndale specifically because of its high unemployment. Once a solid working-class neighborhood, North Lawndale had been home to the Sears, Roebuck world headquarters prior to the construction of the Sears Tower. As Sears and other major employers moved out, however, many longtime residents followed, leaving desolation behind.

In 1994 the median household income in North Lawndale was $12,570. Only 37 percent of residents were employed; 49 percent lived below the poverty level, including 73 percent of children under age 5. Of the 50,000 area residents, 96 percent were African-American.

"I wanted to give the inner city people an opportunity to come in and work, where they may not have had opportunities in the past," Hubka says. "I knew I had a training program to offer for men and women who hadn't had an opportunity to get the kind of training they need to get an income. . . . The people here are interested in working. They need work. And I need employees."

Hubka's approach was risky. Her company, her livelihood, even her home would be riding on a lot of people with marginal employment histories. To make it work, she would not only have to recruit workers but also to foster a professional attitude among people who had never before held "responsible" positions.

TRAINING, PRIDE, PROFESSIONALISM

In 1989, Hubka bid for work with the Chicago Board of Education, and was awarded a contract. With only two months remaining before the start of the school year, she needed to recruit a reliable pool of fifty drivers. As Hubka had hoped, by plastering her inner-city location with "Drivers Wanted" signs, she did attract a number of new applicants who had not previously considered school bus driving. But the location also brought a new set of problems.

Despite the high unemployment in North Lawndale, the neighborhood did not yield enough qualified applicants to fill all the available driver slots. The deep troubles in the area, particularly the prevalence of drugs, meant that many local residents could not meet the strict regulatory criteria for school bus drivers. Moreover, the high crime rate made some potential drivers wary of walking to the bus company, even from nearby homes or bus stops.

One of Hubka's solutions was to set up a shuttle bus system to transport drivers from public transportation stops. Drivers from anywhere in the city can be shuttled directly to Rachel's without having to walk or drive alone through any neighborhood in which they do not feel comfortable. The broader, long-range solution, however, was a thorough and thoughtful recruitment and training program.

Rachel's Bus Company offers drivers with no experience a comprehensive, free training program that guides them through the entire screening and licensing process. In addition to providing training in defensive driving and school bus certification, the training process at Rachel's orients new employees to the company's strict work culture of pride and professionalism.

This culture is demonstrated in many ways, large and small. Buses are kept impeccably clean. Drivers must carry route clipboards and wear ID badges that help identify them as representatives of the company. Each also must adhere to the dress code of white shirt, dress slacks, and tie, a very unusual requirement in the school bus industry.

Hubka and others in the company stress that the dress code is more than an arbitrary or cosmetic requirement. It is a significant step toward establishing the bus drivers—both to themselves and to their customers—as reliable professionals worthy of repeat business. For those drivers who embrace the requirements and maintain a positive, professional attitude, Hubka has created opportunities to build their part-time driving jobs into full-time careers.

TEACHING EMPLOYEES TO BECOME ENTREPRENEURS

"The reason I feel that the employees like working at Rachel's Bus Company," Hubka says, "is that I try to teach them how to become entrepreneurs within the workplace." For drivers, that means a charter incentive program that encourages them to bring in their own business. If a driver draws in a new, first-time customer, the driver receives a commission of 10 percent of the revenue for the first trip, which could consist of one bus or a dozen buses. The driver also has first choice at being assigned to that customer's initial and subsequent trips, for additional driving revenue.

All drivers who qualify to drive charter routes are given personalized business cards to distribute to current and potential customers. Whenever they drive a charter trip, they can leave their card and ask the client to request them for future trips. A driver who impresses customers can build up his or her own clientele to ensure a steady income. "We tell the drivers," says charter manager Carolyn Braggs, " 'Make sure when you go out and drive a trip, you leave your card. Because if you do a good job, people are going to call back.' "

Hubka, too, emphasizes this aspect of the driving job:

> A lot of our drivers that have bought into the program are really making incomes at Rachel's Bus Company that would equal what they could make full-time anywhere else. . . . They learn that through proper dress and proper behavior, they are seeing a lot more money on the bottom line. And that's what we are all about. Seeing a lot more money on the bottom line.

Yet as driver Napoleon Moore notes, money isn't all that is at stake. "I know if I was chartering a bus," says Moore, "I would like to see a bus driver looking professional, acting professional. . . . I feel that I bring to the industry a person that's a caring person, a professional person, a safe driver. I say something to the industry, that school bus drivers are professional people."

This attitude is appreciated by the clients Rachel's Bus Company serves. Dr. Corla Wilson-Hawkins, a Chicago educator, the founder of the Recovering the Gifted Child program, and one of Hubka's loyal customers, says:

> The reason I like the drivers at Rachel's is the continuity of their spirit. I don't have to pick a particular driver, and I don't have to say, "Carolyn, I want this or I want that." Any driver that I get from Rachel's, I can depend on them to be very courteous. Very nice to my children. Very respectful. Hold a basic conversation with the children.

> I am really proud of the fact that they realize . . . that on the bus are thirty or forty or sixty future leaders of their tomorrow, and they are all in their hands. . . . So that is really powerful to realize that it is not a demeaning job. It's not just, "I'm a bus driver," but "I'm a bus driver with pride, because I got *all* of your future in the palm of my hand while I got this motor running."

THE REAL GROWTH OPPORTUNITIES: CHARTER BUS TRIPS

The bus drivers' pride and professionalism is their route to full-time hours, but it is also the company's route to growth and stability. While Rachel's Bus Company has steadily increased its volume of contracts with the public schools, it is Hubka's stated goal to build the charter business to 50 percent of the company's total revenues. The tightly constrained economics of school transportation make this an imperative. Public-school contracts in Chicago are centralized, awarded for two-year periods on the basis of competitive bidding with the Board of Education. Thus, even the highest-quality operators have limited control over the growth of their basic school business from term to term.

Dr. Robert L. Johnson, who served as assistant superintendent of schools and director of transportation for the Chicago Board of Education from 1989 to 1995, explains:

Schools have no real choice of provider for their basic A.M.–
P.M. service. The providers are assigned by the Board based
primarily on geography. But for midday service—field trips
and the like—it's open season. So some companies, because
they develop a reputation for courteous, responsible, well-
trained drivers and clean, well-maintained buses, that
makes a school say, "This is a company that I want to hire
to transport my children."

"You can only get those extra routes, those full-time opportunities," Johnson continues, "if you've developed a great reputation. Rachel is able to provide that for her employees because
her training and reputation are so good. It makes for lots of extra
business."

GIVING EMPLOYEES THE CHANCE TO GROW—AND LEAVE

The standards Rachel Hubka sets are high, and her rules can be
tough, but they are combined with a candid, fair-minded management style. "I've had employees leave here and go to other
companies," says Hubka. "The majority of them come back in a
very short period of time and say, 'Would you please let me
come back? I really didn't enjoy working at another company.
And I really like the structure here.' "

Hubka's door is always open, to her office and garage staff
and to her more than one hundred drivers. "If you have a problem," says Napoleon Moore, "you can always go in and talk to
Rachel. You don't have to go through this chain of command to
get to her. You can go in and talk to her, and she will listen to
you. Not that you're going to win all the time, but she'll give
you the time to sit down and talk. And if there is a problem, she
will try to work on it and come to a satisfactory conclusion."

Joanne Ivory, safety director for Rachel's Bus Company,
echoes Moore:

> If there's a question or a problem or concern, we can sit
> down and discuss it. She's open to other ideas. I think that
> she learned how to be a good boss from years of working in
> the work force herself in other positions, and interacting

with the other employees. You know, you tend to say, "Well, when I own my own business, I'm not going to do this, I'm not going to do that." I think that she took all of those ideas and she took them to heart.

One hallmark of Hubka's approach has been to stay on the lookout for skills that employees have which they might be able to utilize in some capacity at Rachel's Bus Company. One driver with carpentry skills was hired to build partitions for the office; another driver who was picking up extra income by fixing co-workers' cars was offered supplemental work in the maintenance shop.

For employees who show drive and talent, Hubka offers them opportunities to expand their skills and their responsibilities. "For instance," says Hubka, "I have employees that may have come from a factory background, and have come into our office and fit in very nicely. They have been able to do work. They've been able to move up and really perform at much greater levels than I think they might have expected they could do."

Ladell Johnson is one such person. For seven years before joining Rachel's Bus Company she had held a factory line job. "I worked for Borden's Food in Northbrook," Johnson recalls. "I was a machine operator. I made Soup Starter cans."

Yet Hubka was impressed when she interviewed Johnson for an office position. Johnson began as an administrative assistant, but was soon promoted to personnel supervisor. Then, just eighteen months after arriving at Rachel's with no personnel experience, Johnson became personnel manager for the entire company.

Rachel Hubka calls Johnson "the best person I've had in that position, anywhere, anytime. . . . She knows how to relate to the drivers, to make them feel very good about Rachel's Bus Company, about being here. And she can go to a meeting and represent our company with the chairman of the Board."

"It was a big challenge," Johnson says of her promotion. "I think [Rachel] has given me a chance to grow. She has exposed me to a lot of things that I wouldn't have gotten exposed to if I hadn't been here."

Joanne Ivory originally joined Rachel's Bus Company as a field supervisor (the head of a driver team). But she had previously managed a body shop, and when Hubka became aware of Ivory's skills and knowledge, she quickly offered her a more responsible position.

"I stayed at the job for maybe a month in the position that I actually applied for. And then from there I was promoted three different times," Ivory recalls. As safety director, Ivory is now responsible for driver training, safety incentive programs, accident reporting, and insurance adjusting. "Rachel definitely gave me an opportunity, personally. She took a lot of interest in it. She did something that very few company owners do, and that is she actually took the time and read through my résumé. A lot of companies take it and gloss over it. She checked all of my references. She gave me an opportunity."

A TEACHING ENVIRONMENT, AN INCUBATOR FOR ENTREPRENEURS

For some ambitious employees, Rachel Hubka has done more than help them advance: She has actually helped them leave. "I wanted my own company," Hubka explains, "and I think if someone has that attitude and that desire, they should have the same opportunity. In fact, I've let them use this company to learn the things that they needed to know about the school bus industry."

Wallace Johnson, a former general manager with Rachel's Bus Company, had developed custom computer programs to fit its specialized scheduling and accounting needs. Johnson hoped to start his own consulting firm to market such software to other small businesses, and Hubka not only supported his decision but helped him through the complex process of becoming certified as a Minority Business Enterprise by the city of Chicago. Once Johnson began his own operations, Rachel's Bus Company became his first client.

Another former Rachel's employee, Charles Hardy, was exceptionally motivated from the moment he joined the company. When Hubka first leased the garage for Rachel's Bus Company,

Hardy, the newly hired terminal manager, "came in his dunga-
rees and his sweatshirt and helped scrub the floors, because they
were thick with grease and sawdust. . . . They actually cleaned
this place down so it was fit to work in," Hubka recalls.

Hubka knew that Hardy had always dreamed of owning his
own company, and she wanted him to have that chance. "An
opportunity came up for a new company to start as a school bus
company, and I was asked if I could recommend anyone who
had the background and experience to run an operation if they
were given an opportunity. And I recommended Chuck Hardy."
Hardy is now the owner and president of Hardy Bus Company,
which specializes in the transportation of special-needs students. As in the case of Wallace Johnson, Hardy's first contract
was with Rachel's Bus Company.

Hardy has credited the "teaching environment" that Hubka
creates with helping him develop the skills he would need as an
independent businessperson. "Rachel's been in the business for
a long time," he says. "She gave me a lot of insight on things,
and things that she told me—they panned out later. And that's
what really gave me the belief that I could be successful in this
business." Hardy now strives to emulate Hubka's empowering
management style in running his own company.

Hubka sums up her entrepreneurial and empowering philosophy:

> I've known for many years that you can't depend on a com-
> pany to provide income for you, you have to depend on
> yourself. So if you have to depend on yourself, there is a
> point in time that you need to start doing that. And if your
> dream is to own your own company, then that is what you
> should try to do.
>
> Where I have employees here that I see have potential, if
> they are not interested in their own company but they are
> interested in moving on or having an opportunity to work
> in a different department, we try and give them that oppor-
> tunity to see if they can excel somewhere else.

"I think she is a very good role model," says Ladell Johnson.
"She gives me aspirations that *I* can do something, too. Because

she worked—like she'll tell you all the time—she started just like I did, and worked her way up. If she can do that, I can too."

THE SHARED FRUITS OF PROSPERITY

Rachel's Bus Company has given fresh starts and real opportunities to dozens of people whom most businesses would prefer to ignore. It has also offered a glimpse of hope to an entire neighborhood.

"[Rachel's] provides a sense of stability for the neighborhood," says Joanne Ivory. "It is thriving economically. The neighborhood needs this so that other businesses will see that, since she has been here for six years, that businesses can come into the neighborhood and thrive and prosper."

Hubka herself puts her motives in simple terms. "I am doing this business," she says, "running a school bus business, very simply because it is a business I know. It gives me an opportunity to help other people.

"I am very proud of what I have done," Hubka admits. "I have a marvelous staff that has come in and worked with me and shown me a lot of loyalty. That gives me a lot of gratitude and a lot of pride."

7

Lou Krouse and the National Payments Network

A CREATIVE ALTERNATIVE FOR THE "UNBANKED"

Call him Jim Foster, a New Yorker whose household income, including that of his wife, Edith, is only $9,200. Because the Fosters do not have a checking account, Jim spends an entire day each month paying the household bills. When the welfare check arrives, Foster leaves his small apartment on 178th Street and goes to a check-cashing outlet, where he pays a fee of 2 percent or more of the check's face value—at least $7—to get cash. It is a long wait, because everyone's welfare checks come at the same time.

Then for $3.00 round trip, Foster hops on a bus to 125th Street, where Con Edison and the New York Telephone Company both have in-person payment centers. Again . . . long lines. To pay three additional monthly bills that cannot be paid in person, Foster buys stamps at the post office to send money orders that he bought for $2 apiece from the check casher.

By a rough calculation, the Foster household spends nearly $17 a month, or $202 a year, to pay routine bills—plus $36 in bus fare and twelve days of errand running.

For most Americans, the convenience of checkbooks and credit cards is a fact of life, something taken for granted. But for nearly one in five American households—or more than thirty million Americans—banks might as well be on Jupiter. For the vast population of "unbanked," cash is king. Checking accounts are just too expensive, impractical, culturally alien, or unavailable.

The denizens of the cash economy, chiefly the poor, the elderly, and indigent blue-collar workers, would hardly seem to be a promising clientele for a new business. Except to Lou Krouse, a resourceful man who saw a rich business opportunity where everyone else saw only dismal demographics.

Telling tales of his midlife passage into entrepreneurialism from a staid corporate bureaucracy, Krouse radiates a boyish enthusiasm. With gleeful hyperbole, he tells tales of "jumping onto tables" when pitching his business and of tense encounters with roomsful of check-cashing agents wearing pistols strapped to their ankles. It seems weirdly logical that this man would risk his life savings and incur massive credit card debt in order to found a new financial services enterprise dedicated to the downscale consumer.

By the time he was through, his company, National Payments Network, was handling over 3.5 million transactions per month via terminals in nearly 3,000 retail locations, serving twenty-six utilities in nineteen states. Company revenues exceeded $26 million in 1989, enticing Western Union to acquire the company for nearly $30 million: a rich reward for creating a new market niche that serves an important social need.

THE GOUGING OF LOW-INCOME CONSUMERS

Serendipity planted the seeds of the National Payments Network in 1982, when New York Telephone assigned Lou Krouse, then a forty-one-year-old internal systems troubleshooter, to find out why the company was having such difficulty getting low-income customers to pay their bills on time. Could anything be done?

Krouse quickly discovered that the real problem was not so much utility bill paying as the scarcity of the most basic financial services for low-income households. At the time, the U.S. General Accounting Office (GAO), the investigative arm of Congress, estimated that more than 17 percent of all U.S. households did not have checking accounts, a number that has remained fairly constant since then. Among low-income households, more than 58 percent did not have checking accounts in 1989, according to a survey conducted by the Consumer Federation of America (CFA).

Krouse quickly realized the implications of these statistics:

> Figure that you're living hand-to-mouth. Friday, you get a paycheck. What do you do with the paycheck? The bank's closed. You have to feed the kids today. You need cash. So you go to the check casher—and often pay an exorbitant fee.

Bills get paid on the last possible day through personal visits to public payment centers, where long lines are common.

In depressed inner-city neighborhoods, heavy-security storefronts that cash checks and sell money orders are the poor person's alternative to conventional banking. The starkly lit, linoleum-tiled outlets are usually mobbed on paydays and at the end of the month, when Social Security and public assistance checks arrive.

What may look like a small-time operation is in fact big business. In 1990, some 4,500 check-cashing enterprises nationwide issued 150 million checks worth $45 billion. Their annual income: $800 million.

In competitive areas like New York City, check-cashing fees can be as low as 1 or 2 percent, but in states like California check cashers may charge as much as 10 percent of a check's value. Fees of 3 to 6 percent are the norm, according to the CFA survey, which means that a $500 Social Security check is cashed for a fee of $15 to $30. Despite recurrent reports of fee gouging, there is no federal regulation of check-cashing fees. Only four states have set maximum fees, on the order of 1 to $1^1/2$ percent, but spot checks have found that these caps are frequently violated with impunity.

For poor people consigned to the cash economy, the cumulative premium paid to conduct routine bill paying can be significant. According to the CFA survey, a worker who cashes fifty $320 payroll checks a year and buys six money orders a month spends between $272 and $518 a year—a substantial sum for families earning less than $20,000 a year, who constitute an esti-

mated 83 percent of the unbanked. (Some 57 percent of the unbanked have household incomes of less than $10,000.) New
Yorkers alone pay about $100 million in fees to check-cashing
outlets, or about $2 million per week.

WHY THE POOR DON'T OPEN CHECKING ACCOUNTS

Why don't more low-income consumers open checking accounts, given their clear cost advantages? There is no simple answer. Certainly minimum balance requirements and monthly
service fees discourage many people, despite the indisputable
long-term savings of checking accounts over check cashers.

But that is just the point: People living on the edge of desti-
tution often have trouble planning for the long term. Their lives
and incomes are usually too volatile to permit them either to
maintain a $250 minimum checking balance or to afford
monthly checking fees.

The issue goes beyond affordability, however. Many elderly
persons who lived through the Great Depression remain suspi-
cious of banks. Some aliens and immigrants prefer to avoid en-
tanglements with officialdom. And the poorly educated may feel
intimidated by banks.

Consumer groups and bankers, each marshaling their own
survey data and interpretations, sharply disagree about the se-
verity of banking problems for low-income people. For years the
two sides have been at loggerheads over legislation that would
require federally chartered banks to offer "lifeline banking"
(low-cost basic accounts) and to cash U.S. Treasury checks for
free.

Whatever its merits, lifeline banking would not necessarily
help millions of low-income consumers living in poorer neighborhoods, from which banks, pinched by the cost-cutting pressures of deregulation, have fled—or decline to enter. In the late
1980s, certain banks in New York City refused to open checking
accounts for people who did not live or work within ten blocks
of the branch, making it particularly onerous for low-income
minority consumers to open checking accounts.

LOU KROUSE'S CREATIVE ALTERNATIVE

As Lou Krouse contemplated the banking problems of the low-income consumer—and how they affected New York Telephone's ability to collect on its bills—he saw the glimmer of a solution: *Why not build an electronic funds transfer (EFT) network that would link up customers, utilities, and neighborhood stores?*

Customers could pay their bills in cash at a nearby mom-and-pop deli; New York Telephone would get customer payments within two days; and the stores would reap a modest transaction fee and increase customer traffic. The system had the added advantage of being free to customers, a feature that public utility commissions would almost certainly have demanded.

In the scenario Krouse envisioned, which he later implemented, a retail clerk collects payment from a customer and punches the data into a special point-of-sale terminal. The customer's phone bill is stamped, becoming a receipt for payment, and the terminal's payment data are sent to a central computer every day. Under this system, a customer's utility account was usually credited within forty-eight hours, instead of a week or more. For low-income people, who often pay when service cut-offs are imminent, this rapid crediting of accounts can be particularly important.

The EFT system for bill collection also enabled banks to stop serving as collection agents for utilities, a role that state regulators had pressured them to accept. Banks estimated that it cost them between 65 cents and $1.20 to process each utility payment, a sum that often exceeded the fees paid them by utilities; meanwhile, the costs of their teller services were soaring. Not surprisingly, several major New York City banks informed utilities in the mid-1980s that they would no longer serve as collection agents.

New York Telephone was bristling at the rising operating costs of its own in-person payment centers. Some 7.2 million payments were made in person each year, at a cost of $1.21 apiece—versus 34 cents for a mail payment. To the utility's disappointment, a remarkable 30 percent of its customers preferred to pay their bills in person in 1983—and a whopping 46 percent in downstate New York. Nationwide, approximately 30 million

Bell System customers were paying in person each month (a number that excludes customers of independent telephone companies).

Curiously, numerous attempts to persuade these people to mail their payments had failed. Even when one utility, as a test, gave customers a stamped envelope with which to pay their bills, most continued to pay in person. Krouse's EFT system, however, promised to change the unshakable habits of a significant market segment, saving money for everyone in the process.

THE TEST OF AN ELEGANT IDEA

Krouse formally proposed his idea to New York Telephone's marketing operations in a February 1982 memorandum, and was soon authorized to launch a pilot project. By October 1983, several supermarkets in and around Albany, New York, were collecting utility bill payments with special EFT terminals.

The system worked exactly as predicted. A Monday payment was credited to the utility's bank account by Wednesday, and the customer's account was credited within a day. Utility customers who had never been comfortable going to starchy banks in the first place were only too happy to pay their bills at the courtesy desk of the supermarket. And banks were just as happy to redirect nonbanking customers elsewhere.

Marketing of the new system was virtually nil. Krouse describes how it worked:

> We put up small posters that said, "Pay your telephone bills here." That's all we did! That's why I saw such opportunity. If we could get 1.2 million people [who paid face-to-face] in one state to change their habit of doing a financial transaction by doing nothing except telling them to go from here to there—imagine what you could do if you promoted it!

"We estimated that we saved about $13 million in 1985," says Krouse. Payments were credited to the utility within two days instead of four. Labor costs associated with processing paper bills and checks were slashed. Deadbeats who under the old system could delay service cutoffs for six weeks—through excuses claiming "I had no warning" and "the check's in the mail"—could be cut off within a day. And customers who had actually paid would not be mistakenly terminated.

The company saved hundreds of thousands of dollars by avoiding the cost of thousands of dunning calls, the mailing of suspension of service notices, and the execution of more than 1,000 erroneous service cutoffs and subsequent reconnections each month.

Buoyed by the initial success of the project, Krouse had an even grander idea. Why not have New York Telephone develop the EFT network as a freestanding business venture? Utilities could pool their in-person payments systems through a non-profit "utilities cooperative."

Or better yet, an array of consumer financial services for a mass market could be offered through a new national EFT network; New York Telephone would make money from the call volume moving over its "electronic railroad," which could host a range of financial data transactions and services. The potential of a national market, Krouse breathlessly predicted to his boss, "is incalculable."

The marketing administrator to whom the memo was addressed scrawled on Krouse's memo, "Great idea. After EFTs, it's the idea of the decade."

But despite her backing, nothing came of Krouse's proposal, even after he went around his boss to pitch the idea to the NYNEX director of marketing. "I gave the presentation, and I was very animated—and the guy was near falling asleep. . . . That's when I went—ugghhh!—like a bagpipe with the top off," says a dejected Krouse, slumping into his chair. "That's when I decided I was going to do this myself."

At a party honoring Krouse for twenty-five years of service to the company, he impulsively announced that he would not be returning to work the following day—or ever. The revelers roared with laughter. But Krouse was serious.

THE RISKY BEGINNINGS OF NPN

Krouse never did return to New York Telephone. In June 1986, Krouse formally began National Payments Network as a partnership. A neighbor who was an attorney, Mark Perlberg, became his general counsel and minority shareholder. David Dorlen, a manager who had been through several company start-ups, became executive vice president of operations.

One of Krouse's first challenges was to find a vendor to conduct money-transfer and banking functions. He turned to Goldome Bank FSB, a Buffalo-based bank that was then the largest mutual savings bank and the eighth-largest thrift in the country. Goldome's wholly owned subsidiary, Datek-InstaCard, had worked with Krouse and New York Telephone in developing the pilot bill-paying project. Its automatic teller machine (ATM) network, Instabank, was the largest in the state, and its executives were eager to expand.

The partnership seemed ideal. Krouse, an expert in the utility business, could secure contracts with utilities and build a network of retail collection agents. Goldome would take care of the back-room accounting, auditing, and cash management services, and serve as a relatively passive partner in the business.

What was still missing from the business, however, was sufficient capital financing. When the venture capital he found proved too expensive or was fraught with unacceptable terms, Krouse ran up $40,000 in cash advances on several personal credit cards while desperately trying to sign up the first utility. Six months after launching the business, bankruptcy loomed only weeks away.

Then, with storybook timing, New England Telephone agreed to take a chance on Krouse's idea. A five-year contract for $24 million gave National Payments Network its first real momentum. By using EFT payments, New England Telephone estimated that the utility saved about 2 cents per transaction, or about $3 million, over the old collection system.

NPN's CRACK SALES TEAM: MORMON COLLEGE STUDENTS

Apart from gaining new contracts, perhaps NPN's biggest challenge was to assemble a new network of collection outlets and to automate existing ones. This was no mean feat, considering the sales turf: low-income, sometimes dangerous neighborhoods where English was often not spoken. "You go to a place like Bayonne, New Jersey, it's all Portuguese," Krouse sighs. "What do you do?"

Here again, Krouse and his operations chief, David Dorlen, hit upon an imaginative solution. They recruited dozens of recent graduates of Brigham Young University—an alert, clean-cut, self-confident crew. "I used to brag that I had the largest percentage of Eagle Scouts of any company in the United States," Dorlen chuckles.

"The Mormon kids all do missionary work for two years or more," explains Krouse. "They've been selling Bibles in Costa Rica, so they're used to rejection. They all speak at least one or two languages, sometimes more. You could just switch them around to different neighborhoods, and they loved it." Salespeople earned a starting salary of about $20,000 plus commission and relocation costs.

NPN set up two condominiums in Boston where the new recruits could get settled and trained. As they gained experience, they were reassigned to line up collection outlets for Bell of Pennsylvania, the Bell Atlantic telephone companies, GTE in California, and others. Eventually the company had a sales force of seventy-five.

For young salesmen like Michael Merchant, the entrepreneurial atmosphere provided an unparalleled career opportunity. Assigned to recruit 350 new collection agents for GTE in California, Merchant exclaims, "I had more than forty people reporting to me, and I was only three or four years out of college!"

There were unexpected problems, however. A gift shop owner on the Upper East Side of Manhattan pleaded for the opportunity to be a collection outlet, only to find herself victimized by uncontrollable pilferage as dozens of utility customers coursed through her small store. Some outlets complained of money-transfer snafus and inadequate technical support from NPN. Some dissatisfied outlets for New England Telephone quit. A spokesman for Hannaford's, a Maine supermarket chain that served as an NPN outlet, tersely explained, "Our experience could've been better."

But there were also many true believers. Sue Cole, who managed the NPN franchise at Shaw's, a New England supermarket chain, exclaimed that the NPN system was "absolutely fantastic" and "virtually trouble-free." At each of Shaw's sixty-eight stores in four states, utility customers were paying roughly 250 bills a day, or a total of 17,000 payments, according to Cole.

Enough utilities saw the merits of the NPN alternative so that by 1989 the company had contracts with twenty-six utilities in nineteen states, using more than 3,000 outlets. The sum being collected, more than $3.5 billion, represented nearly 7 percent of the $57 billion paid nationwide by utility customers each year.

THE DISASTROUS BACK-ROOM SNAFUS

For a start-up venture, NPN's rapid growth had been remarkable. But the entrepreneur's road to success is rarely a smooth one, and the building of NPN was no exception. Two years into the business, in 1988, Lou Krouse got a quick education on how his partner, Goldome, had been performing.

Krouse remembers the day, June 6. "We got a call from Datek-InstaCard. They said, 'Gee, we've got a couple of agents we've got a problem with. One agent owes us about $240,000.' And we went, 'Huh?!' They said, 'Well, we haven't debited them for several months.' " Later, operations chief Dorlen received a phone call from an NPN agent, the owner of a California stationery store, who innocently informed him that $360,000 had been parked in her bank account for four months. "Don't you want your money?" she asked.

While Krouse had been aggressively enlisting new clients and collection agents, the back-office operations run by Goldome were apparently in a shambles. The accounts of collection agents were not being cleared on a daily basis, according to several sources. For many agents, the temptation of idle cash evidently proved too great. "The funny thing is," Krouse says, "they didn't all abscond with the money. They either put it in the wrong bank account, in their own bank account, or they didn't put it in any bank account."

Krouse once sent an NPN salesman to locate funds supposedly being collected by a small food outlet near the Boston harbor. "This agent had never put the money in the bank, ever, and he had been an agent for about a year!" Krouse recalls. It turned out that the shopkeeper had put the money—$100,000—in a box in the back room. Krouse now estimates that "a good 25 percent of the agents had problems. Big problems."

In Massachusetts, as many as forty agents would send their daily collections, totaling several hundred thousand dollars, into "concentration accounts." According to one knowledgeable utility official, one such account had accumulated $1.5 million, yet Goldome had never wired the money out. In another case, an NPN outlet serving telephone company employees had sent $120,000 in utility payments to the wrong bank account, an error that went undetected until reported by the utility itself.

One reason that the mounting collection deficits went undetected and uncorrected for so long, says Krouse, is that Datek-InstaCard had obtained a line of credit from an outside bank to cover its growing deficits. The interest on the loans was then charged to NPN as an undisclosed operational expense, disguising the money transfer and auditing problems.

With their attention focused on signing up new utilities and collection agents, Krouse and his associates believed that the mounting operating expenses were due to the soaring volume of money coursing through the system, and to attendant check-clearing problems. When Goldome's financial troubles in its other banking venues intensified in 1988, however, Datek-InstaCard's lines of credit dried up, precipitating the June 6, 1988, call to Krouse. The money transfer screwups could no longer be hidden.

The root problem, Krouse later said, was Goldome's unwillingness to spend money to upgrade the Datek money-transfer system and give it keen management attention. "We were moving $3.5 billion a year through that little ATM network. It was blowing them out of the water. . . . This little network in Buffalo had to access every one of a couple of thousand of [agent] bank accounts every day—and mobilize the money. It couldn't do it. So they'd start to slip. It'd be every two days, then four days. It came to a point where there were many bank accounts that weren't debited for thirty days!"

Goldome has since gone out of business, making it difficult to reconstruct exactly what happened. But it seems that Goldome, with a raft of larger problems, simply did not give the Datek-InstaCard contract with NPN sufficient attention. Yet NPN's contract with Datek-InstaCard prevented it from seeking out other vendors to deal with the growing volume.

NPN clearly needed a stronger management team, infusions of capital, and better financial oversight and management of operations. By coincidence, Western Union, which had seen a *Forbes* profile of NPN in December 1988, was eager to join forces with NPN. Western Union did not want a mere partnership, however. It wanted to acquire NPN outright.

NATIONAL PAYMENTS NETWORK BECOMES EASY PAY

Although Krouse and his minority shareholders were not eager to sell, it was hard to pass up Western Union's offer of nearly $30 million. The deal, consummated in 1989, gave NPN and Goldome a fifty–fifty split of $18 million in cash and additional payments based on future performance. NPN, rechristened "Easy Pay," was apparently meant to complement Western Union's electronic money transfers and traditional message services.

Western Union chose not to expand the NPN system into additional retail stores, however, but rather to incorporate it into existing Western Union outlets. Its operations have been hampered, also, because of two changes in ownership of Western Union Financial Services, which managed Easy Pay. In 1996, First Data Corporation planned to incorporate Easy Pay into its own utility remittance service.

Krouse charges that Western Union's real interest in acquiring NPN was to neutralize a competitor that could potentially undercut its high fees for electronic money transfers. "I can sell money transfers for $1 and still make money," Krouse contends, "but Western Union still charges $32 to send $150 to your son in Atlanta."

By 1996, Krouse's five-year non-compete clause with Western Union had expired, freeing him to return to the market he knew so well. Using a more sophisticated technological platform and backed by a major financial services company, Krouse plans to introduce "Direct Express" payment machines in retail stores around the nation. The system will initially enable the "unbanked"—and later, all consumers—to pay any bill electronically.

Like NPN, Direct Express aspires to be a win-win-win scenario: Consumers will be able to pay their bills quickly, for free; retailers will reap greater customer traffic and payments for each transaction; and Direct Express will reap fees from companies seeking to improve their cash flow. Krouse hopes to open 40,000 Direct Express outlets within three years.

Krouse concedes that NPN could not have progressed much further than it did with the technology and partners he had. Since the sale of NPN, new generations of computer and telecommunications technologies have opened up vast new fields of opportunities in electronic financial services. Krouse aims to exploit them in order to pioneer a new market entirely.

Krouse learned important lessons from his National Payments Network experience—about reconciling entrepreneurial zeal with managerial rigor; about the perils of business partners and rapid growth; and about the satisfactions of building a business that meets an important social need.

He takes great delight in confounding the cynics and skeptics: "I once had an argument with a banker who said, 'These low-income people just aren't profitable.'" When anybody makes that argument nowadays, Krouse just smiles.

SECTION THREE

DIVERSITY IN AMERICAN LIFE

Introduction by William T. Coleman, Jr.

William T. Coleman, Jr., is a senior partner in the law firm of O'Melveny & Myers. Prior to joining the firm, he served as U.S. secretary of transportation from 1975 to 1977 in the Ford administration. Mr. Coleman's career in law, business, and public service has included advisory or consultant positions to seven U.S. presidents. An ardent defender of civil rights, he was one of the authors of the legal brief that persuaded the Supreme Court in 1954 to outlaw segregation in public schools. He currently serves as chairman of the board of the NAACP Legal Defense and Educational Fund, Inc.

If businesspeople take pride in making decisions that are rational and well informed, there still remains, however, one area of business endeavor in which irrational prejudices are often tolerated: the hiring, development, collaboration with, and promotion of people of different genders, racial backgrounds, sexual orientations, and ethnic heritages. They often ignore the rule that, if we believe in an all-kind Creator, then we must realize that talent is spread throughout these groups without regard to such distinctions.

Although willful, egregious discrimination in public or business life tends to be rare these days, many subtle yet pernicious stereotypes are quietly condoned. Many managers still cling to the myths that women cannot be bold, effective managers; that gay employees are likely to be a disruptive influence; or that African-Americans are not capable of performing as senior managers.

When affirmative action programs were first introduced thirty years ago, such attitudes were treated as moral and legal issues, which they remain. But in recent years, the most progressive-minded and astute business managers have properly recognized the diversity of their work force as a preeminent *business* issue as well. Increasingly, the presence of qualified women, African-Americans, Hispanics, or Asian-Americans at a company is not just a matter of compliance with federal law or political correctness; it is a matter of competitive necessity. Companies striving to succeed in diverse consumer markets and in the global marketplace need to marshal the best talent they can without regard to its ethnicity or gender. They must be able to elicit a broader spectrum of ideas and perspectives from their top managers and employees. For these goals, a homogeneous corporate culture poses a distinct disadvantage.

Reebok, the shoe manufacturer, almost failed to notice the growing popularity of aerobic exercise in the early 1980s—until some of its women managers prodded the company to develop a new line of aerobic shoes for women. The episode convinced Reebok of the tangible benefits of workplace diversity. Allied Signal credits its success in winning a contract to sell brakes and wheels to China Eastern Airlines to its more culturally versatile managers. The Xerox Corporation, profiled in Chapter 25, ascribes its robust, innovative work culture to the employee diversity it carefully nurtures, even in challenging economic times.

Much of the impetus for workplace diversity came from the landmark 1987 report *Workforce 2000*, produced by the Hudson Institute for the U.S. Department of Labor. The report made the startling demographic prediction that only 15 percent of the newcomers to the job market between 1988 and 2000 would be White men; the remaining 85 percent would be women and minorities. While this anticipated shortage was mitigated by the corporate mergers and restructurings of the 1990s—which made many more White male managers available—the basic challenge remains. American business *needs* talented women and minorities, especially as markets continue to fragment into smaller niches in which ethnicity and cultural sensitivity matter.

Section Three profiles four very different companies that have something in common—their appreciation of work force diversity as a competitive strength. As described in Chapter 8, five managers of Inland Steel squarely confronted the subtle stereotyping that was holding back people of color at Inland and developed a creative new program to sensitize all its employees to workplace diversity.

In the construction industry, which has been notably resistant to the hiring and advancement of women, Julia Stasch of Stein & Company, a commercial real estate services firm, implemented a remarkably effective model program for improving equal employment opportunities for women, as described in Chapter 9. The program bolstered the company's ability to secure contracts and burnished its reputation as a fair-minded, socially committed firm.

As the president of one of the largest stock photography firms in the world, Barbara B. Roberts of FPG International defied the conventional wisdom of her industry by promoting nonstereotyped images of women, minorities, people with disabilities, and others. Despite skepticism that this type of imagery would sell, Roberts won new business for her firm with her "real life" photos and became an industry pacesetter.

Finally, breaking ranks with virtually all members of its industry, DAKA International, which operates the Fuddruckers restaurant chain and food services at dozens of institutions, initiated an aggressive AIDS education program for its employees. By showing compassion and candor, DAKA helped dispel public fears and misconceptions about AIDS while attracting and retaining highly motivated employees and nurturing a cooperative work environment.

As these profiles suggest, American businesses that strive to make their workplaces more diverse will not only help fulfill some basic principles of the American experiment but, in addition, they will make their enterprises more flexible, creative, and successful.

8

Equal Opportunity at Inland Steel

HOW FIVE MANAGERS TRANSFORMED A CORPORATE CULTURE

The numbers are startling: In 1990, decades after the passage of affirmative action and antidiscrimination legislation, White males still held more than 95 percent of the top management jobs at the country's largest corporations.

In response to this continuing inequity, some farsighted companies began to look beyond the hiring process to reconsider their entire approach to "managing diversity." What these astute managers found is that the key to successful workplace diversity lies not just in modifying policies but in molding cultural change—change that demands creative effort, commitment, and bold resolve at all levels of business.

At Inland Steel Industries in Chicago, four African-American employees took the risk of initiating such change. Their efforts, with the aggressive support of a White general manager, triggered deep and lasting cultural changes within their very large and traditional company. Their story is one of hope and perseverance in achieving the actual, often untapped potential of a diverse workplace.

A PROUD HISTORY, AN UNMET CHALLENGE

Inland Steel Industries is the fifth-largest integrated steel producer in the United States, accounting for approximately 5 percent of the nation's steel production. Companywide sales for 1995 totaled $4.8 billion.

Throughout its hundred-year history, Inland had been an industry leader in equal opportunity hiring. It was the first steel company to have an African-American outside sales representative and, in 1954, became the first to secure a nondiscrimination clause in its basic labor agreement with the United Steelworkers Union—eight years ahead of any of its competitors. Inland executives were leaders in Chicago United, an early, forward-thinking coalition of business and community leaders dedicated to racial equality. The company was also among the first to have an African-American on its board of directors.

But even at Inland, and as late as the 1980s, minority and female employees did not feel fully comfortable in the workplace, nor confident that they enjoyed an equal chance to advance within the company. As of 1987, only 11 percent of Inland's officers and managers were minorities, and less than 5 percent were women. With each passing year, a homogeneous management force continued to preside over an increasingly diverse labor pool.

Already, minorities made up 40 percent of Inland's total work force, and the Hudson Institute's landmark 1987 study, *Workforce 2000*, forecast that only 15 percent of net new entrants into the U.S. work force through the end of the century would be White males. In this environment, Inland, like all major companies, would be relying on a highly diverse talent pool to build its future.

THE SPUR TO CHANGE

Around this time, four of Inland's young African-American professionals were independently becoming discouraged by the lack of opportunity they felt within the company. Tyrone Banks, Robert Hudson, Jr., and Scharlene Hurston of the sales department and Vivian Cosey of the human resources department were troubled by the continuing dearth of minorities and women in upper management. The situation suggested their own limited career horizons at Inland. None of the four felt that he or she had a minority mentor within the company; each felt like an outsider.

"When I first started at Inland," recalls Robert Hudson, "I felt as though I had to prove my competency day in and day out. No matter what I did, no matter what I said, I always felt that people questioned my ability. . . . It was a very frightening and discouraging environment for me."

"Whenever you were involved in meetings," adds Scharlene Hurston, "you always felt like you were not part of the group . . . that you were invisible. Although you would speak up and you might have an opinion that seemed to be reasonable to you and to others, your opinion was discarded. But when someone else brought up the same issue, then it was a good idea."

Inland's minority employees constantly sought the advice of Vivian Cosey, the only African-American professional in the general office's human resources department at one point. Yet Vivian herself recalls receiving a poor performance evaluation for "not reaching out more to White people." She was even instructed to make more of an effort to sit with Whites in the cafeteria. "On the one hand," Cosey remembers, "you were highly visible, but on the other, you were invisible. The visibility was not a positive one."

Tyrone Banks sums up the group's collective disappointment: "We were taught by our families to work hard and get ahead, only to find that the doors were closed."

Despite their frustrations, all four employees liked and respected many of the people with whom they worked. They realized, too, that the barriers they faced were not unique to Inland. "Many times I was asked, 'Why don't you just leave Inland?' " Hurston recalls. "But based on my friends' similar experiences [elsewhere], I thought 'Why jump from the frying pan into the fire?' That was really the impetus to stay at Inland and fight the battle."

Although each of the four had broached the subject of Inland's race relations with others in the company, none had made any headway independently. Finally, in 1987, Banks gathered Cosey, Hudson, and Hurston together one Saturday morning outside of the office to discuss the issues. "We found that with a group approach, we were there to protect each other," recalls Cosey. "We covered each other's backs. We kept each other enthused about what we were doing. . . . We strategized together. Each of us thinks differently, and as a collective unit, I think that enhanced our effectiveness."

After meeting privately for several months, discussing common experiences and possible strategies to move the company forward, they decided to bring their concerns to someone with the authority to take action. "We had decided we needed to go to a White manager," says Banks, "because we had all too often complained about what was going on among ourselves—and none of us had the power to do anything about it."

Adds Cosey: "We needed someone to help us and guide us through the maze of how to . . . deliver the message in order to get the best result. We finally found one person who was risk-oriented and action-oriented."

WOULD STEVEN BOWSHER UNDERSTAND?

The group decided to approach Steven Bowsher, the new general manager of sales at the Inland Steel Flat Products division, and an eighteen-year veteran of the company. Bowsher's reputation as an innovator and risk taker was already well established, as was his image as a fair and sincere leader.

"He was the fairest manager I'd ever had," says Hurston. "Steve didn't like traditional thinking and had shown a willingness to take risks on business issues," adds Hudson. Several years earlier, Hudson recalls, Bowsher had spoken out in response to a companywide affirmative action survey. In a letter to his boss, he frankly explained that his employees thought that Inland was not doing enough to ensure equal opportunity and racial understanding in the work culture. To air their concerns, Banks, Cosey, Hudson, and Hurston decided to invite Steven Bowsher to dinner after work.

"We told Steve about minority employees never getting the opportunity to succeed in a job," remembers Tyrone Banks. "We told him about being called names, racist jokes, different people in high levels of the organization making derogatory comments.

. . . We gave him a variety of typical things that minorities have experienced in the organization where diversity and affirmative action are not appreciated."

"We really dumped our frustration on him," recalls Bob Hudson. "He sensed our emotion, but he couldn't interpret what we were saying. . . . I think he was really boggled because Inland had had a very profitable year, so it was probably disconcerting to him that, here the company has a record year, but yet employees are disgruntled. And what we were trying to say to him was, 'We can multiply this profitability twice if we had all our people in power to move ahead . . . particularly our minority employees.' "

Vivian Cosey laughs, looking back. "In that first meeting we probably fried his brain," she admits. "He was sitting there writing frantically and continuously questioning us, as though he really didn't understand what we were saying."

"When I got home that night," Bowsher agrees, "I didn't have the slightest idea what it was that I'd written down. It didn't make any sense to me. It didn't seem to fit any sort of pattern. I really didn't understand what it was that they were trying to communicate to me. And it was at that point that I knew we had to have this meeting again."

After several meetings resulting in the same fundamental lack of understanding, Banks, Cosey, Hudson, and Hurston began to despair of any progress. "In retrospect," says Hudson, "it was impossible for Steve to understand our message. We were asking him to be Superman, because he didn't have the perspective of the victim. His experiences in life were not being oppressed."

Bowsher's Epiphany About Race

Struggling to find a way to help Bowsher gain that frame of reference, the four continually funneled him news clippings and articles about race relations and workplace diversity. When Tyrone Banks sent along a brochure about the Urban Crisis Center in Atlanta and its race relations seminars, Bowsher thought it might be as good a program as any.

On his own time and his own money, and telling no one but Vivian Cosey of his plans, Steven Bowsher flew to Atlanta to attend a two-day workshop sponsored by the Urban Crisis Center and directed by the Reverend Charles King, Jr.

Dr. King, now deceased, began fighting for civil rights as a young pastor in Indiana, and went on to become a nationally respected expert on race relations. "The two-day workshop," Bowsher recalls, "was Dr. King. He talked about his experiences in the White world, he talked about his experiences with society and what it meant to be Black, and it was the most difficult two days that I personally ever went through."

As the only White upper-management person in attendance, Bowsher joined a group that was half African-American and predominantly female. He remembers the experience:

> For two days, they basically ignored me. They would not respond to my questions, they wouldn't listen to me. And throughout this, I was listening closely to King, because I was now perhaps in the same position that women and minorities find themselves in in everyday life. Without question, it was the single most important training I've been through.
>
> It clearly opened up my thinking so that I could understand what it was that Scharlene and Bob and Tyrone and Vivian had been telling me. . . . The other thing it did for me: It said that I had to lead some change.

Robert Hudson smiles as he remembers Bowsher's return from King's workshop. "I recall going up to his office and seeing about fifteen copies of this book, *Fire in My Bones* [Dr. King's autobiography], with a big Black man on the cover. I said, 'My God, Steve, what do you have on your desk? What's going on?!' And he said, 'I've had a traumatic experience . . . I think I can understand you now.' And I remember walking out of that meeting saying, 'Oh my God!' "

Scharlene Hurston recalls the effects of Bowsher's transformation:

> Suddenly, we weren't talking at each other, we started to talk *with* each other. [Bowsher] started speaking in the "we"

framework, recounting the experiences that we had told him in the first person, as if he had gone through them himself. I think having gone through that seminar, he got the sense of what it was like to be a minority in an oppressed environment. And as a result, he was ready to move forward.

Bold Steps to Change Attitudes and the Culture

Bowsher's first move was to direct his entire team of managers to attend Dr. King's class and to return and demonstrate, within his department, that they had learned the lesson he had learned. Although Bowsher believes that some people above him in the organization were concerned that the training was unnecessary, he shook it off: "We just blasted through that."

"We did not allow this to be a vote," he recalls. "People did have to go. And they did have to come back and demonstrate organizational change. . . . We moved enough people forward that the next step started to become a little easier. There was a better support mechanism for change within the company."

Bowsher's initiative soon penetrated other departments of the company. "It became a necessity for communication with everyone in the organization," says Cosey. "And as a result of that, it started to cascade throughout the organization, below the management ranks, as well." By the end of 1987, over a hundred Inland personnel had experienced King's seminar.

Bowsher himself moved swiftly to apply the lessons he had learned. He established an aggressive affirmative action plan for his own department and began promoting minorities to levels more commensurate with their years of experience. "We started to look for high-quality opportunities," explains Bowsher. "We started to take what I think some of my counterparts in the organization thought were high risks, but it was simply the same risk we'd taken with [White] employees, by accelerating some people's careers."

Bowsher immediately mandated career planning within his department, drawing up five-year plans for all employees, regardless of race. Bold diversity objectives were made a part of the general business plan and a requisite part of annual reviews and evaluations.

At a companywide business planning meeting, Hudson recalls, "Steve gave a 'Sermon on the Mount' about what the sales department was doing in the area of affirmative action. The whole hall was galvanized by his intensity and his commitment to it. And the rest of the organization, not wanting to be shown up, at their next business plan meeting talked about affirmative action in their business plans. It really got the ball rolling."

INLAND'S PRESIDENT JOINS THE EFFORT

In 1988, Bowsher approached the president of Inland, Robert Darnall, about the company's diversity shortcomings. Darnall agreed to attend Dr. King's workshop with two African-American employees with whom he had worked for a long period of time. "Bob's reaction was quite similar to mine," remembers Bowsher. "He was not only touched by the emotional impact of it, but he saw the business imperative that was part of this."

Darnall recalls what he learned:

> I thought before that I was pretty progressive and pretty sensitive, but I did not recognize some of the behavior that I had provided and the negative impact it had had on some of the minority employees. . . . It was truly a moving experience for me. Both Dr. Charles King and the way he forced the White male to feel like the minority and get the understanding of what the minority individual is going through. . . . There's no question I was different when I came back from the seminar.

"Shortly after Darnall returned from Atlanta," Steven Bowsher recalls, "he called a meeting of his top officers and asked me to sit in and help them think about what he should be doing to drive this new information and feeling that he had into the organization. We spent two and a half to three hours talking about this around the table, and it was pretty clear to me that his officer team really wasn't on the same wavelength.

"Finally, at the end of the meeting, Bob went around the

room and asked people what they thought he should do. He finally got to me. I said, 'Well, the first thing I wouldn't do, Bob, is ask this group of people what I should do. This group of people, these managers, this management structure you have is the problem. And the group that I would ask are the people who best understand it—perhaps our focus group, perhaps the women and minorities in our company.

"The silence was deafening at that point," Bowsher recalls. "That group of management was not very excited to hear me say that. I guess at that point, I was as far out on a limb as Scharlene and Bob and Tyrone and Vivian found themselves when they first approached me."

Fortunately, Darnall remained supportive of Bowsher's efforts. "Bob provided me with the personal encouragement to go forward and kind of blaze the trail," says Bowsher. "I think his hope at that point was that I would bring others along with me."

THE AFFIRMATIVE ACTION FOCUS GROUP

As momentum built and Bowsher's employees and other general managers began to get on board, Banks, Cosey, Hudson, and Hurston, along with Bowsher, found themselves at the center of intense discussions. Up until this point, the group had continued to meet to discuss issues and strategies but had refused to do so on Inland time or Inland property.

Tyrone Banks remembers Bowsher saying, "We're working on a problem that Inland needs to address, so let's take it in-house and start working on it formally on Inland time. It will send a clear message to the organization that this is important and it's serious."

Formalized as the Affirmative Action Focus Group (AAFG), the team by its efforts and influence began to spawn similar task forces in other areas of the company. These new groups participated in the business planning process within their units, recommending initiatives in career planning, outreach activities, and recruitment.

By 1991, more than 800 Inland personnel had attended some type of diversity sensitivity training. The AAFG drafted

Inland policy statements concerning memberships at exclusionary business and country clubs. The group also made the suggestion, later implemented, that the president of every Inland business conduct a corporate affirmative action audit each year.

SOME BACKLASH—AND MORE PROGRESS

Despite much success, Bowsher admits, not everyone at Inland Steel was pleased with the new initiatives. "I started to gain a reputation in the organization as being someone who was stirring up this problem rather than this opportunity. I did get phone calls to my home, I did get notes that scared my family."

The four minority employees even received some criticism from other women and minorities, who were convinced that Banks, Cosey, Hudson, and Hurston were out only for their own advancement. "Criticism from those whose best interests you feel you have in heart and in mind really hurts," says Hudson.

Fortunately, Bowsher and his colleagues were not discouraged by such tactics. They continued to work together closely. "Steve helped us understand how White males approached problems," says Tyrone Banks, "and how to deal with the issues that they would bring up . . . how to circumvent some of those issues and how to present arguments for others."

Together, the group initiated hiring plans for women and minorities, stepped up recruiting efforts, and created a summer intern program for the sales department. Over a two-year period, minority hires in their group increased from 10 percent to 64 percent of the total hired. Gradually the AAFG grew in reputation and began to provide support for minorities throughout the company to air grievances, with Bowsher often mediating disputes.

USING DIVERSITY REFORMS AS A
TURNAROUND STRATEGY

In January 1990, Steve Bowsher was unexpectedly named president of Ryerson Coil Processing Company, an Inland subsidiary division that processes and distributes steel. Ryerson was a troubled unit with a history of mediocre performance—in Bowsher's words, "underperforming, underachieving, and not well organized." Before Bowsher took over, the unit had lost money for the five years it had been in operation.

Even though it was headquartered in the predominantly minority Pullman neighborhood of South Chicago, Ryerson Coil had not been affected by the affirmative action and diversity efforts that were spreading throughout Inland.

Bowsher explains how he handled this:

> When I arrived, the first thing I did was announce to my direct staff that [workplace diversity] was going to be one of our key business imperatives. I announced this ahead of making a profit. I announced this ahead of lowering costs. I announced this ahead of getting out and getting new customers.

> Now certainly all of those were important, but I set the tone right at the very beginning. . . . We sent people to King's program. We had King come here to Chicago and do some training and we started right at the beginning. We didn't allow any time to slip by.

> There were some people who thought I was kidding about this subject, who thought that perhaps this was the project-of-the-month. We asked those people to learn again and retrain again if necessary, and some made the adjustment. There were a few who didn't. Unfortunately, they're not with us anymore. It was so important that we have everyone pulling in the same direction on this.

Demonstrating his commitment, Bowsher appointed Wright Bozeman, an African-American, as his new general manager. Bozeman was an Inland Steel Company veteran of twenty-eight years and had held nearly every lateral position beneath that of general manager, but he had never been given the opportunity to have the top seat. Poised for retirement, Bozeman was lured back by Bowsher. He became the first African-American general manager in the history of Inland Steel Industries.

Part of Bowsher and Bozeman's approach was to change company protocol to show greater respect for employees at all levels. They immediately revoked the long-standing policy that had made the plant's carpeted office area, adjacent to the immense processing plant, off-limits to workers. They also ended the invidious tradition of plant employees wearing red hard hats while office employees wore white.

Next, Bowsher and Bozeman initiated an ad hoc sexual harassment awareness campaign at the company. "Girlie pictures" no longer adorned Ryerson Coil's walls, and women were hired and trained for jobs they had never held before. "It was very, very important for us to demonstrate through some specific, strategic moves that it was okay to be a minority in the company, and that we were going to balance the scales just as quickly as we could," says Bowsher.

In one highly visible move, he named Mary Vodisek the first female plant manager in Inland's history. "It's significant to see not only that a female has the position but that she's performing well," says personnel director Bill Lowry, "especially running an operating situation. She can lead men as well as women. And that she can add to the bottom line in the same way that a man can."

Andy Villanueva was another first at Ryerson Coil. Once a plant superintendent with Ryerson, Villanueva had become discouraged by the lack of opportunity for himself and other Hispanics, and left the company. Shortly after Bowsher became president, Villanueva was rehired as plant supervisor—and, later, plant manager—of Chicago Select Steel, one of the six units that make up Ryerson Coil. He became the first Hispanic to hold such a position at Inland.

DIVERSITY AS A KEY TO COMPETITIVENESS

"Managing diversity well is increasingly important to an organization such as Inland," says Bob Darnall, who became chairman in 1992.

Forty percent of our employees at Inland are minority, and unless we manage our diversity very, very well and much better than we have in the past, I don't believe we can create the energy and excitement to be as competitive as we otherwise would. . . . We need to stimulate, lead and get the best efforts out of our entire work force in order for this company, in a very tough business, to be competitive in the years ahead.

Ryerson Coil's bottom line bears witness to the effectiveness of this approach. The subsidiary, which had been losing money each month before Steven Bowsher took over, was turned around in less than two years. During the last quarter of 1991, Ryerson Coil Processing was profitable for the first time in its history.

Bowsher himself attributed the recovery to his focus on employees. "We've taken something that perhaps our competitors view as a problem and we've turned it into an opportunity. It's to our competitive advantage. . . . Our problem-solving capability here is much better, I believe, than that of others whom we compete against. And I believe it's because we have gotten everyone involved and everyone feels good about being involved. . . . It's been very healthy for our company."

Inland's Pride in Its New Trajectory

"The veil of discomfort that previously existed for females and minorities operating within this company is diminishing," says Scharlene Hurston:

I'm not going to say that it is completely gone, but it has certainly been dramatically reduced. That has a lot to do with the fact that females and minorities are now being evaluated in terms of how they perform based on a different set of rules—rules that are based on competence, skills, ability, and potential. . . . As a result, people are operating with much more creativity, much more input into the organization, and much more enthusiasm.

Tyrone Banks takes pride in the fact that his group's work has helped to "awaken a feeling in the minority populace that things are changing. A feeling that I have a place here, that my ideas will be appreciated, that my performance will be rewarded. Heretofore, that wasn't there. It has released the power of the people at Inland to try to make our company successful."

While Inland has come a long way, adds Banks, "we have a long way to go." But he is optimistic about the future. "With the commitment of the employees that we have, and the management staff that we have, we can do it. We can demonstrate to the world what a successful, diverse company—where *all* the people feel fully appreciated—can be."

9

Julia Stasch of Stein & Company

FIGHTING GENDER BARRIERS IN CHICAGO CONSTRUCTION

Any decent person would shudder at the stories told by women construction workers. There was the time that a male worker standing at the top of a ladder urinated on a female electrician standing on the bottom rung. The woman had already suffered a fractured jaw after rebuffing a foreman's sexual advances.

If other forms of harassment are less dramatic, they can be equally demeaning: pornographic posters at the work site, hurtful snubs from the male work crew, systemic barriers to women wanting to improve their skills.

Yet still thousands of women seek to join the construction trades each year. Why?

One answer is money. The U.S. construction trades provide about five million high-wage jobs paying an average of $14.45 an hour in 1993, according to the U.S. Bureau of Labor Statistics. These jobs, 98 percent filled by men, are generally much more lucrative than "traditionally female" pink-collar occupations such as cashiers, child care workers, bookkeepers, secretaries, and clerks.

Many influential voices, including those of several U.S. presidents, have called for change. Richard Nixon declared in 1973 that "affirmative action" efforts should expand beyond racial

minorities to include all women. Jimmy Carter in 1978 set a specific gender-integration goal for the construction trades: that
women should constitute 6.9 percent of workers on government-
sponsored projects by 1980.

Despite such action, gender discrimination in the construction trades has persisted. Women face difficulty in obtaining
union apprenticeships. Recruitment by employers has been half-
hearted. Antidiscrimination enforcement by government agencies is often ineffective. And even when women are lucky
enough to find these jobs, unfair treatment as well as sexual harassment is common.

Julia M. Stasch was determined to change this dismal record. The president and chief operating officer of Stein & Company, a major Chicago-based real estate developer, Stasch has
pioneered a comprehensive new approach that leverages the
power of the contractor to achieve tangible results. The program
has not only dramatically enhanced gender equity in an industry
notoriously resistant to such change; it has also bolstered Stein &
Company's business performance in securing contracts and establishing its reputation as a fair-minded, socially committed
firm.

When Stein Met Stasch

Stein and Company was founded in 1971 by entrepreneur Richard A. Stein. Initially, the firm handled mostly small ventures,
such as rehabilitating town houses. Although it employed only
four people through 1976, Stein & Company came to provide a
full array of real estate services by the early 1980s—from development and construction consulting to tenant and landlord representation, brokerage, leasing, marketing, asset management,
and program management. The company gained a Fortune 500
clientele and managed the construction of major structures for
AT&T, USG Corporation, the University of Chicago, the Chicago
Board of Trade, the owners of the Chicago Bulls and Black-
hawks, the McCormick Place Hotel, and the U.S. General Services Administration (GSA).

Honors and recognition followed. Stein was named "Real

Estate Entrepreneur of the Year" by Ernst & Young and *Inc.* magazine in 1989. *National Real Estate Investor* ranked the firm as the twelfth most active in the country in 1990. By 1995 the company employed 240 people and earned $25 million for consulting services and projects worth more than $1 billion.

Much of its success dates back to a fateful day in 1976 when Richard Stein bumped into an old acquaintance, Julia Stasch, then a high school history teacher.

Stasch had been reared in the Chicago suburbs in a socially conscious family before entering Antioch College in Ohio. But in the spirit of the times, the 1960s, Stasch dropped out to join the federal VISTA program (Volunteers in Service to America), working on the Papago Indian reservation in Arizona. After a stint in San Francisco during its countercultural heyday, she returned to Chicago to obtain bachelor's and master's degrees in history, and then went on to teach.

When Stasch's friend Richard Stein said he needed a secretary in his small start-up firm, she readily traded her teaching career for a higher salary and a shorter commute.

Stein handled the finances and overall business strategy, while Stasch came to manage day-to-day operations. As the company grew, Stasch quickly moved up the ranks—from secretary to project coordinator, executive vice president, and, in 1988, chief administrative officer. In July 1991, Stasch was made president and chief operating officer, with an equity stake in the company and ultimate responsibility for the profitability of all of the firm's services.

It was a role she handled with aplomb, leading a Chicago business magazine to call her "tough, hard-hatted and totally driven. Within five seconds of meeting her, it's apparent there's no bull about this top-notch executive." The Chicago Women's Hall of Fame inducted her into its pantheon in 1991, and the following year *Business Week* ranked her among the "50 Top Women in Business."

Stasch remained openly committed to a civic and social agenda of "racial justice and gender equity." As she put it, "I decided that business could be a vehicle for social change when I realized that I was in a position to do things that I had always thought were only possible outside the business environment."

STASCH PUTS HER IDEALS TO WORK

Stasch's first real opportunity to put her ideals to work came in 1984, when the city of Chicago asked Stein & Company to include an affirmative action component in a small project on which it was bidding. Stein & Company plunged into the task with fervor, much to the amazement of city officials accustomed to token support for affirmative action.

A year later, Stein & Company was seeking to become the developer of a $360-million regional headquarters for AT&T, the telecommunications giant. Aware of AT&T's own attempts to support minority-owned vendors and suppliers, Stasch suggested internally that Stein & Company distinguish its bid by including a strong affirmative action plan. Stein welcomed this strategic combination of business and social objectives, and urged Stasch to follow through.

Stein & Company won the bid. An AT&T vice president later told *Commercial Property News*, "Julia's leadership on the affirmative action program was one reason we chose Stein & Company for our headquarters."

Now came the hard part: making the program work. Since construction projects require the harmonious interaction of dozens of participants, Stasch realized that everyone's involvement would be crucial. Aided by mentor and consultant Joe Williams, she assembled a task force composed of clients, developers, contractors, subcontractors, consultants, unions, laborers, and regulators.

On April 29, 1987, when the "AT&T/Stein Partnership" unveiled a scale model of what would be Chicago's fifth-largest building, it announced some aggressive goals. A full 25 percent of the aggregate construction dollars on the project would go to minority-owned firms, exceeding, on an entirely private-sector job, federal government goals for public works. Five percent would go to women-owned firms.

What some critics portrayed as favoritism, Stasch saw as a helping hand. "We need to help [minority- and women-owned firms] grow to the point that they can stand on their own without affirmative action programs," she argues. Such companies, she says, are excellent contractors; they just need the chance to show that they can truly compete in the marketplace."

To help minority- and women-owned firms submit acceptable bids, the task force issued a handbook detailing bid submission procedures and special resources available to them. Stein & Company's consultants held orientation sessions for women- and minority-owned firms; helped them get requisite certification, bonding, and insurance; and maintained a database of eligible firms so they could be readily referred to prime contractors.

Once work began, the task force collected numerical reports from all majority contractors to assess their affirmative action performance, double-checking them against contractors' work records. When goals were not being met, the task force encouraged creative, voluntary solutions. In one instance, a prime contractor divided a large contract into smaller parts so that minority- and women-owned firms could participate. In rarer cases, the task force temporarily withheld payment from recalcitrant contractors.

By the time the AT&T Corporate Center was completed on June 29, 1989, more than 100 minority- and women-owned contractors and subcontractors had worked on the project. About $37 million, or 23 percent of the aggregate construction dollars, went to these firms. Chicago Mayor Richard Daley exclaimed, "Your model partnership sets the tone of cooperation that I would like to see throughout the city of Chicago."

An important reason for this success, Stasch told a reporter, was Stein & Company's willingness to take a public stand: "It's been important in setting a different tone regarding affirmative action within the small development community."

THE NEXT CHALLENGE: HIRING MORE WOMEN CONSTRUCTION WORKERS

This success only whetted Stasch's appetite to do more, particularly for women construction workers. After the offices of top-level management, construction sites are one of the most gender-exclusive workplaces in the United States. Men often insist that it is lack of physical strength and aversion to inclement weather, not gender discrimination, that prevents women from working on construction jobs. It is an argument that ignores the importance of family, friends, and union connections in excluding women from some of the best-paying blue-collar jobs available.

Those women who do manage to land jobs often face a catch-22: If they perform well, they are considered exceptional for their gender, but if they perform poorly, then the industry's stereotype of women's inferiority is affirmed and the exclusion seemingly justified. Stasch herself has encountered similar evasions when contractors claim that their jobs are open to women and they are eager to hire them but the unions simply do not have any women. Then the unions go through the same act, claiming they would love to have women union members but the contractors just won't hire them.

The discrimination is hardly benign. A 1992 study by the advocacy group Chicago Women In Trades (CWIT) found that 88 percent of local tradeswomen on the job were subjected to pictures of naked or partially dressed women; 83 percent experienced unwelcome sexual remarks; 80 percent either had no toilets or only dirty toilets at work sites; 60 percent were given the heaviest or dirtiest assignments; and 57 percent had been touched inappropriately or asked for sex.

Yet many women still seek construction jobs—for the same reasons men seek them: "We have families to support," says Lauren Sugerman, a former construction worker and now executive director of CWIT. "We have lifestyles we want to support. The wages of the construction industry are very appealing. It is not just the wages, though. What comes with the job in the construction industry is full training. And it is on-the-job, paid training."

Stasch pragmatically cites demographic trends. Male construction workers are an aging group, and more than one-half of the current laborers [as of the early 1990s] will be retiring within fifteen years. The now-famous 1987 study by the Hudson Institute, *Workforce 2000,* forecast that about three-fifths of new entrants into the labor force by the end of the twentieth century will be women. Even if there is no net job growth in construction, it is in everyone's best interest to hire and train women now, Stasch argues.

A NEW MODEL: THE FEMALE EMPLOYMENT INITIATIVE

If Stasch was eager to find new ways to hire tradeswomen, she got her chance when Stein & Company won the GSA contract for the Metcalfe Federal Building project. The firm won this plum contract in part by using its signature technique: distinguishing itself in the area of affirmative action. This time it added a twist by agreeing to forfeit $1 million in fees if 28 percent of the contract was not performed by minority-owned firms and at least 7 percent by women-owned firms. The firm also promised to strive to hire the same respective percentages of minority and women workers.

Among these four goals that Stein & Company ambitiously set for itself, perhaps the toughest one was the decade-old federal goal of 6.9 percent female laborers on construction projects. An official with the U.S. Department of Labor's Office of Federal Contract Compliance Programs (OFCCP) remembers thinking of Stein & Company's pledge as "a dream."

Stasch knew that only a well-funded and carefully executed initiative could achieve serious results. So for the Metcalfe project Stasch built upon the lessons learned with the AT&T Corporate Center. She created a standing committee, the Female Employment Initiative (FEI), to bring together all participants on the project. But this time she also invited other key players such as community and women's advocacy organizations and the apprentice coordinators of trade unions.

Stasch saw the chief imperatives as building working relationships among everyone involved on the project; creating a sense of collaboration or voluntary compliance rather than one of forced compliance; and achieving a critical mass of female workers at construction sites so that their presence would be accepted as ordinary. Her personal leadership, most observers agree, was also critical. "When you are in a power position," explained Stephanie Stephens, now a vice president at the firm and a former tradeswoman herself, "they have to listen to you and they are very receptive to what you say, because they know how much it plays upon their entire future."

To keep efforts focused, the FEI committee drafted a mission statement with four key objectives: (1) to become a recruitment, counseling, and referral source for tradeswomen; (2) to follow up and monitor all individual referrals, women hired, and conditions on the job site; (3) to conduct orientation and training sessions for all parties involved; and (4) to explore new ways to recruit, hire, and retain women in the construction trades.

A formal calendar was prepared to assess progress on both a quarterly and an annual basis. The FEI committee also prepared a database referral system and began to ask contractors why they did or did not hire tradeswomen. To underscore FEI's importance, Stasch sent a letter to the chief executive officers of all firms involved on the project.

When it came to awarding contracts, bidders were not only required to declare their support for FEI's goals; they also had to supply work force projections enabling precise estimates to be made of the number of potential "female openings"—and this information would have to be updated as labor patterns changed. Armed with these work force projections and the database of interested women, FEI never lacked for names of women to recommend for apprenticeships or other construction jobs.

Did Stein & Company coerce contractors into accepting its goals by denying lucrative business to those who refused to endorse FEI? Stasch replies:

> If people say that they . . . won't get the next contract because they don't sign on to our social agenda, maybe that's not so bad. Contracts are awarded on a variety of bases. But I would say that you do like to do business with people that you are comfortable with. You like to do business with people who share your values.

Stein & Company, in fact, seeks the low bidder on all occasions; only if there is a tie or a near-tie between two bidders may the bidder with a sincere commitment to FEI have an edge. On the Metcalfe project, only 60 percent of the sixty-five contractors actually ended up hiring women, which demonstrates that the FEI agenda was not forced upon the unwilling collaborators.

PUTTING TEETH INTO AFFIRMATIVE ACTION

As construction got under way, FEI swung into action. To recruit female job applicants, a special trailer was moved onto the construction site and community-based organizations such as the Coalition for United Community Action put out the word. FEI even organized "mini-orientation sessions" to let potential applicants learn what construction work entailed.

Instead of simply accepting women into apprenticeship programs, FEI prodded the unions to help these women succeed. For example, when a coordinator from the masonry trade noticed a high dropout rate among female students, he helped FEI set up a two-day program to orient women to the nature of masonry work before they signed up.

Because contractors had signed legally binding work agreements that included affirmative action commitments, inadequate results could constitute a contract violation. Once, in late 1991, Stasch sent a strong letter to an Otis Elevator official that concluded, "Disappointment in this initiative makes me reluctant to invest time, energy and, more importantly, expectations in another joint effort." On a few occasions Stein & Company withheld paychecks for several days in order to force contractors to do a better job.

Given the dynamics of a construction site, Stasch knew that winning the cooperation of (male) supervisors would be critical to FEI's efforts. Toward that end, FEI convened after-work meetings over pizza and beer to assess progress and talk through problems and prejudices. When one superintendent argued that women construction workers should take aerobics classes to get in shape, an advocate for tradeswomen explained that physical conditioning was already part of the pre-apprenticeship training program, and that most tradeswomen do work out regularly.

One foreman complained that it was not fair to recruit women for construction jobs in a time of high unemployment. Stasch's tart response: "Look at the statistics that talk about how

many families are headed by women. Look at the statistics that
have shown, year after year, that women have been isolated into
the low-paying jobs. Look what economic power women can
have when they have jobs that pay well, that they are proud of,
and I would say that your argument is weak." About one-half of
the respondents to the CWIT survey indicated that they were the
sole wage earners in their households. More than two in three
were the primary wage earners.

FIGHTING SEXUAL HARASSMENT

Getting women into the jobs was half the battle. The other half
was helping them to succeed on the job, a challenge that required special support services.

For example, FEI representatives posted special notices at
the job site to remind all workers that sexual harassment is a
crime. It also organized sexual harassment workshops for both
men and women and informal support group meetings, counseling, and special events for tradeswomen. FEI even helped
women learn the informal folkways of construction work, such
as where to buy heavy boots and other equipment—tips that
men usually conveyed to new male workers as a matter of
course but that many men deliberately withheld from tradeswomen.

Once a fourth-year apprentice, a woman, was given a full-
fledged skilled job only to be replaced later by a first-year man.
The woman was relegated to housekeeping chores that the man
should have been doing. To help deal with such problems, FEI
representatives made unannounced visits to job sites every week
or two. A tradeswoman confronting a pornographic poster at
the job site every day, for example, could get a site-walker to
intervene and get it taken down. FEI also made sure that female
workers had access to separate rest rooms and changing facilities.

Finally, when tradeswomen leave a Stein & Company project, they are asked to answer a lengthy questionnaire as part of
their exit interview. For all departing women employees, Stein &
Company is eager to find out: Was she treated properly? Was

she asked to do things that were unsafe? Were there practices that were offensive to her? Was she not given the opportunity to work? Was she just sent to a corner and not trained?

As might be expected, the women hired through FEI have been keenly appreciative. Kari Moffett, an apprentice-level oiler who keeps a crane oiled and clean, says, "I love it. It means that I can afford a few extra things and that my husband has a chance to go to school and stuff like that, so that we can get a little farther ahead." Francine Williams, a third-year carpenter who puts up scaffolding, has welcomed FEI's backup support: "If you are laid off, they contact you. They want to know why you got laid off. Is there any more work? Did you have any problems?"

Not to be overlooked is the deep personal satisfaction that construction work gives to many women. "You can look back and say, 'I worked here and I worked in this building,'" says Yvette Cruz, a laborer. "I mean, I can't wait to come back here with my kids and say, 'This is where Mommy spent all of her time working.' This is going to be here for over two hundred years. It feels good."

FEI has given a big boost to the veteran tradeswomen of Chicago as well. They can realistically expect future work, and not simply cling to an abstract hope that contractors will not discriminate. The mere presence of more tradeswomen has also been affirming. "Everybody is so excited to be on a site where there are over ten women," says CWIT's Sugerman. "You know, you can go to lunch with another woman. You could meet somebody after work for a beer. You can share experiences. You are not alone on the floor."

FEI's Impressive Results

The Metcalfe Federal Building was completed on August 7, 1991. The final figures released by Stein & Company showed that 85 out of the 500 workers, or 17 percent, were women. Some 6.6 percent of "skilled-worker hours" and 7.7 percent of "laborer hours" were performed by women, who earned more than $1 million in wages. More than 30 percent of the business went to minority-owned firms and more than 7 percent to women-owned firms.

Stein & Company met all four of its affirmative action goals. In October 1990, months before these final figures were in, this performance prompted the U.S. Department of Labor's OFCCP to honor the company with its Exemplary Voluntary Effort Award.

Stein & Company soon deployed the FEI model at other locations as well. On its Chicago Stadium project, women completed 5.8 percent of the hours worked, compared with a nationwide average of 2 percent women's participation. For Stein & Company's development of McCormick Place, the largest exhibition and convention center in the United States, women accounted for 10 percent of the work force.

Why is FEI so effective? Sugerman explains:

> FEI works when other programs haven't because of its collaborative nature. It brings all the key players to the table—and it does it prior to ground-breaking. Before you even begin to work, you start to set your goals, you start to set up your plan of activities, you start to figure out where you are going to have gaps and specific needs.

Everyone also credits Stasch's passionate leadership, not just in pursuing such a vision but in grappling with the complex realities of construction work and using the implicit power of her position.

FEI has already served as a model for similar local and national efforts. Cook County has embraced the FEI model for all its large-scale construction and renovation projects. And, in October 1992, Congress passed, and President Bush signed into law, the Women in Apprenticeship Occupations and Nontraditional Occupations Act. The legislation, directly inspired by FEI, provides technical assistance and support to help women enter occupations historically dominated by men.

Since that time, however, shifts in the political climate and community pressures have forced an evolution of the FEI model into a "cooperative work environment" program that helps *all* trades workers, not just women. A backlash soon emerged against women construction workers, in part because of the special attention they received through FEI. For example, many men, resentful that tradeswomen had convenient changing facilities with running water and portable heaters, vandalized the facilities. Many women, for their part, were not comfortable with such special treatment.

As a result, the special programs of the FEI program—the database of available construction jobs, on-site mini-orientations about construction careers, and preapprenticeship training programs—are now open to both men and women. Workshops addressing sexual harassment have been expanded to address race and gender discrimination as well.

Also, a new director of the state's apprenticeship and training bureau reinterpreted the Civil Rights Act of 1991 in a way that prevented Stein & Company from using FEI program participants ahead of others already on waiting lists. Stasch complains, "This inability to move [women] to the head of the list for entrance into a union has taken away one of the critical tools used by FEI to accelerate the entrance of women into the union and onto the construction site."

Even with these modifications, Stein & Company continues its commitment to do what it can. And its progress in hiring tradeswomen remains impressive—223 in 1994 and 291 in 1995.

THE BUSINESS BENEFITS OF FEI

"People always ask us why we do this," says Stasch.

> They want to know if there is any business benefit from FEI. . . . The answer is yes. If you create an image of a company that is open and fair, the best people—women, minorities, the best people—are going to beat a path to your door. And if that isn't a business imperative, I don't know what else is.

Stasch has always stressed that this commitment is not simply an altruistic proposition. "They call us with business opportunities," Stasch says. "It's a two-way street." Stein & Company has shown, in short, that aggressive commitment to equal opportunity can *attract* significant business.

> A major portion of our client base are Fortune 100, Fortune 500 companies, and many of those companies have made very specific efforts to have a commitment to diversity and things like that. . . . What we found in several instances is that companies want to work with others that share this culture. We share that culture, and it's increased our client base.

Despite a severe construction slump in the early 1990s, with Chicago office vacancies surpassing 20 percent, Stein & Company has stayed nimble, active, and profitable. It has carved out a niche for itself in government-sponsored construction projects, which appreciate rigorous affirmative action plans in bids.

In May 1993, Stasch left Stein & Company when President Clinton asked her to become the new deputy administrator of the General Services Administration, the property manager for the federal government. As the number two administrator at GSA, Stasch managed an annual budget of $10 billion, 20,000 employees, and a portfolio of 160 million square feet of federally owned or leased work space. President Clinton praised Stasch as "exactly the type of aggressive and innovative businessperson this administration needs as it seeks to re-invent the way government works."

When she returned to Stein & Company in 1995 to become managing director, Stasch called upon many of the same skills to continue reinventing the gender relations of Chicago construction.

10

Barbara B. Roberts and FPG International

THE POWER OF THE IMAGE

The temper of the times, in all its rich nuances, can be found hanging in the hallways at FPG International. From offices just off New York City's Union Square, FPG makes a thriving business of acquiring and selling photographs—lots of them. With an archive of more than seven million images in 1996, and still counting, FPG is the second-largest stock photography firm in the world.

Each evening FPG's shipping department sends out a blizzard of photos to a huge cross section of businesses worldwide—advertising agencies, magazines, TV shows, banks, travel companies, retailers. Within weeks the images will sprout up in hundreds of ads, articles, greeting cards, periodicals, brochures, and billboards. The impact is at once trivial and profound. A fleeting glance will take in dozens of images, ignoring many of them while also absorbing other deep, subconscious messages.

This is the world of stock photography, an industry of some 150 agencies in the United States that together sell about $500 million worth of photos each year. It is a business that creates perennial images designed to be used by dozens if not hundreds of different clients. If "assignment" and fine-art photography have historically been the aristocratic show horses of the business, "stock" has been the stalwart workhorse. Bred for versatility and endurance, stock photos have traditionally had more to do with mass appeal than artistic vision. They are meant to be iconic popularizations, a visual vocabulary for defining social reality.

But over the decades, in catering to the most diverse clientele possible, stock photography has tended to idealize White, affluent, mainstream America while virtually ignoring ethnic minorities, women on the job, the disabled, gays and lesbians, and the elderly. Social issues such as homelessness, sexual abuse, teenage pregnancy, or crime have been totally off-limits.

This misrepresentation had long bothered Barbara B. Roberts, an unabashed advocate for women whose soaring career on Wall Street stalled when she encountered the invisible sexist prejudices of her White, male bosses. From 1990, as president of FPG, a business that in essence sold stylized stereotypes, Roberts yearned for depictions of American life that were more authentic.

Where, she asked, are the African-American families doing daily tasks together? Where are the sports-loving elderly people, the interracial teenage couples, the gay couples one sees on the street every day, and the harried single working mothers? After attending countless industry gatherings, populated almost entirely by White males, Roberts realized that stock photography was not about to embrace multicultural imagery anytime soon.

And yet, as a dedicated student of the zeitgeist and of demographic statistics, Roberts was convinced that the actual diversity of the American people could not remain underground much longer. Its most plausible future was to explode upon mainstream national consciousness.

Yet given widespread skepticism, the real issue was whether the idea could be made commercially viable. Would advertisers really be willing to embrace more socially realistic, multicultural images of American society? And even if they were, how could FPG begin to acquire a new archive of nontraditional photos? Why was this seemingly obvious idea being ignored?

Few people in the industry were better equipped to investigate these questions than Barbara Roberts.

A TROUBLEMAKER WITH A SENSE OF HUMOR

Sitting in her airy office overlooking the green canopy of trees in Union Square Park, Roberts is brisk, personable, and funny. She often punctuates her sharp analyses of the stock photo business with gales of laughter and confessional asides. If Roberts exudes a sense of command, it has less to do with her six-foot height than with her unabashed passion, self-assurance, and sheer energy. She deftly combines her appreciation for things aesthetic and emotional, which are so important to photography, with strong management, financial planning, and strategic marketing skills.

Roberts's ability to span diverse realms may have a lot to do with being one of the first women to carve out a serious career on Wall Street. Fresh out of Goucher College in 1969, Roberts began at Blyth Eastman Dillon (which later merged into Paine Webber) at a time when women employees were literally required to use the back staircase. In the early 1980s she joined Dean Witter, eventually becoming senior vice president for marketing. She ran the firm's internal radio and video production facility, launched major marketing campaigns, and became a member of the Dean Witter board.

Roberts recalls that she was "a troublemaker with a sense of humor. I'd try to call things straight out, raising consciousness without too much confrontation." One example is a photocopied cartoon pinned to her office wall: "The Evolution of Authority," reads the headline over four black footprints—of an ape, a human foot, a man's dress shoe, and a woman's high heel.

After a few years, the promotions stopped coming, and the reasons given had a distinctly sexist ring. "At one lunch, I was told by a key senior executive that he would not recommend me for an executive vice president position because he wasn't comfortable making decisions with a woman in the room," Roberts recalls.

> Although I had a spectacular career on Wall Street for eighteen years, I always felt that I was an outsider who was one to two steps behind where I could have been if I were a man. I felt that the institutions that I worked for were not really allowing or encouraging me to be the best that I could. It left me with an extraordinary sadness and feeling of alienation. I went in one Monday and quit.

Roberts's experience apparently inspired the coinage of the term *glass ceiling*, when *The Wall Street Journal* published a special report on "The Corporate Woman" in March 1986. One article featuring Roberts's career troubles was entitled "The Glass Ceiling." The term gained much wider currency a few years later when President Bush's secretary of labor, Lynn Martin, made a major speech about sexual discrimination in the workplace.

After leaving Wall Street in August 1985, Roberts set up her own consulting firm, specializing in strategic business planning and marketing. Several years later, Roberts learned that FPG was searching for strong financial and management leadership. In 1990, Jessica Brackman, the thirty-year-old daughter of FPG's founder, hired Roberts as chief operating officer and then, within a matter of months, made her president.

MODERNIZING A VENERABLE ARTISTIC BUSINESS

FPG, an acronym for its original name, Freelance Photographers Guild, was started in 1937 by Arthur Brackman, a former reporter and photographer. Launched when picture magazines like *Life* were at the height of popularity, FPG served as a broker between photojournalists and magazines, and as a supplier of generic-looking photos for advertising agencies and calendar companies. The company's heyday was in the 1940s and 1950s, when it established some of the most enduring traditions in stock photography with romanticized portrayals of the postwar White middle class: the suburban idyll, the marvels of technology, the consumer paradise, the beaming nuclear families.

By the 1980s, however, FPG's future had grown more problematic. Arthur Brackman died in 1982, leaving the firm to his family. Although his wife had played an active role in FPG's business affairs, she was inheriting a business that had changed little in its fifty years of existence despite sweeping changes in the stock business, not to mention in American culture. For example, although FPG then had an impressive archive of five million photos, it had done little marketing. Clients were not always aware of its holdings, and the company's market identity had grown fuzzy. Meanwhile a growing number of niche stock agencies, specializing in travel photography, celebrities, and sports, had entered the trade, taking bites out of FPG's business.

Certainly FPG's internal systems did little to help it compete. All transactions were still performed by hand and typewriter, even throughout the 1980s. Data about customer needs, previous orders, and even sales, payment records, and client lists were not computerized. In such a low-tech environment, it was difficult to control costs, improve employee morale, boost productivity, or enhance customer service. Although it was a profitable agency with a proud past and considerable artistic talent when Roberts joined FPG in 1990, it clearly needed serious management reforms.

Roberts quickly moved to modernize FPG's operating procedures, more clearly defining employee responsibilities and opening up new lines of communication. She initiated daily meetings with top managers, started monthly lunches for all new employees, and began regular communications and meetings with employees.

She also sought to develop a new corporate culture, one based on cooperation, civility, and diversity. To help spur this, she moved the company into new offices and inaugurated a new set of employee policies and benefits that included liberal leave benefits, flextime, and active recruitment of people of all backgrounds. By 1995 about 70 percent of the company's top managers were women and 30 percent of employees were minorities.

The moves were motivated not just by her social ideals but by her small-business priorities. "If you create an environment of diversity and respect, people will go the extra mile, they will give the extra service and care about quality," explains Roberts. She notes that small businesses have a special stake in fostering work force diversity. "We can't offer the same salary levels as the large corporations in New York City," says Roberts, "so we have to be able to appeal to 100 percent of the job applicant pool. Particularly since we are growing so fast, we can't afford to lose employees because of incidents in which they feel they are not treated well by managers or fellow employees."

Roberts instigated some sweeping operational changes, including a $2-million computerization of FPG's vast archives and operations. The investment not only improved the reliability and speed of service; it also helped boost revenues fourfold with only twice as many employees. Roberts also developed more aggressive marketing strategies to better serve clients and increase sales. She pioneered the use of CD-ROMs and online services to market and distribute FPG's photographs.

Within two years of her joining FPG as president, annual revenues began to nose upward, from $7 million to $12 million, and FPG's staff grew from seventy to ninety people. The company was showing a new assertiveness in the stock photo world. The question, now, was not whether FPG could compete successfully, but what new directions in stock photography it would choose to pioneer.

THE ORIGINS OF REAL-LIFE PHOTOGRAPHY

As a business that lives off its archives, stock photography has a long tradition of looking more to the past than to the future. Its identity is more invested in great photographs already on hand than in the more difficult work of acquiring new, contemporary imagery that could prove transient. This cultural conservatism is perfectly logical because advertisers and magazines, stock's primary clients, have traditionally wanted photos for mass audiences, which tend to be averse to anything too daring, ethnic, or experimental.

Curious about which photos were selling most frequently, in 1992 Roberts asked her sales manager to compile a list of the fifteen best-selling FPG photos. This was the kind of basic business analysis that many stock firms simply do not conduct. It was no surprise that the list included photos of a glorious sunset, a romantic couple lolling on a Caribbean beach, and the Statue of Liberty—images as basic to stock photography as "Blue Suede Shoes" is to rock and roll.

But what really captured Roberts's attention was the fact that *five* of the fifteen photos featured interracial children and youth. Previously no photos of non-White people had ever shown up among FPG's best-selling images.

The top seller was a poignant photo by Ron Chapple of three four-year-olds—an African-American girl flanked by a

Caucasian and a Latino boy—with their arms linked around each other's shoulders. The photo was once used in an Ad Council billboard campaign, with the tag line: "It's time we started acting their age. Stop the hate." Since it was first offered by FPG in 1991, more than 120 different clients have bought this photo for various uses, generating more than $100,000 in licensing fees for FPG.

The appeal of multiracial photographs was a pleasant surprise to Roberts. Just a year earlier, FPG had published a marketing catalog whose cover featured an Asian woman in colorful garb. "This caused some minor commotion in the industry," recalls Roberts, "because no one had ever put a non-White person on the cover of a stock photography catalog, except in travel photos."

Indeed, photos of African-Americans were fairly scarce in stock catalogs, and those that did exist tended to reflect White, middle-class norms. In one memorable incident in 1993, a top competitor of FPG put no images of African-Americans in one of its marketing catalogs. The oversight stirred derision among advertising clients, enraged some of the agency's employees, and prompted some of its photographers to switch their affiliations to other stock firms.

THE UNTAPPED GROWTH MARKET: MULTICULTURAL IMAGERY

Despite the neglect of diversity within the industry, Roberts believed that multicultural stock imagery could generate considerable revenue for FPG. The most compelling evidence for her belief was demographic projections. Harvard demographer Harris Sussman, for example, avers that ours is the last generation that will live in a United States consisting mostly of White European ethnic groups. By the year 2000, White men—currently 37 percent of the population and 42 percent of the work force—will make up less than 25 percent of those entering the work force. Sussman also points out that one in four Americans is not White. Within thirty years, this non-White population will double in size while the White population is expected to remain proportionately the same size.

For the first time in U.S. history, there are more people over age 65 than under 20. The average age in the United States, 33 [in 1994], is the oldest in its history, and the average married couple has more parents than children. One in six Americans is disabled as defined by the Americans with Disabilities Act. In fact, *Business Week* estimated in 1994 that the forty-three million Americans with disabilities earn a total income of $700 billion, making them a huge untapped market.

Anecdotal evidence from FPG's clients confirmed these statistics. Barbara Riches, an art buyer for Ogilvy & Mather, the advertising agency, said, "I have noticed that in the past four years or so, my art directors want more realistic situations—interactive groups of children from different backgrounds, more realistic families, families who aren't rich." FPG's director of international marketing, Karen Bernstein, heard similar messages from FPG's foreign affiliates: "I kept hearing from our agents that American photographs looked too slick. They are not believable."

Roberts realized that new media technologies—cable television, specialty magazines, desktop publishing, and direct mail—were helping advertisers to reach discrete demographic audiences in cheaper, more flexible ways than were possible through mass media. They offered more customizable, cost-efficient means to reach targeted groups of customers.

Roberts also saw that the ascendance of CD-ROM, computer software, and desktop publishing technologies was creating an entirely new clientele for stock photos. Furthermore, these new clients, as well as existing ones, were no longer clustered in New York, Los Angeles, and Chicago. These businesses were springing up in Seattle, St. Louis, Dallas, and scores of other places. The fragmentation of the advertising industry and the geographic dispersal of FPG's clients were profoundly changing FPG's market, Roberts believed, and this would require new kinds of photos.

Roberts's feminist sensibilities were also influential. "I definitely had a strategic direction and saw that the demographics were changing," says Roberts, "but my first motivation was women." It was also inspired by her intimate familiarity with immigrants, another marginalized group. "All of my grandparents were immigrants," Roberts says. "As a child, I had to translate for them whenever we went shopping. . . . So getting rid of stereotypes has always been important to me."

THE BIRTH OF A NEW MARKET NICHE

What Roberts had in mind was a new market niche that would combine the artistic quality and panache of assignment photography with the lower cost and mass appeal of stock photography. As it happened, the economics of advertising in the early 1990s were starting to blur the lines that once separated these two traditions in commercial photography.

Once the recession of 1990–1991 arrived and the bottom fell out of the publishing industry, advertisers and magazines began to think twice about expensive assignment shoots, especially if stock photos would suffice. A single assignment shoot can cost $20,000 or more, while stock photos generally cost only several hundred, or thousands, of dollars, depending on the particular use. (Most fees are negotiated.) Better yet, stock photos are available overnight. It was not surprising that art buyers at ad agencies began to look to stock agencies for creative work previously done in-house.

Rather than see this shift in the market as a threat, Roberts saw it as a rare opportunity to meet an emerging market demand for multicultural stock imagery. After all, there were promising demographic projections; an increasingly fragmented advertising market that favored targeted, lower-cost ad campaigns; new technologies that were spawning new clients for stock photos; and an increasing cultural demand for multiracial photos, as shown by FPG's best-sellers in 1992.

All that was missing was a new inventory of real-life photos themselves.

Roberts figured: Why not work with FPG's photographers to shoot this new genre of photos? Why not inject a new realism, and even tension and edge, into the tired iconography of stock?

Despite the compelling reasons, the idea also entailed considerable risks. Sure, the market had stampeded for several exceptional multiracial photos. But would it buy a broad new inventory of them? Would clients embrace a new catalog that overturned some venerable stock traditions and essentially declared the need for a new stock style?

A few stock firms were waking up to the nascent market demand for multicultural imagery and for more artistic, authentic photographic styles. But FPG did not want simply to tiptoe into this potential market. It wanted to develop it into a major niche that would become identified with FPG itself. The next challenge was to bring this vision to fruition.

CREATING AND MARKETING THE NEW PHOTOS

FPG could not just assign various photographers to go out and shoot pictures of "Hispanics" or "disabled people." Good photography, like good journalism, is generated by professionals who have a wide range of established contacts and a sophisticated feel for the subject.

In any case, stock photography has a demanding and peculiar aesthetic that even accomplished commercial photographers must learn. FPG photographer Seth Joel explains:

> Stock photography has to be a generic enough image that can be captioned twenty different ways, often in many different languages. Working closely with the FPG photo department, I have learned how to simplify an image—to remove a lot of the information and just focus in on the concept and make it as clear and clean as possible, without a lot of distracting elements that might normally enhance but, in the case of stock, take away from it.

The easiest solution might have been to hire experienced stock photographers who had access to America's diverse subcultures. Unfortunately, there are few such people in commercial photography, long a preserve dominated by White males. So FPG began a vigorous search for promising talent, contacting professional societies, trade organizations, and even local high schools and colleges.

FPG's photo editors began working closely with the firm's existing stable of 500 photographers to come up with appropriate assignments. This can be an intense, complicated process because each assignment must be carefully matched with the style, temperament, and personal contacts of each photographer.

Another way that FPG "primed the pump" was by adding new ideas to its "needs list," a constantly changing enumeration of photos being sought for the archives. The idea was not about political correctness, but about acquiring photos that provide a deeper, more complex portrayal of Americans, beyond the stereotypes of skin color, disability, age, sexual orientation, and gender. The need for a fresh approach, says one FPG photo editor, is suggested by the practices of a stock agency she once worked at: It filed pictures related to homosexuals under "Psychology."

In developing the new photo genre, Roberts's commitment to hiring a diverse work force now had a tangible payoff. Knowing that its employees were familiar with diverse cultures and interests, FPG asked them to help suggest appropriate photos, locate appropriate models, and identify potential clients. The entire work force understood, and helped actualize the acquisition and marketing of the real-life photos.

As the inventory grew, Roberts seized the occasion to issue a new "Sensitive Subject Policy" that appears to be unique in the industry. Its three key provisions: FPG will not sell any photos to, or work with any companies doing business with, magazines or tabloids it considers pornographic or sensational, such as *Playboy*, *Penthouse*, and *The National Enquirer*. FPG also refuses to work with companies that produce work it considers racist, sexist, or generally defamatory of any group of people. Some magazines, irritated by this policy, have sought to negotiate a compromise, but Roberts has refused, easily forgoing tens of thousands of dollars a year in revenues by her estimate.

Finally, FPG requires that no photos dealing with sensitive subject matter (such as alcoholism, smoking, AIDS, child abuse, homosexuality, and contraception) can be sold unless the models used in each photo provide permission for each intended use. This legal provision is important because the photos depict ordinary people, not professional models, who may or may not want to be associated with certain issues.

Originally, Roberts simply wanted to generate a larger archive of socially realistic images. But when enough high-quality photos had accumulated by late 1993, Roberts, with the approval and assistance of Jessica Brackman, decided to publish the new, separate catalog. Since this move would cost $500,000 or more, it represented a serious long-term marketing investment that would make a major statement about the company's identity and directly affect future sales.

The catalog that emerged in 1994 represents a landmark in the history of stock photography. Never before had stock clients been offered such bold yet sensitive depictions of social reality by top photographers: AIDS, drug addiction, Alzheimer's disease, depression, battered wives, and even child abuse and date rape were all covered. But the catalog also served up striking images of volunteerism, recycling, safe sex, adult education, alternative therapies, and interracial friendship.

To underscore the realism of the images, Roberts laced the catalog with dozens of concise demographic facts. For example: One of every three Americans is involved in a stepfamily relation. One in ten babies is exposed to illegal drugs in utero. Half of all women over age 65 are widows.

Most reactions to the catalog have been enthusiastic. "Exactly what should be done in stock photography," raved one particularly fussy, difficult client. An art buyer at a Chicago ad agency wrote, "Being one of the 9 to 14 percent of gay people in the world, I was thrilled to finally be represented in a positive way. As usual, your new book is beautifully designed."

Not everyone welcomes the new images, however. An Arlington, Texas, firm wrote FPG: "Please take me off your mailing list. This [a page with casually affectionate gay men and women] disgusts me and I don't want to see this." It was signed "Respectfully," from a "happily married father, husband, and advocate of the way things ought to be."

Because of its wide distribution to diverse clients, the "Real Life Collection," as it is called, is likely to have a significant impact. Unlike assignment photos, which are used for a single ad campaign, the stock catalogs that FPG sends out by the thousands become standing references for ad agencies and magazines for years. When FPG publishes international catalogs for its thirty-six foreign affiliates, it refuses to purge the "diversity" photos, as some affiliates in Japan and Europe once requested. Karen Bernstein, director of FPG's international marketing, explains: "This is an international world, and we are becoming more and more multicultural. This is a message we want to communicate very strongly."

By 1995 the Real Life Catalog had grossed more than $500,000, a strong showing for a relatively small catalog. Moreover, interest continues to grow, especially among editorial and textbook clients. As multicultural imagery moves into more mainstream venues, Roberts already sees real-life photos as "not just a statement, but an ordinary part of our business." It is a strategy, Roberts emphasizes, that has distinct business benefits:

> I believe companies and managers who celebrate diversity will have a major competitive advantage over the next five years. In addition to being the right thing to do, celebrating diversity leads to tremendous marketing opportunity for Latinos, women-owned businesses, and other groups; better, more creative ideas; and the ability to attract a wider pool of top talent as employees.

THE SPIRIT OF ENTERPRISE

Why has Barbara Roberts been so fiercely committed to developing real-life photography when it entailed so many risks, costs, and uncertain payoffs? Because, for Roberts, a person's social passions and ideals cannot be severed from one's business life.

Roberts's "diversity strategy" has catapulted the company from the middle ranks of its industry into the second-largest stock agency in the world. In conjunction with a series of management reforms, back-office computerization, new marketing initiatives, and the cultivation of a new corporate culture, Roberts has boosted revenues from $7 million to $35 million in six years. The FPG work force has more than tripled from seventy to more than 220, and the agency has come to be regarded as the artistic, technological, and commercial pacesetter for stock photography.

Barbara Roberts has found that there is more than one way to deal with glass ceilings.

11

DAKA International

COPING WITH AIDS IN THE WORKPLACE

In 1985, as vice president of administration for daka Inc., Allen Maxwell did not have much time or inclination to think about AIDS. Like most people, he had read about its terrible physical symptoms, the medical mysteries, the virtual certainty of death.

For Maxwell, AIDS was an abstract tragedy happening "out there," well beyond the operating concerns of daka, then a $164-million food service company that he had founded in 1973 with five other partners. (Shortly thereafter, daka became Daka food service, a division of DAKA International.)

Then one day Maxwell received a phone call from a district manager, John Lojko, a strapping, athletic man in his thirties who had spent his entire career at the company. Lojko supervised twelve food service operations, and was one of Maxwell's best employees.

With a catch in his voice, Lojko told Maxwell he was calling from a hospital bed. "Allen, I've got to talk to you," he said. "I have AIDS."

Maxwell sat back, stunned. "John was a fine young man," he recalls. "He started out as a cook, then became an assistant manager, then a manager and a district manager. He had been sickly, but I had never ever suspected that he might have AIDS."

The emotional complications ran deeper, however. One of daka's longtime clients, responsible for $300,000 in sales each year, learned of Lojko's condition and insisted that he be fired—or it would take its business elsewhere.

151

Complying with the client's request would be morally abhorrent and probably illegal, since in the eyes of the law an employee infected with the HIV virus is a disabled worker and thus protected against discrimination. Luckily, Lojko agreed to accept a new auditing job at company headquarters, with no change in pay. The arrangement effectively resolved the dilemma.

But it also served as an abrupt wake-up call to daka, which in 1988 became DAKA International, a $320-million company whose chief divisions are Daka food service and Fuddruckers restaurants. Daka food service, with annual revenues of $197 million in 1995, is one of the nation's top ten contract food management companies, serving more than 700 institutions. Fuddruckers, with $116 million in revenues and 168 restaurants, is a midsize "casual dining" chain catering to budget-minded families.

A year after the Lojko episode, a gay rights activist diagnosed with AIDS ran amok at a small Daka-run sandwich shop in Albany, New York. He was protesting what he alleged to be harassment of his wife, a Daka employee, by co-workers who said they feared working with her because of his illness. As it happened, the employee soon quit her job and the issue abruptly disappeared.

DAKA did not need a third brush with AIDS to get the message. Unlike many companies that still close their eyes, hold their breath, and hope that AIDS will somehow pass them by, DAKA management took bold action. It instituted new, flexible sick leave and disability policies; opened an AIDS counseling office; started an AIDS hotline; and required all hourly employees and managers to attend AIDS education seminars.

By actively fighting panic and prejudice with facts, DAKA has largely defused AIDS as a workplace issue. Moreover, the company contends its AIDS programs and policies have helped it attract and retain a more loyal, motivated group of employees, and made the company more productive. Chairman and CEO William Baumhauer, one of the nation's most visible business leaders fighting AIDS, has also discovered that his frank, compassionate advocacy has earned his company great admiration.

Arriving at this higher ground, however, required more

than a little courage and creativity to navigate past the fear and uncertainty caused by the AIDS epidemic.

WHY THE HOSPITALITY INDUSTRY LOOKS THE OTHER WAY

As the AIDS virus began to spread in the 1980s, a great many businesses had simple, direct ways of dealing with employees thought to have HIV or AIDS: Avoid hiring them. Get rid of suspect employees. Act as if there is no problem. And let business continue as usual.

Historically, the hospitality industries—hotels, restaurants, food service providers—have worried that the slightest business association with AIDS could be devastating. "There was this fear that if word got out on the street that my chef had AIDS, my restaurant would probably go out of business," recalls Maxwell, a former president of the New York Restaurant Association.

According to Scott Allmendinger, editor of *Restaurant Business*, "The president of a much-celebrated, well-respected dinner house chain with over 200 units tells his managers to send HIV-infected employees home. This is not a pervasive response," Allmendinger adds, "but it is a typical one. The industry generally thinks that it's not its place to educate people about certain things. It is aware of AIDS, of course, but it prefers to keep quiet or look the other way."

For some restaurateurs, a common strategy for ousting an employee suspected of HIV infection was "to pay his or her full wage in return for a promise to leave town on the next bus," according to a restaurant trade journal. Some businesses openly fired employees suspected of being homosexual, a practice that is still legal in many states.

These reactions have generally been based on gross misconceptions about AIDS. A 1987 survey by the Centers for Disease Control found that 33 percent of the public believed it was "likely" or "very likely" that AIDS could be transmitted through food. One third of hotel employees surveyed in 1990 did not know the difference between being infected with HIV and having AIDS (HIV generally entails little or no disability, whereas AIDS may or may not involve disease symptoms and disability). Nearly 14 percent thought they could get AIDS from cleaning a hotel bathroom used by an HIV-infected guest. And 7 percent feared that clearing the dishes of an HIV-infected customer could transmit the virus.

Because of such misinformation, large segments of the public in 1985 favored overt discrimination against people with AIDS, according to a *Los Angeles Times* poll. Some 51 percent agreed that people with AIDS should be prohibited from having sex, and 51 percent wanted them quarantined. Some 15 percent favored special tattoos for people with AIDS.

THE EARLY BUSINESS RESPONSE TO AIDS

The more farsighted segments of corporate America began to realize in the mid-1980s that business needed to better understand the economic impact, and moral and social dynamics, of HIV/AIDS. Most important, it needed practical, humane responses.

The disease had few precedents, after all. Ten years ago, medical knowledge was still evolving, and there were few guideposts for accommodating employees with the unusual disease symptoms of AIDS. Nor were there established techniques for ensuring confidentiality or squelching AIDS-related rumors and harassment. Not surprisingly, thousands of corporate managers became bewildered, anxious, and fearful when they encountered employees with HIV or AIDS.

The workplace tensions could not only be unpleasant and seriously undermine workplace productivity; they often resulted in misguided management decisions, and worse, expensive litigation. "AIDS has generated more lawsuits than any other single disease in history," says Rosalind Brannigan, director of the National Leadership Coalition on AIDS Workplace Resource Center. (The Coalition has since merged with the National AIDS Fund.) A single wrongful discharge lawsuit can cost $150,000 to $250,000 just to litigate, Brannigan reports.

To be sure, a small vanguard of corporations realized early

on that a concerted business response was imperative. Levi Strauss & Co., Syntex, Wells Fargo, Bank of America, and Pacific Bell, among others, developed some of the first, most farsighted AIDS policies and programs. Yet most other businesses, particularly in the restaurant and food service industries, were none too eager to confront the grim realities of AIDS.

BILL BAUMHAUER TACKLES AIDS IN THE WORKPLACE

Stung by the death of a friend and colleague, and still mindful of the Albany deli uproar, Allen Maxwell was determined to take action. In 1987 the company joined six other businesses in the region to produce an educational video about AIDS for employees. The group went on to create the New England Consortium for AIDS Education, dedicated to sharing AIDS-related research, educational materials, and policy papers. "Business generally likes to make intelligent, educated decisions," Maxwell explains. "Why not here?"

With the help of his administrative assistant, Louise Faucher, Maxwell aggressively began developing a set of flexible, compassionate AIDS policies and programs. The project received a significant boost in 1988 when Daka food service merged with the Fuddruckers restaurant chain. Besides swelling the employment roster to over 9,000, the merger gave the new corporate entity, DAKA International, Inc., William H. Baumhauer, a CPA who had been chairman and CEO of Fuddruckers, Inc., since 1985.

Baumhauer, a gregarious man with a commanding presence, had had his own personal epiphany about AIDS. Only weeks earlier, he had learned that the son of a close friend was infected with AIDS. But in this man's very conservative, midwestern family, nobody was able to acknowledge the son's illness, his homosexuality, or his apparent drug addiction.

"The long and short of it," Baumhauer recounts, shaking his head in sad disbelief, "is that the son tried to kill himself."

> There was a car accident. I found out later that it wasn't an accident. The father told me that his son had been drunk.

Again, denial. Soon afterward, the son died of AIDS. The
family was crushed—crushed in every aspect.

All this forced me to take a closer look at AIDS, to try to
understand it a little more. This happened to be a very
wealthy family. It broke down some of my barriers and mis-
perceptions. It allowed me to understand that this is a real
problem which can affect any of us.

With Baumhauer's ardent backing, DAKA embraced a set
of principles published by the National Leadership Coalition on
AIDS. Among them: to refuse to discriminate against people
with HIV infection and AIDS; to base employment policies upon
scientific facts; to provide AIDS education for all employees; to
ensure confidentiality respecting employees with HIV/AIDS;
and not to require pre-employment screening for the HIV virus.

The new programs and policies were not simply a matter of
humanitarian concern, but equally of sound management. Besides perhaps saving a person's life, they helped ensure a more
positive work environment, free of rumors, hysteria and harassment. As Allen Maxwell explains, "If our associates are unedu-
cated and fearful that someone back in the kitchen is HIV
positive, they are not going to be in the best frame of mind to
serve DAKA's guests."

A TOP PRIORITY: PREVENTIVE EDUCATION

One autumn morning, the chefs, food servers, and other cafeteria staff filed into a meeting room at Clark University in Wor-
cester, Massachusetts.

"You probably never thought you'd be in the workplace
and have somebody talk to you about AIDS," says Jack Orelup,
DAKA's vice president of franchise operations, a plain-spoken
man in his forties. "But that's what we're going to spend some
time talking about today. . . . About 160,372 people in the United
States alone have died of AIDS [by 1993]. That's more people
than died in the Vietnam and Korean Wars combined."

Orelup normally teaches DAKA managers about hiring policies, cash accounting, and other management concerns. Now

AIDS is also a key part of his training portfolio. He proceeds to show a half-hour video, introduced by a prerecorded Allen Maxwell who warns employees that DAKA will not tolerate AIDS-related jokes or harassment. Anyone with HIV or AIDS, says Maxwell, "needs the same respect, concern and support shown to them as you would expect if you or a loved one had a serious, or probably fatal disease." After the video, which features poignant profiles of three employees suffering from AIDS, Orelup invites questions from the rapt audience.

"Are there some kinds of condoms that are better than others?" a twenty-five-year-old kitchen assistant asks.

"Good question," says Orelup. "Natural-skin condoms can be penetrated by the HIV virus, so you should use only latex condoms."

"Can you get AIDS through oral sex?" asks a gray-haired woman in her fifties.

"Absolutely," says Orelup. "Any time there is a transmission of blood or sexual fluids between people, there's a serious risk."

Orelup seizes the occasion to dispense some advice: "If you're not practicing safe sex, please do so. If you're doing drugs, please call the DAKA hotline."

The most important goal of any AIDS education seminar, says Paul Ross, worldwide director of the pioneering HIV/AIDS program at Digital Equipment Corporation, is to "create an atmosphere of trust, where people feel free to discuss their fears, phobias and prejudices. The sessions must be interactive and nonjudgmental. Give managers and employees plenty of opportunity to ask questions and bare their feelings."

Bill Baumhauer explains what happens:

> The initial reaction of employees to AIDS education is, "Why me? Why are you putting me on the spot?" But after they go through it, they generally are grateful. When they begin to understand what happens to a person with HIV and AIDS, they start looking at the human being who is suffering. They have a tremendously different attitude about it.

LIVING WITH HIV AND AIDS IN THE WORKPLACE

The results of DAKA's initiatives have been gratifying. When the company hired Jön Stanley Szumigala III as executive chef at the Smithsonian Institution cafeteria, the opportunity gave him a new lease on life:

> I had just buried a lover who died from AIDS. And at that point there was very little hope in my life. And all of a sudden, I walked into a place that gave me the opportunity to be myself, a gay talented professional with AIDS. And all of a sudden I didn't have time to think about the disease anymore. It was marvelous!

When Szumigala's condition worsened and he sought short-term disability status, he said the company's attitude was:

> "We'll work it out! What can we do? How can we support you? How can we give back anything that you've already given this company?" Which blew me away! I can remember putting that phone down and crying for almost two hours. Because it was off my shoulders. I was out! I was able to discuss this.

Szumigala died in 1995.

One of the primary tools in DAKA's program is a confidential AIDS hotline. The majority of calls come from anonymous employees seeking assurance that their jobs and health insurance will not be jeopardized if they reveal their HIV infections. (The hotline is now operated by an outside contractor, partly to ensure an extra level of confidentiality.)

Louise Faucher, who initially ran the hotline, recalls:

> I got lots of calls from people who were worried. One call came from an executive chef who had waited, out of fear, to disclose his AIDS. By then he was in the dementia stage of the illness. Physically and mentally, he couldn't perform his job, so we suggested that he write menus at home. But at this point he couldn't even do that, so he went onto disability.

Another caller was a young Hispanic man, a pizza maker, who didn't really understand the illness or its medical implications, says Faucher. "It was very hard to deal with that. He was diabetic, a needle user. There was a lot of denial by his parents." Faucher helped the employee obtain proper medical attention.

BAUMHAUER BECOMES A NATIONAL
CHAMPION OF AIDS EDUCATION

One turning point in Baumhauer's evolution as a champion of AIDS education was a keynote speech he gave at the 1989 World AIDS Day Conference in Boston. Afterwards, he reported, "I was overwhelmed by the audience, the press and others, who asked how could I, as a CEO, take the risk to speak out to the public, and go on record and admit in so many words that this disease exists? A lot of people came up to me and said, 'Thank you for your courage.' "

Buoyed by the response, Baumhauer decided to move forward even more aggressively. He did not just want his company to provide nondiscriminatory health insurance and flexible workplace policies. He wanted to change the entire climate of national discussion, to focus on what one commentator has called "the ancient impulse to isolate and abandon others during times of terrible social upheaval."

Soon Baumhauer was seizing opportunities to speak to students at his son's university; to doctors at Massachusetts General Hospital; and to human resources directors at restaurant industry conventions. He began writing articles for trade publications, and joined the board of the National Leadership Coalition on AIDS. DAKA's programs were even featured on the front page of *The Wall Street Journal's* "Marketplace" section in October 1991.

At one conference, recalls Baumhauer, "One of the HR [human resources] people told me that their company had twenty full-blown AIDS cases, and he heard his CEO say that AIDS was not a problem at their company." When the audience at a conference panel peppered him with questions for forty-five minutes, and then surged around him afterward, Baumhauer realized how much business needed to do. "All these HR people were fed up and frustrated, and here they had a forum to speak. The HR people were screaming for help."

Their concern was well placed. In 1994, AIDS was the leading cause of death for the age group that comprises three-quarters of the U.S. work force—people between ages 25 and 44. More than two-thirds of larger companies (with 2,500 to 5,000 employees) had at least one employee with HIV infection or AIDS by 1993. Among small businesses (having fewer than 500 employees), one in twelve companies has had at least one such employee.

Fred J. Hellinger, a leading federal AIDS health care expert, estimates that the direct medical costs of treating AIDS in 1993 were \$5.8 billion, and the indirect societal costs roughly \$23.2 billion. Thanks to earlier medical intervention and medications such as AZT, AIDS has been transformed from a short-term death sentence into a chronic disease, with far-reaching implications for the workplace.

Meanwhile, incidents of AIDS-related fear, harassment, and discrimination were growing. According to "Epidemic of Fear," a 1990 report by the American Civil Liberties Union, there were approximately 13,000 instances of HIV-related discrimination nationwide from 1983 to 1988, many involving employees suspected of being gay, of being HIV-infected, or even of having a friend or family member with AIDS. In subsequent years these rates seem to have declined somewhat, but not disappeared, as public knowledge about AIDS has grown.

Yet the response from American business remains disappointing. By early 1996, only 20 percent of Fortune 500 companies were estimated to have formal workplace policies and/or practices in place for dealing with AIDS. In smaller firms, where most Americans work, the percentage of AIDS programs is negligible. The companies most active in fighting AIDS, especially as it relates to the workplace, have worked together since the mid-1980s, first through the National Leadership Coalition on AIDS, and now through a new, larger coalition, the National AIDS Fund.

Mindful of the human and business toll inflicted by AIDS, Baumhauer has not been afraid to argue his case to DAKA's institutional clients when necessary. At one Massachusetts college, a student became fearful when she saw a dried red sticky substance on an apple in the cafeteria. An editor on the student newspaper planned to write about the "blood," which she feared might be infected with the HIV virus. Allen Maxwell and other DAKA officials immediately met with the editor and the college president, and discovered that the "blood" had been raspberry sauce from a cheesecake, which had accidentally brushed against the apple.

Even though a campuswide panic had been averted, many DAKA staffers worried that Baumhauer's high visibility on AIDS issues would result in a serious business loss or public embarrassment. But when basketball player Magic Johnson disclosed that he had tested positive for HIV, it did a great deal to allay anxieties at DAKA and enlighten the public in its attitude toward AIDS.

Scott Allmendinger of *Restaurant Business* says that industry executives sometimes privately dismiss Baumhauer as "off-the-wall" because of his AIDS advocacy. " 'Let him talk about AIDS, and I'll swoop down and take his business,' is the general tenor of such remarks," says Allmendinger. But few dare to speak openly; none of the top human resources executives at six major restaurant chains returned repeated phone calls that sought their comment on DAKA's AIDS education program.

Baumhauer is unfazed by the scuttlebutt. He has come to realize that a strong AIDS education program is not only a decent and humane corporate policy, it also gives his business a significant long-term competitive advantage—in attracting good employees, in nurturing work force loyalty and morale, and in preempting costly disruptions that might otherwise occur in a fearful work environment.

SHOULD EMPLOYMENT LAW SANCTION PREJUDICE?

DAKA's commitment to fighting AIDS was tested again in 1990 when Congress revisited employment discrimination law, which includes the treatment of people with HIV or AIDS.

Throughout the 1980s the only statute offering significant

protection to HIV-infected employees was the Rehabilitation Act
of 1973. This federal law prohibits discrimination against handi-
capped individuals who are "otherwise qualified" to perform
the functions of their jobs, and who have been discriminated
against solely by reason of their handicaps.

But the Rehabilitation Act covers only federal employees
and employees of federal contractors. Moreover, it did not apply
to HIV-infected individuals until the Supreme Court held in
1987 that employment discrimination based simply on *perceptions* of impairment, with no basis in fact, is illegal. Eventually,
this legal standard was codified in the landmark Americans with
Disabilities Act of 1990.

But not without a fight. While this legislation was pending
in Congress, the National Restaurant Association and others
sought to pass an amendment justifying employment discrimination against HIV-positive individuals. Although the amendment's sponsors did not argue that HIV-infected food handlers
actually pose a health threat, they held that the public's negative
perceptions of HIV/AIDS were justification enough.

An attorney for the National Council of Chain Restaurants
told Congress: "Look, we have to deal with public perceptions,
whether they're accurate or inaccurate." A Chicago restaurant
owner argued in a trade magazine that the "restaurant community certainly does not need to reopen the door to misguided
public perceptions of a need for heightened vigilance. Research
has proven you can't get AIDS by eating out in a restaurant,
period. Why arouse unwarranted fears?"

But if negative perceptions have no basis in scientific fact,
argued the Public Health Service, the Centers for Disease Control, and dozens of other health authorities, then the law should
not sanction them. The U.S. Public Health Service declared, "All
epidemiological and laboratory evidence indicates that blood
borne and sexually transmitted infections are not transmitted
during the preparing and serving of food or beverages, and no
instances of transmission have been documented in this setting."

If food were to be accidentally contaminated with blood—
through a knife cut of a finger, for example—ordinary food sani-
tation procedures would be adequate for dealing with it,
concluded the Public Health Service. The food would be dis-

carded. What many people do not realize is that HIV-positive employees themselves face serious health risks from knife cuts and workplace exposures to communicable diseases, because their immune systems are less able to repel infections.

Charging that the proposed Chapman Amendment "fosters misinformation, condones ignorance and encourages discriminatory behavior," DAKA and other members of the New England Consortium on AIDS Education formally urged Congress to defeat it. In the end, both houses of Congress passed the amendment, but a House-Senate conference committee deleted it from the final legislation.

WHY PROGRESSIVE AIDS POLICIES ARE GOOD BUSINESS

For Bill Baumhauer the rationale for the company's AIDS program is disarmingly simple: Happy employees are more productive employees.

"We're in a service business—people serving people," says Baumhauer. "Many times I'm amazed at how we don't understand that employees need to feel comfortable and happy in the work environment. They need to feel proud of the organization they work for."

Though it is difficult to document, DAKA believes its AIDS program is helping reduce its work force turnover to a rate of 140 percent per year, versus an industry average of 200 percent, thereby reducing a major cost factor. "We find that people stay with us longer," Orelup notes. "In our industry we'll have two million more jobs than people to fill them. So we need to have people stay with us longer."

DAKA executives also believe that the company's reputation as a progressive, caring employer is helping to attract and retain more loyal, motivated employees. Chefs, busboys, and cashiers appreciate their employer's openness and compassion. Says a Fuddruckers bartender: "It's very good to know that the company is going to stand behind their employees if, God forbid, anybody ever gets this disease."

When one employee learned that DAKA planned formally to include sexual orientation in its antidiscrimination policies, and was considering offering domestic partner benefits, the astonished employee exclaimed, "Well, then, I will work here until the day I die!"

The benefits of such employee loyalty may be difficult to measure, but Baumhauer and his senior managers are not only convinced that it exists but that it greatly helps the company.

And what about health care costs?

Like many companies, DAKA has sought to control its health care expenses by moving to a preferred provider plan. But AIDS is only one of many factors pushing health care costs in any case, and is certainly not the driving force. The National Research Council calculates that AIDS consumes about 2 percent of the nation's health care expenditures. At DAKA, cancer and heart disease, for example, represent a signficantly greater health care expense than AIDS.

Corporate Cashflow magazine concludes that "employers can expect to spend a maximum of $32,000 over five years for an HIV-infected employee—much less than the estimated $85,000–$120,000 total cost of treatment from date of diagnosis to death." Hence the cost-effectiveness of prevention. "If one person, through our education program, took precautions and didn't contract AIDS," says David Terhune, the former chief financial officer for DAKA, "I'd assume it would pay for the program for five years."

DAKA's performance since Baumhauer took the helm has been impressive. Between 1993 and 1995, DAKA's revenue grew at a compound annual growth rate of 32 percent, reaching $321 million in 1995—nearly double the revenue of ten years earlier. At the end of 1995, after DAKA's stock had doubled in value over the preceding sixteen months, the Smith Barney brokerage firm rated DAKA's stock as the best-performing among sixty-three restaurant chains for 1994.

Baumhauer finds that honoring one's humane impulses in the face of a terrible epidemic generates lots of tangible and intangible benefits that, over time, come back to invigorate the company. "I find that taking care of people, especially people who work for you," says Baumhauer, "goes a long way toward making money for your company."

SECTION FOUR

UNLEASHING THE BEST IN EMPLOYEES

Introduction by Douglas A. Fraser

Douglas A. Fraser is a professor of labor studies at Wayne State University, and the former president of the United Auto Workers. Mr. Fraser first joined a UAW local in 1936, and held a series of positions at all levels of the union before his election as president in 1977. His ground-breaking accomplishments included his election to the Chrysler Board of Directors as a representative of the company's workers. In 1994, Mr. Fraser served on the Dunlop Commission to review federal labor law.

In the fiercely competitive marketplace of the 1990s, too many companies are failing to understand that a business enterprise is not just a collection of assets and machines. It is a living human community. It is not enough to introduce advanced technologies or more efficient operational systems. Close attention must also be paid to the personal, emotional, and social well-being of employees, and to the organizational culture.

Why? Because increasingly a company's competitive success depends upon unleashing the latent personal talents of every employee. A company's values and ethos are not discretionary humanistic concerns, but vital business assets.

A company is likely to become more competitive if its workers are personally resourceful and innovative, and if they are empathetic and friendly, particularly in service industries. As job responsibilities shift, employees must be able to handle diverse responsibilities with aplomb and to think strategically. They must have a fierce personal desire to contribute their best, and work as a team to achieve shared goals.

If the emphasis sometimes differs—employee empowerment, the values-driven workplace, the healthy corporate culture—the general point is the same: Market success requires assiduous attention to the personal needs of workers and the integrity and openness of a work community. In the most progressive quarters of corporate America, employee/management relations have moved beyond the pitched adversarialism of the past to embrace a more enlightened, fluid collaboration.

The five chapters of Section Four depict some remarkable innovations in management/employee relations. What is most striking in the five stories is the fact that no single model or management philosophy emerges as best. There are an unexpectedly diverse number of approaches that, in disparate ways, foster competitiveness while giving employees new dignity and respect. The empowering of workers, including giving them an effective voice in company affairs, also affirms the principle of democratizing the workplace.

The story of Jack Stack and the Springfield ReManufacturing Corporation is, by now, the stuff of legend. Stack, the originator of "The Great Game of Business," has produced enormous productivity gains by trusting workers to use their own intelligence and judgment. By teaching all employees how to read and use the company's financial data as part of their daily work, Stack was able to stimulate cost-cutting reforms on the shop floor that any command-and-control manager would envy. The phenomenal growth of Stack's company owes much to its spirited work community and quarterly bonuses for collective performance.

Similar lessons can be learned from Rick Surpin, president of Cooperative Home Care Associates, a worker-owned and -managed enterprise providing home health care in New York City. Surpin has demonstrated that employee ownership and participation can yield remarkable results, even among unskilled workers of the South Bronx. Not only did Surpin provide a career track and decent wages to minority women, most of them on public assistance or in dead-end, low-wage, transient jobs, he led a work force of such employees to set new standards of care in the home health care industry. This business model is now being replicated in several other cities.

Hal Rosenbluth, president of Rosenbluth International, the

third-largest travel agency in the world, has demonstrated that eliciting the best from employees is particularly important in technology-dependent service industries. While computer and telecommunications systems helped his company offer more responsive, reliable service, they also made the creativity and commitment of frontline reservation agents more critical. Precisely because Hal Rosenbluth understands the human needs of his employees, and the community dynamics of his organization, Rosenbluth International has been able to offer consistent, top-notch service.

Another pioneering figure in contemporary management/labor relations is Howard Schultz, chief executive officer of The Starbucks Coffee Company. While many employers are shifting more work to part-timers in order to *avoid* paying benefits, Starbucks gives full health benefits and even stock options to its entire work force, two-thirds of whom are part-time employees. The resulting rise in insurance premiums has been offset by a much lower turnover rate and a corresponding decrease in recruitment and training expenses. By nurturing his most important competitive asset—his employees—Schultz, like Rosenbluth, has built a corporate culture renowned for its high-quality service, which is the basis of the company's superior productivity.

Finally, Section Four examines a company that understands the business benefits of resolving tensions between work commitments and family life. Rather than ignore this tension, Fel-Pro, Incorporated, a manufacturer of gaskets and engine sealants, has created one of the most comprehensive work/family benefit packages in American industry. It not only offers on-site child care and flextime, but also tutoring for children, college tuition support for employees' children, elder care for employees' parents, career counseling, and more.

These programs have engendered a great deal of employee loyalty and trust. Workers, in turn, have eagerly cooperated with management, showing flexibility and enthusiasm in meeting the fierce competitive challenges of automotive manufacturing.

If there is any common denominator in the stories told here it is that in an era of flattened hierarchies and intensified competition, employers need workers who are resilient and resourceful, empathetic and enterprising, competent and creative—a set of skills, in short, that was once demanded only of managers. The following five examples suggest some highly successful ways to craft work cultures that are both competitive and humane.

12

Jack Stack and the
Springfield ReManufacturing Corporation

WHEN WORKERS PLAY THE
NUMBERS GAME

There is an innocent enthusiasm and openness about Jack Stack that always seems to disarm the big-city visitors who trek to this remote corner of southern Missouri. With a freckled, round face and sandy hair that is always drooping over his forehead, Stack's boyish looks and natural modesty belie an extraordinary business savvy.

Exactly how, visitors wonder, did this genial, self-deprecating midwestern kid, at age 33, orchestrate the most highly leveraged buyout in American history, then rally a demoralized work force to buy and transform their cash-dry, poorly performing engine factory into an economic powerhouse? How did the 119 workers and managers, with hardly any financial expertise, a small customer base, and low productivity, multiply the value of their company's stock by 18,300 percent within six years, building one of the most competitive and respected small companies in the nation?

The "secret," Stack likes to tell his listeners, did not come from an ivy-covered university or a big-time management consultant. It came from the employees themselves—the cam rod grinders, the inventory clerks, and the purchasing agents at the Springfield ReManufacturing Corporation (SRC). Working with trust and candor, workers and management together invented a highly original way of running a business that combines "business education" for all employees with active participation and employee stock ownership.

The heart of the system is what Stack calls "open-book management," in which every numerical assessment of every part of the business is made available to every employee. The radically decentralized system has not only helped SRC constantly to improve its performance. It has turned the company into a cohesive community that thrives on enthusiasm, hard work, and *fun*. Which is why the folks at SRC call it "The Great Game of Business."

In many quarters, The Great Game is hailed as a homegrown answer to the renowned teamwork of Japanese businesses. The SRC factory has become something of a mecca for students of innovative management, attracting a steady caravan of business executives and journalists. Visitors from India and China, middle managers from Xerox and Allstate, people with small businesses from everywhere—they all come to ask employees like Cindy Jacobs, a cam rod rebuilder wearing a T-shirt and safety goggles, how she tracks the company's weekly cash flow and overhead absorption rate, and why she cares.

THE LESSONS JACK STACK LEARNED AT INTERNATIONAL HARVESTER

Expelled from both college and a seminary for disciplinary reasons, and fired by General Motors for playing poker while on duty, Jack Stack got a fresh start when he took a mail clerk job at International Harvester. He was eighteen years old, and it was 1968. During the next fifteen years, in ten different jobs within Harvester, Stack saw in wrenching detail how a seemingly impregnable company—once the largest in the world—could actually fail.

The 4,000-employee Melrose Park factory of International Harvester, with twenty-six acres under one roof (one mile in each direction), was a living archetype of another management era. Steeped in traditions of secrecy and bureaucratic hierarchy, that management style dictated work parceled into discrete functions. People did their jobs, nothing more, nothing less, and no one was encouraged to consider how the enterprise as a whole might be functioning. That was for the top managers to know.

"I was the only person, apart from the plant manager, who actually had permission to visit any department in that organization—because I was the *mailboy!*" Stack quips.

Stack saw the disastrous consequences of contemporary versions of Taylorite "scientific management." It became clear when Stack, at age 28, was made superintendent of machining, the least productive of Harvester's seven divisions. It was a rough environment in which 500 unionized workers grumbled at the daily grind and were often careless about quality, despite the harangues of five general foremen.

No matter how hard management tried to improve productivity, the division consistently underperformed Harvester's other divisions. So Stack devised his own guerrilla management solution: wacky competitions.

After learning that the division was capable of delivering a productivity rate of $10 a person higher than it usually did, Stack challenged his work crew to exceed its top performance rate the next week.

> I told everyone on the assembly line, if you beat your all-time high, I'll buy all of you coffee. And if you beat it a second week, you'll get coffee and rolls. And if you beat it a third week, I'll have everyone over to my house for pizza and beer.

> At the end of three weeks [*Stack deadpans*], my wife and I entertained 200 people—the entire first shift—[in small groups] over a two-week period of time. It was the first time that anyone in management had ever gone to the organization and actually told them how they were really being evaluated.

What made his little trick work, Stack realized, was its appeal to people's latent desire to do something that made them feel proud: "People just love to have little wins. They love to play little games and feel good about what they're doing. And they will contribute—if you trust them." But this means that management must give employees the whole, unvarnished truth, not weave a tangled web of half-truths or manipulations.

Stack put this insight to work when he learned, at a confidential management meeting, that the company would soon pay a huge cash penalty for every day it went beyond an October deadline for shipping hundreds of tractors to the Soviet Union. Stack recalls:

> We only had about twenty days left. We were 800 tractors short, and we were making about five tractors a day. Going at that pace, we would have wound up about 700 tractors short of our goal. At the meeting, everybody was saying that heads were going to roll, and people were talking about covering their own backsides. They felt it would be better if we kept the whole mess to ourselves.

Stack had a different idea. He told his assembly line the truth, and posted a sign outside his office, reading: "Our goal: 800 tractors." When line workers, accustomed to meeting the bare demands of their narrowly defined jobs, were suddenly presented with a collective goal that made their individual performances matter, productivity took off. Freed of rigid job descriptions and inspired by a tangible challenge, Stack's workers rallied to the challenge, and began cranking out fifty-five tractors a day, a tenfold improvement. By October 1, 808 tractors had been assembled and shipped, to Moscow's and Harvester's great surprise.

It was on the basis of such episodes that Stack began to build his own people-driven philosophy of management: Treat employees as whole human beings who want to give of their intelligence, creativity, and energy.

HARVESTER SENDS STACK TO A TROUBLED OUTPOST

As Stack turned the machining division upside down in the late 1970s, Harvester brass began wondering if his talents might be usefully deployed at its troubled engine remanufacturing plant in Springfield, Missouri.

The Springfield ReNew Center, a remanufacturer of Harvester's heavy-duty engines, was bleeding $300,000 a year on $21 million in sales. Its 170 workers were so demoralized that two unions were vying to organize them. While the tiny facility was no jewel in the crown of an $8-billion, 100,000-employee company, Harvester executives figured that the ReNew Center might be a useful learning experience for the brash and clever Stack. With an assignment to turn the factory around or close it down, Stack, his wife, and two babies departed for Springfield in 1979.

The Springfield ReNew Center had been started by Harvester in the late 1960s to gain a share of the flourishing used-engine market. Unfortunately, it had never been given serious attention by corporate headquarters or managed with any rigor. When Stack first visited the plant, he found the shop floor in a shambles and the inventory in a state of gross disorganization. Productivity was abysmal, contributing to a backlog of orders. Employees were so disgruntled that they had invited both the Teamsters and United Auto Workers to organize the plant.

Remarkably, Stack succeeded in avoiding unionization. "We got down on our hands and knees and begged them to trust us," Stack recounts. "We groveled!" His sincerity won the day, and workers, although still dissatisfied with their jobs and the company, voted 3 to 1 against unionizing. Employees sensed they had a different breed of manager to lead them.

Slowly, in fact, things did change. The most basic problems, such as safety, inventory control, and production routines, were addressed. Improvements were made in delivery time, inventories, quality, even profits. A new discipline took root. But as a near-forgotten appendage of the Harvester empire, the ReNew Center could not get the capital investment or management attention it deserved.

This was partly because Harvester was going through some serious turmoil of its own. After a disastrous strike by the United Auto Workers that lasted six months, Harvester's losses were so great that it was eventually forced to shed its farm equipment division and other subsidiaries and to lay off nearly 90,000 of its 100,000 employees. To avoid bankruptcy and liquidation, International Harvester was reorganized and reborn in

1986 as Navistar International Corporation, a maker of heavy-duty trucks.

Throughout this period, workers at the nearly forgotten Springfield ReNew Center were paralyzed with fear and uncertainty. Stack recalls the atmosphere:

> Every single day when the employees of this factory came to work, they would come up to me and ask, "Should I buy a car? Should I get married? Should I have a kid? What am I going to do with my life?" Unemployment was running at around 11 percent. The company froze wages for a long period of time. We saw other factories close. Everybody was scared.

Realizing that he might soon be commanded to lay off everyone before being "taken out to a field and shot" himself, Stack and his fellow managers, hanging out one evening in a basement rec room, came up with a crazy idea: *Why not buy the plant ourselves?* The idea was born of pure frustration and the dismal prospects for change.

Stack and his buddies drafted a five-page purchase proposal and sent it to Harvester in May 1981. Harvester's swift, decisive response was to send six internal auditors to the Springfield plant, unannounced, to investigate possible financial shenanigans. Why else would its managers want to buy such a woebegone operation? Even though the auditors found nothing amiss, Harvester did not follow up on the managers' buyout proposal.

It did galvanize Harvester to shop around for other buyers, however. Two years later, Stack was shocked to learn that Dresser Industries, a competitor, had purchased the Springfield ReNew Center as part of a larger purchase of properties from Harvester.

On the Thursday before Christmas 1982, however, the chief negotiator for Harvester informed Stack that the Dresser deal had fallen through. "Would you be able to come up with $1 million more than their offer [a total of $9 million]?" the negotiator asked. "We'll sell the plant to you."

Stack groans in recollection of that crazy Christmas. "I had to try to raise equity, float a loan, and find an attorney, all by January 1, 1983, when they wanted to close the deal."

Since first offering to buy the plant, Stack had been on a cross-country odyssey trying to find a bank to finance the deal. "We were turned down in excess of fifty times for loans," Stack recalls. "One thing we learned," he sardonically adds, "is, when you've got a bad loan, don't go to the safest bank in America. Look for a bank that is in serious trouble. Because they're the kind of banks that will make risky loans."

His perseverance paid off: On February 1, 1983 (the original January 1 deadline had been extended), a West Coast bank agreed to finance the $9-million deal. With eighty-nine parts debt ($8.9 million) to one part equity ($100,000), and an interest rate of three percentage points over prime, which then stood at 15 percent, the deal represented the most highly leveraged buyout in corporate history. (Leveraged buyouts generally have a 2:1 debt/equity ratio.)

The Birth of "The Great Game of Business"

It was the brave beginning of a new company, the Springfield ReManufacturing Corporation, or SRC, which consisted of an unremarkable 68,000-square-foot plant and its inventory—and only 60 percent of its previous customer base. Dresser Industries, previously a client, abruptly withdrew its business after its attempt to acquire the factory fell through.

Thirteen manager-investors whose largest previous individual financial obligations had been monthly mortgage payments of $350 or so, now collectively had to come up with $90,000 a month in interest payments alone while meeting a $3-million annual payroll. The firm's only working capital consisted of $100,000 in cash. The smallest misstep could wipe out the company and, with it, the life savings of the managers and the jobs of 119 people.

"We didn't have time to go through TQM [total quality management] or quality circles or just-in-time production," Stack explains. "We didn't have time to write mission statements or value statements. Our mission statement was simple: Don't run out of cash. Don't destroy the firm from within."

During his two-year search for financing, Stack learned that the financial performance of a company is paramount. So why not make sure that all employees and managers could read their company's income statement, balance sheet, and cash flow statement? There was too much on the line for management *not* to give employees the truth, the whole truth, and nothing but the truth. Besides, as Stack had seen at Melrose Park, the truth could liberate employees to do their best.

Starting with a few simple benchmark numbers and moving on to a full-fledged training program for reading corporate financial statements, SRC quantified almost every element of the company's operation—from amounts spent on receptionists' notepads to the amount of overhead absorbed each hour by a person grinding crankshafts. "We constantly measure material costs, overhead, hourly rates," says Stack. "Labor ratios [labor costs as a percentage of overhead] are calculated on a daily basis—by supervisors, group leaders, department managers, and the hourly people themselves."

The numbers are not disembodied abstractions. Everyone at SRC knows the human faces, production methods, and market relationships that give rise to a given number. At workstations throughout the plant, grease boards proclaim the numerical goals and actual performance for every day and week. Employees become even more familiar with the numbers at weekly meetings known as the "Great Huddle," in which companywide numbers are reviewed by top managers and then discussed in small groups of employees.

Stack explains how the numbers "game" works:

> Cost control happens—or doesn't happen—on the level of the individual. You don't become the least-cost producer by issuing edicts from an office, or by setting up elaborate systems and controls, or by giving pep talks. The best way to control costs is to enlist everyone in the effort. That means providing people with the tools that allow them to make the right decisions. Those tools are our magic numbers.

Suppose we're paying $26 an hour for labor and overhead, and a guy decides to rework a connecting rod, which would cost us $45 new. If it takes him one hour, the company makes money. If it takes him two hours, we lose money. And it has to be his judgment call, because no two salvage jobs are exactly the same.

Purchasing agent Jack Bain says production people use the numbers to make the most accurate estimate of inventory needs, rather than make unnecessary purchases. "When you deal with the number of parts that we do, that represents an extremely large amount of dollars," says Bain. "Every individual has a brain. Let them use that brain—because sure as the world, they will come up with an idea you never thought of that is going to improve your bottom line."

In conventional companies, close quantitative oversight of people's work might lead to resentment. But at SRC, people take great pride in how they can meet or exceed goals. They consider it not only a useful and fair accountability tool but also a way to look after their own future. They understand how their individual productivity contributes to the company's overall financial performance, and how they share in the wealth they help create through quarterly bonuses and an employee stock ownership plan, or ESOP.

The Game helps employees see the interconnections of all parts of a business as well as the long-term implications of management choices. They see how the performance of purchasing agents can affect the production line; how the production line's work can affect warranty claims and subsequent sales; how the quality of sales projections can affect cash flow and, in turn, capital investment decisions and dozens of other choices. By seeing their company as an organic whole, and not as a collection of conflicting fiefdoms each striving for their own advantage, the company moves forward in a more coordinated, mutually supportive way.

SRC management is not the least bit worried if competitors somehow get hold of the company's numbers. Engine remanufacturing has few proprietary secrets, and is based on least-cost production principles. In theory, anyone, can enter the business.

What really matters in this labor-intensive business is the productivity- and quality-consciousness of the work force.

Perhaps the key reason that The Game works so well is that it satisfies two basic needs of any enterprise: It helps make the organization more responsive to changing marketplace conditions while providing a tremendous inner satisfaction to employees. People are participating in something larger than themselves, something that has a powerful meaning, both individually and collectively. One employee says of The Game, "To me, it means that I'm not just a name on a time card. I'm a person, and what I have to say means something. I matter."

In its second year of operation, 1984, SRC increased sales by 20 percent, to $15.5 million. The next year, as sales grew to $23 million, the company hired 100 new employees, swelling the work force to 225. Quality soared as well. Fewer than 1 percent of SRC's products are returned for any reason, compared to a 6 percent return rate in the industry.

Success builds its own momentum. SRC was soon able to offer some of the best warranties and most competitive prices in the industry. And this soon induced General Motors to give SRC a three-year contract to remanufacture Oldsmobile diesel engines, which generated 150 new jobs and $40 million in revenues.

ONE FOR ALL, AND ALL FOR ONE

One reason the entire work force buys into The Game is that everyone shares in a bonus plan based directly on companywide productivity. Managers and professionals can earn up to 18 percent of their regular annual pay; everyone else can earn a maximum bonus of 13 percent of regular pay. To keep employees interested in ongoing improvement, bonuses are distributed quarterly, in a steadily rising percentage, if goals are met. The psychology of The Game is key: Bonuses are not arbitrarily bestowed as gifts from management but rather as rewards that have been demonstrably earned.

The whole system of open-book management, number-based assessment, and companywide participation helps root out the company's weaknesses. After a few flush years in the mid-1980s, for example, Stack and his managers suddenly realized that the "charge-out rate," the companywide average cost of one person's labor, had jumped from $32 to $39 an hour. So the company offered to give everyone a 6.5 percent bonus if the charge-out rate was reduced back to $32. At the end of the year, the rate had plummeted to $29 an hour.

One year, employees nearly lost their bonuses when health care payments unexpectedly came in at $60,000 over budget. "It was the first time that employees really understood that some insurance company wasn't paying their claims; that it was really coming out of their sweat and their equity," says Stack. "People got a sense of ownership that they could in fact control health care and could make a difference."

Not only does SRC's bonus program tend to eliminate structural weaknesses in the company; it also helps to bring everyone together as a team. After all, no one can win a bonus unless everyone works together toward a common goal. That is precisely the message the company wants to send, that everyone is dependent on everyone else.

Nowhere is this more evident than in the building of the long-term equity value of the company, which is another bounty shared among workers. At present, 35 percent of the company's stock is owned by the Employee Stock Ownership Plan (ESOP). The original manager-investors own 59 percent, and the remaining 6 percent is held by individual employees and directors. Because the company is still privately held, the value of SRC cannot be truly established. But employees, knowing that the theoretical value of the company increases approximately tenfold for every $1 it earns in after-tax profits, can reap some impressive equity rewards through their own productivity improvements.

The fact that employees can clearly see the trade-offs between their own short-term gratification and long-term investment has created some interesting dilemmas. Once, when everyone at SRC had gone without a bonus for six consecutive quarters and the latest quarterly statistics were within thousandths of a decimal point of meeting the bonus goal, SRC's top executives were inclined to fudge the results in order to grant a bonus for the quarter. "We decided that people could really use a little morale boost," says Marty Callison. But when the question of whether to grant third-quarter bonuses was brought to the shop floor, the vote was virtually unanimous in favor of not taking the bonus lest it jeopardize the end-of-the-year ESOP contribution.

For Stack, informed debate about company dilemmas is exceedingly healthy. Line employees are assuming responsibility for their own behavior. Through The Game, they have a practical means to transcend the counterproductive "me boss, you worker" mentality that has prevailed for the past 130 years in American business. Stack is not opposed to unions per se. But he is opposed to the needless adversarialism and inequities that can thwart opportunities for wealth creation—opportunities that he believes are possible only when management and labor work together in good faith.

THE GREAT GAME SPAWNS A MOVEMENT

Judging by the economic performance of the Springfield ReManufacturing Corporation, Stack's faith in The Great Game is well founded. The thirteen managers' original equity investment of $100,000 is now worth about $23 million. An employee who started with SRC in 1983 has seen the value of his or her stock soar from 10 cents a share to more than $18 a share, generating a nest egg of as much as $45,000.

From revenues of $16 million in 1983, the company's business has grown to about $100 million in 1995. The number of employees has soared from 119 to more than 800. Stack says:

> I'll never forget walking through the fuel injection department one day. Somebody sweeping with a broom came up to me [and said], "You guys are always teaching us business and financials. I was looking at the balance sheet the other day and 76 percent of your receivables are in one marketplace, and that marketplace typically has a recession every seven years. If you really believe in job security, what are you going to do about it?"

And I went, "God Almighty! He's absolutely right!"

Another time an employee approached Stack and said, "You know, we've got an ESOP program here, and I've heard that eventually you've got to pay off an ESOP program. And in order to pay off an ESOP, you've got to sell the company or take the company public. So how are you going to pay off the ESOP?"

Again, Stack was stopped in his tracks. "That's a really good question," he replied.

The solution to these dilemmas was to identify new business opportunities that could generate new revenues. SRC decided to provide venture capital and management supervision to start the enterprises, each of which would be staffed by SRC employees eager to run their own businesses. The idea was to build up the value of the spin-off ventures and then, twenty or thirty years down the road, sell them and use the proceeds to pay off ESOP obligations. Already, several spin-offs have greatly appreciated, giving SRC ample surplus assets to pay off any employees who want to cash in their ESOP holdings. In addition, the profits from one SRC subsidiary can help out others in times of need.

To date, SRC has founded sixteen subsidiaries that manufacture a variety of automotive products (power units for engines, cylinder heads, electrical components, starters and alternators, kits of engine components) and operates a warehouse distributorship in Canada. One of SRC's most flourishing lines is The Great Game of Business itself, chiefly as a result of Stack's book by that name (Doubleday Currency, 1992). Over 100,000 copies have been sold, with four printings at last count, and it has been translated into Russian and Chinese.

Capitalizing on this success, SRC started a special division headed by Stack to teach The Great Game, as well as two "coaching divisions" to assist businesses in implementing its management system. There are now two-day training programs held every month of the year, a separate division selling training products, and an annual Gathering of Games conference. The Great Game of Business division earned about $850,000 in 1995. Over 2,500 people have toured the company since 1990.

The Great Game's success even prompted the government of Zambia to ask Stack to personally teach The Great Game to the 55,000 workers of the ZCCM copper mine, the fifth-largest in the world. Within the first twelve months the ZCCM mine generated more than $10 million in incremental cash, net of all expenses, primarily through increased production, with some mines setting new production records. Employee morale is soaring, and absenteeism, accidents, and disciplinary problems have all decreased.

Given his impressive achievements at age 47, Stack's current circumstances may pose as big a challenge for him as the Springfield ReNew Center once did. What does a man of such unquenchable idealism, business sophistication, and faith in people do for an encore? While Stack's professional options are plentiful, one suspects that he will find his true path in helping people rediscover "hopes and dreams," as he often puts it. "That's what our country is all about."

13

Rick Surpin and Cooperative Home Care Associates

UP FROM WELFARE AND INTO THE BOARDROOM

Talk to some of the 300 employees of Cooperative Home Care Associates (CHCA) about their company, and the same word seems to crop up every time: *family*.

"Everybody here is so warm," says Bibi Yusuf, a shy but poised woman who came to the South Bronx from Guyana five years ago. "I had never experienced anything like this *anywhere*. You can talk to anyone at any time, and everyone treats you so equal. You are *special*."

Working at CHCA, agrees Joanne Poue, another aide, inspires "pride and dignity. Pride, because the company has come as far as it has come. I feel the dignity has come within myself, because I'm a part of something that's beautiful."

CHCA's remarkable esprit de corps thrives under unlikely circumstances: in jobs that pay only marginally more than welfare; in a business that has been described as a revolving door of low-wage temporary labor; and in the South Bronx, one of the most distressed urban areas in the nation.

The sense of family at CHCA is not simply a pleasant amenity. It is the guts of the business, and is the primary reason that the company's employees have become renowned for their high-quality service. As the nation's first major worker cooperative in the health care field, CHCA has demonstrated that worker participation and worker ownership need not be matters of naïve idealism and dubious economics; they can be a highly successful business strategy. In 1995 the company had its seventh consecutive profitable year, with gross revenues of $6.5 million.

Not only has the company become profitable in the highly competitive New York City market, it has become a "yardstick corporation" demonstrating that higher levels of performance can be achieved in an industry better known for fierce cost cutting than for quality service. CHCA has used its reputation as a successful, socially minded business to push for sweeping reforms in the home health care industry and in Medicaid and Medicare policies. Its ultimate goals are the professionalization of home care jobs and improved pay and working conditions.

How to Foster Professionalism in Dead-End Jobs

As an industry, home health care hardly existed fifteen years ago. But in the early 1980s, changes in the reimbursement structure of Medicare and Medicaid encouraged hospitals to discharge patients as soon as possible. Home health care emerged as a cheaper, more humane alternative to institutional care, combining medical care with social service. Aides typically oversee patients' modest medical needs, help with their personal hygiene, prepare meals, perform light chores and errands, and provide companionship.

It is a fairly intimate relationship, and not simply a job. One client described her relationship with an aide as "almost like a marriage." For the worker, continuity with a single client can be one of the most satisfying aspects of the job. For the client, the same continuity can be critical to his or her emotional well-being and recuperation.

Unfortunately, the very thing that makes home care so attractive to the health care establishment—its lower costs—have historically made it an unappealing job. Wages usually hover a little above the minimum wage. Full-time permanent work is rare, as are health care benefits and paid vacations. Aides must work in isolation, without direct supervision or worker support, and they must travel to remote and sometimes dangerous neighborhoods. Training is minimal to nonexistent, and the opportunities to advance into better jobs are virtually nil. It is not surprising that the industry has an annual turnover rate of 40 percent.

Economists call home health care "a marginal secondary labor market." The minority women who toil on this bottom rung of the health care ladder have more colorful words to describe these sometimes dismal, dead-end jobs. Because many home care businesses operate like temporary employment agencies—as clearinghouses that match aides with short-term job assignments—the emphasis is often on getting "warm bodies" to job sites. The actual job satisfaction of workers or the personal needs of patients frequently take a backseat.

RICK SURPIN'S GAMBLE: WORKER OWNERSHIP AND MANAGEMENT

In 1983, Rick Surpin, an experienced community development activist in New York City, realized that the quality of home health care would not improve unless the jobs of aides were also improved. But acting on this insight seemed virtually impossible in a market governed by Medicaid and Medicare fee structures and administered by state and local governments. The home care industry was thriving precisely because it was based on low-cost, part-time jobs offering no future advancement.

Surpin's innovative but risky idea was to revamp the job of the home health aide by creating a worker-owned and -managed business: "We thought that if we could create a business that was owned by the workers, the profits that would normally go to a single owner or the shareholders could be used to maximize wages and benefits for workers." In Surpin's vision, better pay and working conditions would attract better employees. Motivated, well-trained employees would provide better-quality care, which in turn would help the company succeed in the marketplace.

But Surpin did not merely want to create a competitive, profitable company. He wanted to upgrade and standardize the professional norms of the occupation. He even wanted to erect a career ladder that could help the working poor move from home health care into nursing and other helping professions. The low-income minority women of the South Bronx, many of them single mothers accustomed to shuttling between welfare and minimum-wage jobs, did not need Horatio Alger stories, Surpin realized. They needed training in practical skills, on-the-job experience, and a supportive environment that could nurture self-confidence and hope.

Surpin had spent years chasing government and foundation grants, only to see good ideas wither on the vine for lack of sustaining support. Pursuing the same goals through a business enterprise had great appeal because it would give him greater autonomy and control while allowing him to serve social needs more creatively. The engine would be profits wrung from the marketplace. And so it was that Rick Surpin and several associates started Cooperative Home Care Associates in 1985.

THE GREENING OF A SOCIAL ENTREPRENEUR

Surpin's temperament and work experience made him ideally suited to this challenge. Since 1982 he had worked for one of the oldest and largest social service agencies in the nation, Community Service Society (CSS), where he experimented with "enterprise development"—the creation of businesses that would create "good jobs" for unemployed or underemployed New Yorkers. He had previously directed both a Staten Island community action agency and the Mutual Aid Project, a community organizing and economic development organization.

Associates describe the forty-seven-year-old Surpin as a remarkably creative conceptualizer and aggressive initiator, as well as an attentive listener and decisive executive. His commitment to social justice was complemented by entrepreneurial virtues learned through his family's wholesale food business.

As he explored possible venues for a socially minded business in 1983, Surpin had a few prerequisites. He wanted to employ more than a hundred people who had few marketable job skills. He also wanted to enter an expanding industry that would allow for the creation of "decent jobs," defined as salaried positions of $15,000 a year offering benefits and a career ladder.

Home health care quickly became a promising candidate because it met all Surpin's goals except one: The jobs were not "decent." The prevailing wage for home care aides at the time was only $3.75 an hour, with no benefits whatsoever. This amounted to only $7,800 annually, approximately half of Surpin's original goal of $15,000 per annum plus benefits. Worse, there appeared to be little chance of building a career ladder in such a low-wage industry.

Another drawback was the limited prospects for improving wages and working conditions in such a tightly regulated industry. The New York City market has always featured a baroque array of home care programs, funding systems, and disparate occupational definitions. These circumstances would make it difficult to redesign the transient, part-time jobs into permanent, full-time positions, which Surpin regarded as the essential challenge in improving the work life of aides.

Despite these disadvantages, home health care was also one of the fastest-growing segments of the human service system in New York City, serving approximately 113,000 clients each year. The city government was spending more than $850 million on home care programs at the time, 1988, with 85 percent of this sum coming from Medicaid and Medicare. In an increasingly cost-conscious health care system, home care was expected to flourish.

A BOLD EXPERIMENT BEGINS

To explore whether Surpin's business plan could truly become profitable, a team of CSS leaders began meetings with the ICA Group (formerly the Industrial Cooperative Association), a Boston, Massachusetts, consulting firm and financing source that advises on the start-up and management of worker cooperatives. Surpin points to the basic paradox he was wrestling with:

> A typical home care company would focus on high value-added services like nursing, physical therapy, and infusion therapy—things that will make you more money. But that would not benefit the people who we set out to help, the

people who do paraprofessional work. In traditional business thinking, our business plan went against the grain of a
high-profit business.

CHCA did not aspire to make the maximum possible profits in
its field; it wanted only adequate profits so as to achieve its social
goals and possibly fuel expansion.

For Surpin, a worker-owned business structure offered both
economic advantages and disadvantages. On the one hand, any
social goal that raised the margin between the company's costs
and its prices—for example, better wages, more generous benefits, and work circumstances that cost more—would create a
competitive disadvantage. On the other hand, democratic ownership and control of a well-managed company could help to
improve worker morale and boost quality and productivity. For
both competitive and idealistic reasons, Surpin bet that the latter
scenario could succeed.

In launching CHCA, then, Surpin's task was to find a major
institutional contractor—a hospital or nursing home—that
would agree with his basic premise, that upgrading home care
jobs would improve patient care. Surpin got a big break in October 1984 when the Bronx's Montefiore Medical Center agreed
to subcontract some of its home care assignments to the new
enterprise.

Since conventional lending sources were unwilling to help
finance such a high-risk enterprise, Surpin and his associates
had to approach foundations, charities, and other unconventional sources for loans and grants. In the end, they assembled a
total package of $350,000, consisting mostly of debt, with equity
stakes of $30,000 from CSS and $50,000 from the United Hospital
Fund of New York.

The final business plan called for full-time jobs for 70 percent of the employees, versus the industry norm of 30 percent.
Starting wages would be $4.25 an hour, 50 cents higher than the
industry average. Also, the company would provide an allowance of $100 per year for uniforms. Surpin's ambition to provide
benefits like paid personal days and health insurance, however,
were dashed against hard financial reality. They were as yet simply unaffordable.

COMMON PITFALLS OF WORKER COOPERATIVES

Perhaps the most problematic idea behind CHCA, from a traditional business perspective, was its reliance on a worker cooperative structure. Even though co-ops have proved to be a strong, resilient social and economic model in several European nations and parts of the Third World, their presence in the United States has been fairly marginal. The reasons for this anomaly are varied and disputed. One oft-cited reason is the lack of equity capital to finance the creation and development of co-ops, a problem that was remedied to some degree in 1980 when Congress created the National Consumer Cooperative Bank.

Another reason lies with co-op management. Although there have been some notably successful producer co-ops in the United States—for instance, agricultural, rural electric, and plywood co-ops—a great many others have been guided more by ideology and idealism than by strong management. This is particularly nettlesome in enterprises simultaneously pursuing egalitarian work practices, employee satisfaction, quality output, competitive success, profitability, and a larger social impact. By contrast, conventional businesses tend to measure their success by one yardstick: the bottom line.

A more familiar form of worker ownership in the United States is Employee Stock Ownership Plans (ESOPs), in which employees receive part of their wages or benefits in the form of stock, thus gaining equity ownership in their businesses. Since 1976, federal tax law has encouraged companies to establish ESOPs, on the theory that they help increase productivity, create more jobs, and encourage better management/labor relations. ESOPs also allow companies to tap into a lower-cost source of capital (workers' wages) than conventional stock offerings do. In the late 1970s there were about 300 ESOPs in existence; by 1995 there were about 10,500.

CHCA shunned the ESOP model and less formal systems like "quality work circles," in which management solicits workers' suggestions and gives them modest influence over working conditions. Surpin did not want home health care aides to have merely legalistic ownership of their company, with no active participation in the business. Nor did he and his team want workers to have only a limited and revocable influence over workplace decisions. They aspired to create the purest—and riskiest—form of worker-owned business, in which workers would not only have full ownership but actual control over major business decisions.

CHCA's Troubled First Years

The first two years of CHCA's existence proved to be calamitous. The first CEO hired backed out just before starting the job, and the second CEO had to be released from his contract after failing to show the requisite leadership. It turned out that the company's contract with Montefiore Hospital functioned only as a license to subcontract home care service; the power to make actual job assignments remained with the hospital's coordinators, who continued to make job assignments much as taxi dispatchers divvy up jobs to their favorite cabdrivers. Consequently, CHCA could not obtain enough job assignments, let alone enough assignments to remake them into full-time work.

As CHCA entered 1986, it was reeling from a vacancy at the top and a shaky administrative structure, growing worker dissatisfaction with unkept management promises, an extremely tight cash flow, no immediate prospects for additional institutional contractors, and increasingly anxious lenders and foundations. By the end of the year, the entire business apparatus, with 130 employees and revenues of $1.5 million, was careening toward collapse, as losses totaled $77,000 for the year.

Could this unconventional experiment be salvaged and made profitable?

Surpin started by offering to leave CSS and become the new chief executive officer of CHCA. While CHCA's lenders had some reservations about someone of Surpin's modest business experience taking charge of a $1.5-million company, they did not have any better options. So Rick Surpin, the default candidate, formally assumed the CEO post, and quickly proved to be the right person for the right job.

As a first order of business, CHCA's entire management

needed to be revamped and rationalized. Surpin fired many of the administrative staff and hired new personnel; began to establish new management systems; and became more personally involved with the company's home health aides. He secured several more home care contracts that not only erased the operating losses but allowed the company to offer a more generous benefits package, which now included life insurance and five paid personal days off a year.

Dissatisfied with the uneven instruction provided by the local community college, Surpin assigned a former colleague, Peggy Powell, to start an in-house entry-level training program for aides. Instead of blackboard lectures, Powell's program featured hands-on instruction dealing with the real-life situations that aides encounter.

Kathleen Perez, later appointed training director, describes some of the scenarios that CHCA aides would commonly encounter:

> What do you do if someone says, "Get your Black hands off of me!" Or: "Go play my numbers for me." Or: "Go get my liquor for me." What do you do if the wheelchair doesn't work? What do you do if you're accused by someone of stealing her soap?

Powell and Perez would help aides play-act the appropriate responses to such common problems.

On Friday afternoons, when aides came to the company's offices to pick up their checks, they met to swap horror stories, and CHCA trainers got firsthand reports from the field, which would be integrated into subsequent rounds of training.

The training not only made CHCA aides more skillful and resourceful on the job, it helped build their personal self-confidence and professionalism. Aides were not being blindly dispatched to strangers' apartments in crack-infested buildings to deal with all sorts of unexpected medical, personal, and social problems—the alcoholic mother, the drug-addicted brother, the sexually harassing boyfriend. They were rigorously trained to deal with such situations.

MANY ARE CALLED, FEW ARE CHOSEN

As much as CHCA wanted to help unskilled women in the South Bronx, the company realized that its quality standards must come first. Some 90 percent of CHCA job applicants are public assistance recipients, many of whom have never graduated from high school or worked at regular jobs. CHCA's answer was to institute a rigorous screening process that focuses on the person's maturity, motivation, and sense of responsibility; the actual job skills could be taught. In the end, only one in every four applicants is hired.

The thorough screening has paid off. While the rest of the home care industry loses 40 percent of its employees each year, staff turnover at CHCA is about 20 percent—and two-thirds of these departures are initiated by CHCA itself when it dismisses unacceptable new hires during their three-month probationary period.

Within months of taking charge, Surpin had begun to turn the company around. Worker morale was improving; the new training program was upgrading the aides' skills and the company's overall standards of care; administrative operations were finally functioning properly; and, as if to verify this heartening progress, the cooperative posted a $98,000 profit for 1987, its third year. But the original goal set forth by Surpin, to build a worker-participatory work culture, remained largely unfulfilled. That became the next order of business.

BUILDING A WORKER-PARTICIPATORY CULTURE

The compassionate, family-like work culture that Surpin and his top managers created not only made the company unusually productive and professional within its industry; it also met some of the most basic needs of home health care aides: for dignity, respect, and a caring community.

For home health aides, who work in isolated, emotionally stressful circumstances, yet have few natural opportunities to meet with their peers, these are particularly important. Bibi

Yusuf was devastated when the 100-year-old woman for whom she had been caring for four years died.

> I just gave her her last cup of tea, about three o'clock in the afternoon, two days before Christmas. And I saw her pass away. It really hit me hard, because you have a relationship for so long, and it's special. When I came here, everyone made it a point of giving me a hug, letting me know how hard it was—"Are you all right?"—and saying I should take some days off.

Surpin and his management team deliberately created opportunities for workers to get together for both social and business purposes. Instead of mailing paychecks, CHCA requires aides to come into the office to pick up their checks. The weekly arrival of dozens of aides on Friday afternoons is an opportunity for them to renew acquaintance, trade gossip, provide mutual encouragement and support, and discuss company business. Four or five times a year, after caucusing in smaller groups of ten or more, all aides meet in companywide assemblies to discuss and vote on major business decisions.

Rick Surpin moves freely and frequently among the company's aides, and is extraordinarily well liked for his soft-spoken, self-effacing manner as well as his visionary leadership. His example sends the message that business acumen alone is not enough; courtesy and respect are essential. CHCA managers take pains to pronounce aides' names properly and not keep job applicants waiting. A training manager was once fired because she routinely issued orders in a high-handed way and failed to treat people with respect.

HOW WORKERS BECAME OWNER-MANAGERS

In the South Bronx, where half the population depends on some form of public assistance, performing a responsible, full-time job with professional aplomb and earning a regular paycheck is a notable accomplishment. Recalls Peggy Powell:

> Anna was a new aide who had been on welfare for years.
> On the day she received her first paycheck, she ran through
> the office with the paycheck and showed it to everyone and
> said, "My paycheck!" It always gives us a good feeling
> when Anna comes in on Fridays.

At any given time about 100 names are on CHCA's waiting list for jobs.

Once the company achieved a positive net worth in 1987 and energies could be focused on building a worker-oriented culture, Surpin inaugurated "ownership campaigns" to recruit worker-owners. Upon payment of $50 toward the $1,000-ownership share—paid in $3.67 weekly increments over five years—an aide secures full voting rights on all major company decisions. At the moment, 260 of the company's 400 employees have elected to become owners.

To help workers make informed management judgments, Surpin and his team sponsor formal workshops. "We work with very simple figures and then build up to the more complex aspects of financial statements and business projections," explains Powell. At companywide assemblies, Surpin outlines the choices that must be made and the likely consequences of each.

Although CHCA aides clearly must learn much about how to manage the business, their control is not a charade. Worker-owners on the board are active and informed and communicate regularly with their fellow aides. The board also conducts periodic evaluations of Surpin's performance as CEO. "For me, that was one of the best moments in the life of this company," Surpin recalls. "It was the most rigorous evaluation that I had ever had."

By October 1989 the company's growth allowed it to begin fulfilling its original ambition of creating a professional career ladder for home health aides—the only such program in the country. The Home Care Associates Training Institute pays for tuition, textbooks, and release time for twenty aides to attend classes to become licensed practical nurses. Although the company may lose some of its best employees through this program, Surpin believes that offering a career ladder, and by means of it engendering hope, is more important to the company over the long term.

CHCA AS A "YARDSTICK CORPORATION"

By the early 1990s, CHCA had achieved its original goal of becoming a "yardstick corporation." Wages at CHCA now average $7.50 an hour, among the highest in the industry, and the average aide works more than thirty hours a week. Besides medical and dental insurance, paid vacations, and sick time, CHCA aides typically earn bonuses of $250 to $500 each year.

Surpin's founding hypothesis has been borne out: Upgrading the quality of jobs *will* produce higher-quality care.

"Life has changed since we started using CHCA," says Peg Sweeney of the Dominican Sisters Family Health Service. "The difference is in the quality and dependability of the employees. We used to work with four vendors. Now our only contract is with CHCA." Several of CHCA's major contractors, including Montefiore and the Visiting Nurses Service of New York, have named CHCA as their highest-quality provider. All three of the industry's trade journals have featured CHCA for exemplifying "best practice" in home care.

Surpin has aggressively leveraged this credibility to push for reforms in an industry riven by deep disagreements among entrenched factions—unions, legislators, government regulators, home care providers, and consumer advocates. Citing its own successes, CHCA argued that better wages and working conditions did not help workers alone; they helped patients as well. Furthermore, a more satisfied, professional work force could improve on the reliability and cost efficiencies so important to health care providers. With these arguments and the help of health care unions, CHCA helped boost Medicaid reimbursement rates from $4.50 an hour to $6.50 an hour in 1989.

Surpin then convinced historically antagonistic players in the city's home care industry to sit down and try to hammer out a common agenda for reform. It was a remarkable, unprecedented move that resulted in the coalition's producing a landmark 1990 report. It called for standardized job titles for home care professionals, uniform professional training and certification, a uniform client complaint system, and flexible, collaborative government oversight.

Surpin has leveraged CHCA's success in other directions as

well. In 1993, with foundation support, CHCA started a replication program that has established home care businesses in Philadelphia and Boston—and soon, two midwestern cities—based on the CHCA model; expansion into other cities is being contemplated. Inspired by CHCA, foundation officials are exploring similar "sectoral development" projects in child care and food processing.

After many false starts and setbacks redeemed by rigorous management and sheer determination, Surpin's ambitious vision of a new cooperative business model for the United States has finally taken root. Its fruits are likely to continue for years to come.

14

Hal Rosenbluth and Rosenbluth International

PUTTING THE CUSTOMER SECOND—AND THE EMPLOYEE FIRST

Tom Peters called it "Service Company of the Year" in 1989. Intel named it a "Preferred Quality Supplier." *CIO Magazine*, the professional journal for chief information officers, recognized it for top customer service. Experts, peers, and customers are declaring Rosenbluth International one of the best service companies in America.

Among the travel agency's offerings are an exclusive database technology that provides agents with a wealth of information to search and manipulate; customized reporting to give clients detailed accounts of their travel expenditures; and a worldwide computer network granting agents instant access to travel and client information.

Yet for all this pioneering technology, it is the attitude of Rosenbluth frontline staffers that industry observers, and countless Rosenbluth customers, appreciate most. They are "relentlessly upbeat," eager to help, and ready to deal with last-minute changes. They even take the trouble to call and inform travelers about breaking weather conditions or airline problems.

Any service company—indeed any company at all—would relish that kind of employee commitment and enthusiasm. How it all came about is a story of one manager's special vision and determination to make his company an "oasis" for both customers and employees. Rather than treating technological progress as an opportunity to squeeze out his company's human touch, Hal Rosenbluth envisioned how the two sides of the business, personal and technical, could invigorate one another.

The Evolution of Rosenbluth Travel

The early history of Rosenbluth Travel reads much like a history of the American travel industry. Marcus Rosenbluth, a Hungarian immigrant, opened his steamship ticket office in Philadelphia in 1892. During the early years, Rosenbluth and his sons Max and Joseph specialized in immigrant services, reuniting countless European families in the New World.

Through the decades that followed, the Rosenbluths' children and grandchildren guided their company through a series of transformations that mirrored the evolution of the country around them. In the 1920s and '30s, they branched out from immigrant travel to offer leisure cruises. When World War II brought the travel industry to a halt, the Rosenbluths kept their office open by selling insurance and financial services. In the 1950s, with the immigration boom fading and disposable income on the rise, Rosenbluth Travel focused squarely on vacation packages. The 1960s marked the company's first entry into business travel.

By 1974, when Marcus's great-grandson Hal Rosenbluth looked at the family business, he saw a typical local travel agency doing business in a very traditional way. And he wanted no part of it.

Rosenbluth's first job during college had been teaching literacy to prison inmates. So when he contemplated his postgraduation life, the staid family business hardly seemed the place in which to apply his values and try to "make a difference."

Eventually, but reluctantly, he signed on with the company, and his early experiences did little to change his mind. "At that time I wasn't all that happy within our company, and kind of wandered around to different positions," Rosenbluth recalls.

What discouraged him most was seeing the squandering of potential: offices crippled by internal bickering and negative attitudes. He wanted his work to elevate people. But what he saw around him—not only in this one company, but in many others—was a work environment that stifled creativity rather than nurtured it. It seemed to take from employees more than it gave.

When he encountered his company's fledgling corporate travel department, however, Rosenbluth suddenly saw a future for himself. Here was an inspiring model of cooperation and conviviality, a division where teamwork came naturally and people cared about what they were doing. Throwing away his vice president title, Rosenbluth demoted himself to reservationist and joined the team.

As he answered client calls and brainstormed with his new colleagues, Rosenbluth began to envision a new Rosenbluth Travel—one based on an enthusiastic group of co-workers sharing common goals and an inspiring ethic of teamwork. What he wanted was a robust community of motivated self-starters who would be encouraged to show initiative and creativity—and be rewarded accordingly.

As his formula evolved, Rosenbluth took command of the corporate travel department and charted a new course. In afterwork gatherings, he and his team set forth their modest goal of developing "the best company in America."

HAL SEIZES THE MOMENT

Luckily, Rosenbluth had hit upon a perfect time and place for such grand designs. His industry was about to enter a period of extraordinary turbulence and insecurity, in which the future would be up for grabs. In 1978, the Airline Deregulation Act phased out federal control of airlines and opened the industry to intense market competition.

"Prior to that, air fares were all basically the same," Rosenbluth explains. "Then all bets were off; the rules all changed and the marketplace became very, very confused. In that environment we found a tremendous amount of excitement, because we recognized that if we could take this confusion and turn it into knowledge for companies, we could be very, very successful."

The vehicle for this vision: the growing promise and power of computer technology. Rosenbluth saw early on that as computerization made information more available, his company's services could become more and more flexible and accessible:

> We recognized that we were really in the information business and not the travel business *per se*, and you can do an awful lot with information. . . . You can create strategies to buy better, create strategies to make travel easier for people—and at the same time, radically reduce costs. So, we went from order taker to information broker.

Computer and telecommunications networks, Rosenbluth recognized, would increasingly render physical distance irrelevant. Information entered at any point in the network could become the property of all. This meant that the knowledge travelers relied on need no longer remain the exclusive province of their local agent. Through sophisticated computer databases and telecommunications, an agent in Atlanta could seamlessly step in to serve a customer in Los Angeles, thereby optimizing agents' time and ensuring rapid service even during periods of heavy call volume in a given locality.

In 1981, Rosenbluth put the initial piece of this system in place. The company's Philadelphia reservation center became a centralized site where reservations were handled for multiple corporate clients—an industry first. This pooling of resources lowered expenses and allowed Rosenbluth to make agents with focused expertise (such as Eastern European travel) available to all its client companies.

Over the next few years, the company launched the prototypes of a series of exclusive systems that gave Rosenbluth travel associates an unprecedented flow of information—and unrivaled independence.

Most travel agencies, historically, had relied on the major airlines' proprietary systems for their fare and scheduling information and for critical reporting functions. Rosenbluth's "READOUT" software, which premiered in 1983, offered the first unbiased third-party access to fares and seat availability. At the same time, the company made an enormous long-term investment to develop independent back-room systems, including custom accounting and reporting capabilities.

With this combination, Rosenbluth became the first travel agency to control the information required to truly manage clients' travel expenses. Since travel and entertainment are typically a corporation's third-largest operating expense, the outlook for Rosenbluth was tantalizing indeed.

THE POINT OF NO RETURN

Spurred by the new services and technologies, Rosenbluth's annual sales topped $150 million by 1984. The company had grown from a local agency to a regional one, with business travel now its focus. Rosenbluth even opened satellite offices in Philadelphia International Airport to better serve its business clients.

Hal Rosenbluth, as the architect of this accelerating growth, was poised to become president of the company. But the true watershed was yet to come.

Traditionally, and even into the 1980s, corporate clients managed their travel on a local basis. Each office of a major corporation would contract with a nearby travel agency to handle its ticketing and hotel reservations. But, in 1984, Du Pont shook the entire travel industry by tossing aside the old local model, becoming the first major corporation to seek a consolidation of its nationwide travel arrangements through a single agency. That agency would have to go beyond simple ticketing to work with Du Pont as a travel management partner.

After an extensive, bitterly fought contest, Du Pont selected the small company over the industry giants. It had been impressed with Rosenbluth's aggressive vision, service, and technology. The move stunned the travel trade and put Rosenbluth under a microscope. More significantly, Du Pont's collaboration with Rosenbluth changed the business of corporate travel and catapulted the company into a whole new arena of competition.

TECHNOLOGY TO EMPOWER, NOT DEHUMANIZE

For Hal Rosenbluth, the prospect of this transformation was invigorating, but there were some things about his family business that he did *not* want to change. Throughout the company's growth, Rosenbluth had devoted much attention to making the company a caring, family environment. On the brink of explosive growth and sweeping technological change, the company's business prospects glittered, but its culture was newly vulnerable.

"We knew that we had an environment here, an atmosphere that was something very, very special," recalls Frank Hoffmann, a longtime Rosenbluth executive.

> And what Hal really wanted to do was to make sure that as we grew, not only in numbers, but as we spread out through the United States and started to do business in areas of the country we never had before, that the culture would remain intact—that the best parts of what we had would remain.

Too often, Rosenbluth realized, growth and technology are sources of fear for employees and customers, resulting in a dehumanized work environment and declining service. Workplace automation is presumed to be the enemy of the "human touch." Yet Rosenbluth envisioned an information-driven company that would give frontline service people more responsibility and decision-making power than ever before. The technology would transform passive order takers into skilled travel consultants. Far from replacing human effort, the new systems would place a premium on individual initiative.

Rosenbluth explains:

> When you boil everything down, what we really sell is thought . . . and that is a result of good people who can think smartly and understand what you can do to create opportunities for clientele through this confusion. . . . Processes don't come from a computer. Products don't come from a computer. There are applications obviously that help, but all those things are a result of people.

Remembering the positive teamwork that had first attracted him to the corporate travel division, Rosenbluth was convinced that a spirited company was the only kind of place that could thrive through the stresses of change that lay ahead.

ROSENBLUTH'S PLAN: PROMOTE "HAPPINESS"

Hal Rosenbluth's need—to attract the best people and harness their energies—is a common business challenge. His strategy was far from ordinary, however. Rosenbluth and his colleagues resolved to establish formal programs and policies to promote *happiness*.

The word alone sets the company apart. Most employers care about their employees' well-being, and may track "satisfaction" ratings or try to make work "rewarding." But how many CEOs dare to address happiness in the workplace? Rosenbluth describes why he believes it is important:

> I think that companies today have an obligation to create an environment where people are happy. Because if people aren't happy and they don't like the company they are a part of, if they don't like their leader, then they are really not going to be focusing on the customer. They're going to be focusing on their résumé.

At Rosenbluth, workplace happiness was not merely discussed. It became a central strategic objective. This commitment meant reexamining the large and small ways in which the company affects its employees' lives, from hiring and training to day-to-day management and long-range planning. It meant rejecting the very words *employees* and *managers* in favor of *associates* and *leaders*. "At this company," Rosenbluth proclaims with a contrarian brashness, "the customer comes second"—the title of his 1993 book, *The Customer Comes Second and Other Secrets of Exceptional Service*.

The initial step was to choose the right people. Rosenbluth's team reasoned that the most important part of any employee's working environment is his or her co-workers. A positive attitude and flexibility are indispensable, especially in a dynamic, fast-paced company. So, in recruiting new associates to keep up with growth, the number one criterion, even more important than conventional credentials or job experience, became niceness.

If *happiness* is too soft a word for most business forums, *niceness* is off the scale. Yet it is a concept that Rosenbluth International has taken very seriously. Says human resources director Cecily Carel:

> It's something we look for from the very beginning of the interviewing process. From the moment the individual sends a letter to us or places a telephone call, through the various stages until the actual physical interview. . . . One needs to have that deep-seated sense of really caring about other people and naturally wanting to go the extra mile.

A substantial number of Rosenbluth associates had no experience in the travel industry before joining the company. Rosenbluth has found countless gems by looking past traditional qualifications. As Vice President for Operations Kathy Veit explains:

> We find that it is worthwhile for us to spend some additional time in training on the skills. You can learn skills that you need for a particular job, but you can't usually learn how to be nice. And so we really look for people who will fit well into our company and into our culture.

KEEPING CONNECTED WITH EMPLOYEES

As Rosenbluth won more national contracts and began to recruit and set up offices across the country, its unusual hiring process became even more important to ensure consistent service. The rapid growth also raised some troubling questions for a company that valued its family atmosphere and shared goals. As new people streamed in and the organization spread out geographically, how could the leaders share their vision and philosophies with new recruits?

Rosenbluth addressed this problem by harnessing what he

considered a shamefully underutilized resource: the excitement
and curiosity of each associate's first day of work. He recalls:

> So many times the first couple of days of someone's em-
> ployment are anticipated to be the most exciting. I know
> when I got my first job, I got dressed two days ahead of
> time. I was going to go in there and set the company on fire
> and help determine its destiny. What I ran into was a stack
> of forms to fill out. It was just like the air came out of my
> balloon. And I never wanted that to happen to anyone who
> joined our company.

When new employees join any Rosenbluth International office, their first two days are spent at the company's world headquarters in Philadelphia so that they can experience the
excitement of the company's vision and the depth of its values.
Says Frank Hoffmann:

> We don't spend any time on job skill training. We don't fill
> out benefits forms the first two days. We do nothing but talk
> about the values of the organization, the industry that we
> are in, the status that we have in that industry, and the
> things that are important to us as human beings—the way
> we treat one another.

At orientation, new employees from all levels of the organization cluster around tables, working on small-group projects.
Their tools—crayons, Magic Markers, sheets of newsprint—call
to mind a grade-school classroom more than a typical corporate
orientation. And the projects they tackle have nothing to do with
the travel business—at least directly.

But the enthusiasm in the room is infectious as they plunge
into creative group projects and see links to some of the issues
that Hal Rosenbluth considers most critical to his company's
success, like innovation, openness, leadership.

The next day, the new associates are asked to recall a time
when they encountered poor service, and to act out the experience in a skit. After the hilarious presentations of terrible service,
they discuss how the situation could have been turned around
into a positive one. Then, after acting out the new and improved

version, they are asked to go back one more time and think of ways to push the service up even one more level, from good to exceptional.

The final stage of orientation draws all the lessons together. After a tour of the building, the orientation group gathers for afternoon tea served by Hal Rosenbluth and other top officers of the company. This unusual ceremony, repeated dozens of times each year, is both an illustration of Rosenbluth's service ideal and a warm welcome to the company. Associates leave with the understanding that their contributions will be valued.

THE OPEN, DECENTRALIZED WORKPLACE

The open organization that associates experience during their first days is reflected throughout the workplace. When Rosen-bluth reshaped the company to focus on corporate travel management, he decentralized the decision-making process. Associates at all levels now operate under minimal supervision and have access to all the data they need to make informed judgments.

The result: During the company's explosive rise to the top of the travel industry, layers of hierarchy were actually reduced. Rosenbluth has declared bureaucracy the "archenemy," a stultifying force that strips an organization of its vitality.

"We guard our environment like gold," he says, "because the margins in our business are exceedingly slim. There is no room for anything that would detract from our ability to constantly operate as efficiently and effectively as possible." At Rosenbluth, operating efficiently means motivating each associate to use the best of his or her abilities.

Says Cecily Carel:

> When frontline associates know that they have decision-making ability, they feel part of the organization. They know that how they respond to a client, what they do and say, is ultimately going to form the basis of our reputation. . . . In a lot of other companies, I think one often

needs to be at much more senior levels to really feel that one is making an impact on the organization as a whole.

This open decision-making structure has two sides. Front-line staffers are not only allotted more responsibility; they are also given freer access to upper management to express opinions and offer ideas. "It's not just an open door policy," says Kathy Veit. "It's really sitting down with people, talking with them, creating that environment day to day, where people will be willing to really share what they are thinking about." The company has developed extensive leadership training programs to help managers develop this kind of open environment.

Rosenbluth encourages all associates to offer their ideas on how to improve the company, from procedures in their own offices to worldwide policies and strategies. An annual "idea week" drives the point home, but the working environment offers opportunities to express ideas year-round.

FEEDBACK TOOLS: THE "HAL HOTLINE" AND CRAYON DRAWINGS

One unusual technique is the "Hal Hotline," a voice-mail link that any associate can dial up to leave messages directly for Hal Rosenbluth. Rosenbluth responds personally to every message—and takes each one seriously. The hotline is more than just an electronic suggestion box. It also serves as a means for Rosenbluth to keep in touch with employees' concerns and opinions, even as his company's work force spreads worldwide. "It's an avenue for me to keep my finger on the pulse of the company, which is really the pulse of thousands of people," Rosenbluth says.

Rosenbluth also meets with internal focus groups to ensure that the goals and principles established at headquarters are being realized in all the company's offices. One such group, a representative cross section of associates, holds two day-long meetings with Rosenbluth each year. The subjects of discussion: morale, fulfillment, and happiness in the workplace.

One of Rosenbluth's favorite techniques for eliciting employees' views is asking them to draw how they feel about the company, using crayons. The response, Rosenbluth insists, is far more revealing than what any traditional survey could elicit. "Through those pictures," he says, "you get a tremendous amount of insight into someone's frustrations, and the things that make people very happy." On several occasions a drawing has identified a problem that no one had been willing to put into words. Rosenbluth has even extended this approach to clients, asking them to depict their feelings about his company's service.

Another Rosenbluth trademark is "upward reviewing," a turning of the tables on the traditional review process by asking associates to assess the performance of their supervisors. Hal started the process with himself. "He asked all of the vice presidents that reported to him to review his performance, to review his skills, and to be very honest with him," recalls Frank Hoffmann. The process proved so rewarding that the entire company eventually shifted to a "360-degree" review process, incorporating the evaluations of employees, supervisors, and even clients.

All Rosenbluth associates are encouraged to create "personal development plans" in consultation with their supervisors. The plan outlines skills that the individual would like to develop and career paths within the company that he or she wants to explore. Any associate who is interested in a particular area of the company can learn more about it through a program called "associate of the day." The ultimate expression of open management, this program gives the employee the opportunity to shadow a top executive through an entire workday. Since the program's inception, more than a hundred associates have spent the day with Hal Rosenbluth himself.

Mary Holton, a Rosenbluth reservationist, came to the company after a long career in teaching. She appreciated the chance to start afresh and to grow in her new career. "There is somehow a quality that permeates this company that allows people to develop in ways that you might never have suspected or been able to predict," says Holton.

Associate David Buchholtz, a travel industry veteran, appreciates the contrast with the agencies in which he previously worked. "Everyone just works together," he says, "they all pitch in, they help out when necessary—everybody just seems to get along."

REAPING THE REWARDS

Rosenbluth's fierce focus on its employees' happiness has engendered a rare loyalty and enthusiasm. The company's turnover rate is substantially lower than its competition's, and the majority of the turnover occurs during the first weeks of probationary employment. As the company's good reputation has spread, it has also proved a boon to the recruitment process. "We have received literally thousands of unsolicited résumés and telephone calls," notes Cecily Carel.

Jessica Miller, a newcomer to Rosenbluth's corporate communications department, was among the associates attracted by the company's renown as a good place to work. "I had grown up in this area, and Rosenbluth has an amazing reputation," says Miller. "As far as a career path, it was where I wanted to go." Such dedicated employees have built Rosenbluth's reputation for exemplary service.

A Rosenbluth client, Lisa Piniella, corporate travel manager for Oracle Corporation, has consolidated all her company's travel with Rosenbluth International. She explains why:

> What we look for from a travel supplier is not just a set of order takers. You can basically get that anywhere. What we're looking for are people in a more consultative role. . . . Anything they can do to get my travelers from A to B in the most convenient way possible, but also at the lowest cost possible, I appreciate.

Management expert Jim Kouzes confirms Rosenbluth International's national reputation as a service leader:

> Rosenbluth has achieved this status because of its singular focus on its employees. From his obsessive attention to employee training to his proper service of high tea at all new employee orientations, Hal Rosenbluth lives his philosophy that employees are second to none. . . . He is proof that

when you focus on people, social vision does indeed pay off.

The exceptional performance of Rosenbluth's reservation staff has led to even more exceptional corporate performance by Rosenbluth International. As of October 1995, Rosenbluth boasted 1,000 locations worldwide, 3,500 associates, and $2.5 billion in travel sales—up a hundredfold from the late 1970s, when Hal assumed leadership of the corporate travel division. Even more impressive, these numbers translate to over $700,000 in sales per employee annually—a tenfold increase over the same period.

An industry that was staid and supposedly mature at the time of Hal Rosenbluth's arrival is now being constantly reinvented by his dynamic, fast-growing company. For Hal Rosenbluth, it all comes down to focusing first on the factors that most companies attend to last. "I think that people have to recognize the absolute importance of the human mind and of the human psyche," says Rosenbluth. "There are 3,500 minds in this company. You put them all together, you can do amazing things."

15

Howard Schultz and The Starbucks Coffee Company

EMPLOYEES AS PARTNERS IN GROWTH

On a weekday morning at a retail store in northern California, a line forms, disappears, then re-forms. The employees behind the counter call out to each other; they work together as efficiently as the espresso machine sibilating nearby. Above their heads hang pictures of coffee cups, ingredients sketched to the side like architectural drawings. A *barista* (Italian for bartender) and customer confer quietly: Does she want a dark roast? Is the coffeemaker a drip or an automatic? Is the filter circular or cone-shaped?

Outside, a woman spills an entire caffé latte on the seat of her car. One of the *barista*s helps her clean up the mess and brings her a fresh drink at no charge. Across town a young *barista* at a similar store watches for a regular customer and his guide dog. When he comes through the door, she has his order ready. In the Pacific Northwest another employee spends an hour with prospective customers, patiently demonstrating how to use an espresso machine.

The service is distinctly thoughtful. The atmosphere is distinctly friendly. The store is distinctly Starbucks.

As the chief executive officer of Seattle-based Starbucks Coffee Company, Howard Schultz realized early on that employee motivation and loyalty are critical to maintaining an edge in the competitive retail market. Determined to increase employee satisfaction and give workers a stake in the company's success, Schultz designed a remarkable benefit plan, one so comprehensive that it includes stock options and health coverage for all workers, two-thirds of whom are part-time. As a result of this commitment, Starbucks has built a dedicated work force renowned for its service. Schultz's philosophy has also paid off in explosive growth: At the end of fiscal 1994, Starbucks had opened 399 company-owned and 26 airport-licensed stores nationwide, serving 2 million customers weekly, with revenues of approximately $285 million.

A COMMITMENT TO DO BETTER

Howard Schultz grew up in the Canarsie housing projects, a rough area of Brooklyn, New York, in what he describes as a "traditional, middle-class family." The son of a blue-collar worker and the oldest of three children, Schultz remembers that his father worked as a truck driver, cabbie, and factory worker, never making more than $20,000 a year.

"I guess I really began to realize that there were many things that we did not have access to in terms of privileges," Schultz says of his childhood. "As I got older, I realized that there were things about that childhood that gave me . . . the unique view towards wanting to do something for others because we didn't have it ourselves." Schultz, seeing that a lifetime of hard, honest work did not necessarily guarantee financial security or personal satisfaction, promised himself that if he were ever in a position of leadership, he would do better for his employees.

Schultz attended a traditional city high school with a diverse student body of 6,000. He describes himself as an average student who spent his whole day in the schoolyard "playing ball." His enthusiasm reserved for sports, Schultz found the inner drive to apply himself in school only after he reached college.

He graduated from Northern Michigan University in 1975 with a B.S. degree and, in his words, "a lot of enthusiasm to conquer the world." After graduation, Schultz went to work for the Xerox Corporation in New York City. "I had to make over fifty cold calls a day," he recalls. "We weren't allowed to sell anything; you just had to knock on doors . . . it was humbling, but a wonderful experience in terms of learning how to communicate with people and also earning your stripes."

After three years at Xerox, Schultz was recruited to start an American division of the Swedish-based housewares firm Hammarplast, a company that happened to sell products to the Starbucks Coffee Company. It was on a trip to Seattle in 1981 that Schultz met the original founders of Starbucks.

SCHULTZ RECRUITED BY STARBUCKS

While Howard Schultz was about to enter college in 1971, three academics, English teacher Jerry Baldwin, history teacher Zev Siegl, and writer Gordon Bowker, were opening the first Starbucks store in Pike Place, a Seattle marketplace overlooking Puget Sound. Starbucks, named for the coffee-loving first mate in Melville's *Moby Dick*, opened shop selling whole coffee beans only. By 1982 the partners had built Starbucks into a respectable retail business with five stores, eighty-five employees, a roasting facility, and a wholesale business selling beans to local Seattle businesses. That year Baldwin recruited Schultz to Starbucks as head of retail sales and marketing.

Early in his Starbucks career on a buying trip to Italy, Schultz noticed that the Italians were passionate about their coffee. According to Schultz, there are 1,500 coffee bars in Milan alone, a city about the size of Philadelphia. "No matter what people were doing during the day," he says, "when they entered the coffee bars, there was a feeling of safety, of warmth, of comfort. Almost an extension of their front porch."

Schultz observed the pride with which employees prepared the coffee and provided service. "I think that if you look at the history of retail in America over the last ten, twenty years . . . there has been a fracturing of services and a fracturing of . . . customers feeling special."

He began to envision a new opportunity for the company: Use the sterling reputation of Starbucks for quality to build a chain of coffee and espresso bars. "Starbucks was not doing anything but selling coffee by the pound for the first twelve years of its history," recalls Schultz. "I thought there was an untapped opportunity for us."

In 1984, Schultz convinced the original founders to open a Starbucks coffee bar in downtown Seattle. Though successful, Schultz was unable to convince his colleagues to expand upon the idea. Frustrated, he left Starbucks in 1986 and returned to Italy to do more research. His wife, Sheri, supported the two of them working as an interior designer. "People gave us zero credit and very little respect that we could pull this off," Schultz remembers.

They underestimated Schultz's determination. He wrote a business plan for the company he envisioned and approached over 240 potential investors, including Baldwin and Bowker (Siegl had left the company by this time). The founders did invest, but more than 200 others declined.

Eventually Schultz was able to raise $1.7 million and, in 1986, he opened his first coffee bar in Seattle's Columbia Seafirst Center. He called it Il Giornale after the Italian newspaper of that name, and he served brewed coffee and espresso beverages made from Starbucks beans. The café was an instant success. Schultz went on to open a second café in Seattle and a third in Vancouver, British Columbia.

In August 1987, Schultz and his investors bought out the partners of Starbucks for $4 million. Il Giornale acquired their Seattle assets, and the new enterprise became the Starbucks Corporation.

SCHULTZ TAKES THE HELM

When Schultz officially took control, the Starbucks Coffee Company consisted of eleven stores, eighty-six employees, and a number of restaurant supply contracts. The early years were turbulent. Starbucks incurred losses for three years in a row, losing more than $1 million in 1989 alone. But Schultz held fast to his vision: to marry the existing bean business with retail outlets by building a solid infrastructure.

Starbucks first established a market presence in Seattle and Vancouver before cautiously moving east, eventually opening a store in Chicago. In 1988, Starbucks introduced a mail order catalog, and by year's end the store count rose to twenty-six. The following year Starbucks opened its first store in Portland, and the total number of locations reached fifty.

In 1990, the company's first year of profitability, Starbucks expanded its headquarters and built a new roasting facility. Specialty sales, the department handling wholesale contracts, began operations in Portland and Chicago, and the Starbucks store count rose to seventy-eight.

Schultz continued to seek new markets but was careful to avoid overconfidence and uncontrolled expansion. He wanted the company to enter one city at a time, dominating that market before moving on to the next. Schultz recognized that the challenge would be to ensure that the rapid growth did not undermine quality or dilute the elegance of Starbucks culture and its reputation for service.

In 1991, Starbucks opened its first store in Los Angeles and its first airport location with Host International at Seattle's Sea-Tac International Airport. Horizon Air began serving Starbucks coffee on all its flights, and the number of stores climbed to 112. The next year Starbucks began expanding down the West Coast to San Francisco, Orange County, and San Diego, and east to Denver. The specialty sales division was awarded Nordstrom's national contract; Starbucks was also selling coffee to restaurants throughout the Pacific Northwest, California, Washington, D.C., New York, and Boston.

To fund further expansion, Schultz decided to take Starbucks public in 1992. By year's end the total number of stores reached 165. Starbucks also opened seventy-three café locations within the Barnes & Noble bookstore chain. In 1993, Starbucks completed an $80.5-million convertible debenture offering and, as the company opened a second roasting plant in Kent, Washington, the number of stores swelled to 260.

The phenomenal growth of Starbucks continued in 1994 when its specialty sales department secured a national contract with Sheraton Hotels, and the Coffee Connection became a wholly owned subsidiary of the Starbucks Corporation, adding twenty-three stores to the Starbucks empire. By the end of fiscal year 1995, the number of coffee bars totaled 676.

HOW EMPLOYEE BENEFITS HELP
SPUR CORPORATE GROWTH

Over the past thirty years the nation's coffee consumption has actually decreased by a full third. So, under the circumstances, what enabled the Starbucks Coffee Company to succeed and grow?

"If I am asked as chairman of the company, what is the single reason why Starbucks has been able to achieve its objective qualitatively and quantitatively," says Schultz, "I always recite . . . that our people are making the difference."

To attract dedicated employees, Schultz designed a generous and comprehensive employee benefits package that includes stock options, health care, training programs, career counseling, and product discounts for all workers, full- and part-time.

Part-time workers have generally received little respect in the workplace; in the fast-food industry, employers actually encourage employee turnover, which can reach as high as 300 percent. Schultz never accepted the flawed logic that workers were simply interchangeable components of a business; nor did he believe that high turnover was more cost-effective than providing benefits to employees who contributed value to the company.

The Starbucks benefits package, says Schultz, is "the single greatest advantage we have in our company in terms of a competitive advantage because of the value and relationship that our people have to the company, to each other, and most importantly, to our customers and our shareholders."

"Because we are treated so well . . . it's reflected in the way that we treat our customers," says Heather Dimbat, a *barista* in Seattle.

BEAN STOCK: MAKING EMPLOYEES
PARTNERS IN GROWTH

The most innovative aspect of the Starbucks benefits package is the "Bean Stock" option plan, the first of its kind developed by a private company and offered to all workers, including part-timers.

Why go to this length? Schultz explains: "The two corner-stones of the culture of our company [are] to treat people with respect and dignity, and a manifestation of that was, first and foremost, creating an environment where everybody was an owner."

In order to be eligible for Bean Stock, a worker must be employed at Starbucks from the first of April to the end of the given fiscal year. He or she must have worked at least 500 hours (an average of twenty hours per week), and must still be employed by Starbucks at the time of distribution in January. The number of options granted is dependent on an employee's annual base wage (the target is 10 percent of base pay), the grant price, and the company's profitability. The more profitable the company is, the greater the percentage of base pay, which ranges from zero to 14 percent.

To ensure that employees understand the program, a Bean Stock hotline has been established to answer workers' questions. Starbucks has also spent a considerable amount of time and resources to explain the plan to employees.

"We do a lot in terms of communicating our benefit plans and our Bean Stock plan," says Bradley Honeycutt, director of employee benefits and compensation. She has noticed how employees change their behavior when they realize that "if they do something to achieve savings, it comes back to them in the form of stock options."

Bean Stock took two years to develop and required a special exemption from the Securities and Exchange Commission prior to implementation. Because Starbucks was a private company when the option plan was created in 1991, it was reluctant to publicly report its financial performance, a mandatory regulation for any company with more than 500 shareholders. Instead of granting shares, the Starbucks plan granted employees options, and the rule was waived.

Although some retailers offer workers company ownership through Employee Stock Ownership Plans (ESOPs), Starbucks was the first private company to offer employees stock options. Under ESOPs, employees buy actual shares of a company, but with stock options, the company grants employees the option to buy, in the future, a certain number of shares for a price set at the time the options are granted. A period of time must pass before workers can exercise their options. Employees with as little as six months of service can participate in the Starbucks plan, but the longer one stays with the company, the more options are granted and, potentially, the more valuable they become. Schultz firmly believes the program provides the incentive for employees to remain with Starbucks.

Honeycutt remembers developing the innovative yet untried plan: "Our first obstacle was getting the idea put together in some format that people could understand. The second obstacle was talking to the board of directors."

The Starbucks board, which included three venture capitalists, was skeptical at best. But Schultz remained committed to giving all workers a stake in the company's success, and he talked to each member individually, eventually convincing them that the plan would actually enhance shareholder value.

Matthew Patsky, a vice president with Robertson Stephens & Company in San Francisco, notes that Schultz, by empowering his employees, was able to achieve a customer service level that he believes is the force driving success at Starbucks. Employees are willing to work harder, says Schultz. They feel more a part of the organization because they have a direct stake in the outcome of their labors.

"Because of Bean Stock, I own my own home," says Jani Daubenspeck, who has worked at Starbucks since 1989. The average employee participating in a stock program will, over ten years, amass stock options with a value equal to three times his or her salary, according to Corey Rosen, director of The Center for Employee Ownership in Oakland, California.

Today, employees, or "partners," as they are known at Starbucks, are able to participate in insurance programs after a ninety-day period of employment during which the individual maintains a twenty-hour weekly average. Depending on the type of care chosen, Starbucks generally pays 75 percent after the deductible, with the remaining balance taken from the partner's paycheck. Starbucks covers some vision costs and mental health counseling and up to 100 percent of dental charges depending on the procedure. The company also pays both long- and short-term disability costs.

Employees are eligible to participate in a 401(k) plan after one year with the company. Starbucks contributes 25 cents for every dollar, up to 4 percent of base pay. Workers also receive product discounts, a free pound of coffee each week, and complimentary beverages while working. Starbucks provides paid vacations and holidays to full- and part-time partners, including two paid personal days a year.

Starbucks spent roughly $8.3 million on health care costs in fiscal 1995, which represented 7.6 percent of total payroll costs (which include base pay, bonuses, overtime, and commissions). The company offers a companywide managed care plan that provides 100 percent medical coverage through a list of preferred providers, or 70 percent coverage at out-of-network providers.

Because the mix of employee benefits can vary widely, it is difficult to compare the benefit costs at Starbucks with those at other retailers. But one crude comparison is revealing: Starbucks estimates that in 1994 it paid approximately $1,500 per year per employee versus the $1,700 to $3,000 paid by retailers who do not cover all workers.

REDUCING THE COSTS OF EMPLOYEE TURNOVER

Critics argue that benefit costs at Starbucks are easily supported by the company's huge growth curve and because a college-age work force keeps Starbucks clear of more costly claims. (Contrary to this assumption, the age of Starbucks' average employee is actually a "mature" 26.) Schultz maintains that while insurance premiums have risen, these costs are offset by the lower training costs associated with a lower attrition rate. He justifies the added expense by noting that Starbucks has a turnover rate of less than 60 percent by comparison with the retail industry average, which can reach between 150 and 300 percent.

> I would ask the cynics, how could you afford not to do this?
> We have lowered our attrition rate to such a low level that

it's a glaring advantage in terms of retail workers. . . . The
financial performance of the company, given the growth
rate, is probably second to none of any retailer in America
today.

Bradley Honeycutt adds, "We know that the cost of turnover is much higher than the cost of offering the benefit package
that we do."

Even Wall Street critics appear to have changed their minds
and are now some of Starbucks' biggest cheerleaders in terms of
the plan. Schultz says, "They were the people at public shareholders' meetings, many of whom were very critical in the early
stages of our company. But, there is nothing like performance to
gain trust."

Maintaining a superior work force has the added benefit of
the good ideas that come from dedicated employees. Each quarter, Starbucks executives travel from city to city to conduct employee forums and gather ideas, addressing issues that range
from environmental concerns to marketing strategy. "We have
an open forum every quarter in every region where we have
stores," says Schultz. "We open it up to the 100 or 200 or 300 in
the auditorium . . . to questions, concerns, criticisms, compli-
ments, or just points of view on how we are doing as the keeper
of the key."

To recognize employee service and emphasize involvement,
Starbucks created the Bravo! Recognition Program, in which any
partner may acknowledge another for actions that show initiative or resourcefulness in service, sales, or savings.

Matt Bartholomew, a worker in the midwestern region, was
recognized when he found the extra labor, coffee, and bags
needed to fill a last-minute order for a $1,300 sale. John Stephen-
son, a manager at an Encino, California, store, was given a Bravo!
award following the 1994 Los Angeles earthquake, when he and
his co-workers provided coffee to the Red Cross aid stations in
the area.

THE PROOF IS IN THE COFFEE

Schultz's commitment to strong employee relations is an integral part of maintaining high product quality. Besides keeping

employees happy, Schultz refuses to cut corners or risk losing control of quality by selling franchises. He also staunchly refuses to use artificially flavored beans, a practice common in the coffee business. No coffee bean stays in a Starbucks store for longer than seven days. Each of the thirty distinct blends of Starbucks coffee is created at the roasting plant in Seattle.

Schultz believes that once people realize what makes truly good coffee, they will naturally migrate to Starbucks. To this end, stores carry pamphlets explaining roasting procedures and how to prepare coffee and espresso at home. Workers attend extensive training classes to further their coffee knowledge and product expertise. Every new employee spends about twenty-four hours training in a classroom. Courses include coffee history and a seven-hour workshop on preparing the perfect cup.

The design of each Starbucks store is based on the assumption that every detail matters. "It's not only what the customer sees, it's what the customer doesn't see. If you are going to try and create a product that is . . . the highest quality in the world . . . you can't build a store whose design isn't as elegant as the quality of the coffee," says Schultz.

Author and gourmet coffee expert Corby Kummer agrees, noting that Starbucks pays careful attention not only to packaging, marketing, and presentation but also to store design and traffic flow.

THE ROAD AHEAD

With the goal of having 2,000 stores and $2 billion in sales by the year 2000, Starbucks does not appear to be experiencing any slowdown in company growth (total net sales at the end of fiscal year 1995 were $465 million). Christopher E. Vroom, a retail analyst with the securities firm Alex Brown & Sons, believes that Starbucks could easily top a billion dollars in sales by the end of the decade.

As for the future of the benefits program, human resources hopes within the next year or two to implement a cafeteria-style benefits plan that would give workers the flexibility to select different combinations of benefits and degrees of coverage. Similarly, Bean Stock will continue, adapting to the changing and growing work force. "There's no difference in creatively addressing the changes in our benefits program as we would the changes of our business," says Schultz.

Despite the whirlwind expansion, Schultz stays dedicated to his original vision for the company: "Metaphorically, we have to keep our eye on the rearview mirror as well as the road in front of us." Refusing to let growth weaken the integrity of Starbucks, Schultz hangs on to his desire to "take care of our people . . . and focus on one customer at a time."

16

The Work/Life Programs of Fel-Pro, Incorporated

PORTRAIT OF A FAMILY-FRIENDLY WORKPLACE

It is a dilemma for our time—juggling the often-conflicting demands of a job and family life in an era of overcrowded schedules. Most American workplaces today function as if the two-parent nuclear family were still the norm, with a woman at home taking care of the kids and putting dinner on the table every evening. Yet for growing millions of workers, life is far more complex. They may be single parents; spouses in two-income families with children; or grown children taking care of their disabled or elderly relatives.

So what happens when the children get sick? How can children be assured a safe and nurturing environment when their working parents are stretched to the limit? How can employees cope when a family crisis erupts?

The answer is usually a nonanswer. Businesses tolerate tardiness and absenteeism. Distracted employees make mistakes, miss meetings, and are generally less productive. Sometimes employees quit. And sometimes companies simply refuse to accommodate the troublesome life realities of employees, and fire them.

It comes as a pleasant shock, then, to encounter Fel-Pro, Incorporated, of Skokie, Illinois, a manufacturer of gaskets and engine sealants for over seventy-five years. Instead of just "plugging holes" in the work/life conflicts that most employees face, Fel-Pro has been aggressively proactive. Four generations of Fel-

Pro management have pioneered a wide range of programs and benefits, from child care and special-needs tutoring to flextime and elder care.

Defying the association of work/life benefits with white-collar jobs and corporations, this company is an auto parts and industrial chemicals manufacturer that aggressively strives to help its work force of more than 2,000 employees. Rather than resent the costs or the effort, it bursts with pride at having one of the most motivated, loyal, and productive work forces in American manufacturing. Because employees feel valued and respected, they are not just willing but eager to help their company be the best that it can be.

It shows. Through a period of tremendous change and instability in American manufacturing, Fel-Pro's positive labor-management partnership has helped it maneuver quickly and effectively to meet its clients' changing demands and stricter product specifications. Workers at many manufacturers grumble and groan about changes in work routines or added responsibilities. At Fel-Pro, where strong bonds of trust between management and employees have been assiduously cultivated, workers throw themselves into new challenges and show their own leadership. It is no surprise that while other competitors have faltered, Fel-Pro has enjoyed steady growth and profitability and an unsurpassed reputation for quality.

A STRONG AND SIMPLE MANAGEMENT PHILOSOPHY

"Fel-Pro's philosophy towards its employees is incredibly simple," asserts David Weinberg, Fel-Pro's co-chairman and fourth-generation owner. "What it says is, for good social reasons and for good business reasons, we ought to treat people honestly, equitably, and openly. And, in return, that comes back to us."

This philosophy was established by Fel-Pro's founders, and has continued throughout seventy-six years of family ownership. Hugo Herz, together with his son-in-law Albert Mecklenburger, launched Felt Products Mfg. Co. in Chicago in 1918 to supply felt components to the burgeoning automobile industry. Gaskets and washers for Model T's made up the bulk of their early business. Under Mecklenburger's leadership the company grew steadily and expanded to several sites throughout the city. Then in 1957, Fel-Pro, as Felt Products had come to be known, consolidated all its operations at the current headquarters in Skokie.

Mecklenburger's sons-in-law, Lewis Weinberg and Elliot Lehman, succeeded him as Fel-Pro's co-presidents, guiding the company's further expansion and diversification into lubricants and sealing products. Weinberg and Lehman pioneered new ways to support their employees and enrich the surrounding community, a tradition today carried forward by Lehman's own sons, Paul and Ken Lehman, and Weinberg's son and son-in-law, David Weinberg and Dennis Kessler.

Fel-Pro's commitment to employee-friendly programs reflects not only a genuine social concern but the demanding realities of auto parts manufacturing as well. Over the past decade Detroit automakers have introduced sweeping changes into their production processes by embracing the total quality management (TQM) approach, which encourages all workers to find ways to serve customers faster and better. Detroit's TQM revolution has caused major upheavals for many parts suppliers, however, as automakers demanded wholesale changes in operations virtually overnight. They often demanded quicker turnaround times for certain parts, for example, or asked suppliers to provide quality-control statistics that had never been compiled.

Such changes can be difficult to implement if workers balk at increased responsibilities and higher productivity targets. Yet mutual trust and loyalty between Fel-Pro workers and management have enabled the company to adapt and even thrive during tumultuous times. "In a company where there are hostile relationships between management and the employees," says co-chairman David Weinberg, "I think that those changes come about in a very, very difficult way—with a lot of hostility, with a lot of stops and starts, and a lot of setbacks."

But Fel-Pro employees have been remarkably flexible. Says Weinberg:

> They trust in what we say. They get on board. They learn new skills. They do different jobs. They are really willing to

> change in a lot of different ways. And so . . . it may take us
> a year to make a change that might take other companies
> with relationships that aren't as solid with their employees,
> two, three, four or five years to make those changes.

One key factor in employee satisfaction, of course, is compensation. Fel-Pro's pay scale is highly competitive, the company's stated goal being to remain at the 75th percentile for compensation in its region. A generous profit-sharing plan gives employees a stake in the company's success and helps provide for a secure retirement. The plan is open to all employees who work at least twenty hours per week and who have been with the company for at least six months.

But Fel-Pro has deliberately gone far beyond such basic incentives by creating an ambitious array of pathbreaking employee benefits that complement its egalitarian, participatory work culture. It is hard to argue with the impressive business results.

THE FIRST STEPS OF A FAMILY-FRIENDLY TRADITION

Fel-Pro's tradition of partnership with its employees began in the 1960s, when Albert Mecklenburger's daughter, Sylvia Radov, became distressed that the company's employees, many of whom commuted to the Skokie plant from Chicago, had so few recreational facilities available to them. Chicago's public parks and playgrounds were scarce and overcrowded. And those non-White members of Fel-Pro's diverse work force who ventured to suburban facilities often faced discrimination.

Fel-Pro seized upon the problem as a corporate challenge and responsibility. It purchased a 220-acre tract of undeveloped, unkempt wooded land in Cary, Illinois, then turned it into the Triple R Ranch, a private recreational facility for Fel-Pro employees and their families. A pavilion was built for family outings and company picnics, followed later by swimming and wading pools, basketball and volleyball courts, and a baseball diamond. The lake was stocked with fish, and individual garden plots were made available to employees who wanted to grow vegetables.

The success of the Triple R inspired Fel-Pro in 1973 to create a summer day camp at the ranch for employees' children; for a modest fee, the camp offered sports, arts and crafts, swimming, and field trips. Over 300 children from ages 6 to 15 attend each summer, and receive care and instruction from highly qualified counselors. Unlike public camps, the day camp is tailored to mesh perfectly with Fel-Pro shift schedules; school buses pick up the children at the plant parking lot in the morning and return them just as their parents get off work.

IN THE VANGUARD OF ON-SITE DAY CARE

The Triple R experience quickly sensitized Fel-Pro management to the problems facing families with preschool-aged children. Eager to establish a year-round day care center, the company in the mid-1970s studied its feasibility only to discover that the expense, complexity, and potential liability of a day care center made the idea prohibitive.

By the early 1980s, however, Fel-Pro managers concluded that the lack of quality, affordable day care had reached a crisis stage—for the company, its employees, and the nation as a whole. In most business quarters at the time, quality day care was still below the radar screen of serious concern. Yet Fel-Pro managers saw a slow-motion social emergency: the growing number of single-parent and two-income families who were struggling with an unpalatable set of fragile and costly options.

Then, as now, many working parents relied on relatives or neighbors to care for young children, but often found such arrangements could be scrambled by a caregiver's illness or vacation. Some full-time responsibilities became too burdensome for elderly, infirm, or overextended family members, leaving the employed parent with few, if any, affordable options.

Parents who sought professional care, whether in-home or at day care centers, faced huge expenses and varying levels of care and expertise. Centers were sometimes overcrowded and staffed by ill-trained, underpaid caregivers. The resulting high turnover could have serious emotional consequences for the children. Yet those centers that did provide a stable, stimulating environment typically had long waiting lists. And even those families fortunate enough to find good day care struggled with inconvenient locations and schedules.

Fel-Pro management was determined to respond. Even without formal studies to document it, the company believed employees would be more loyal, committed, and productive if such basic parental concerns were resolved.

The perfect opportunity to move forward arose when a business directly opposite Fel-Pro's parking lot closed its doors. It was an ideal site for a company day care center. Fel-Pro purchased the building, and hired Scott Mies, an expert in early childhood education, to direct Fel-Pro's work/family programs and help design the day care facilities and curriculum. The center opened in 1983, and currently serves forty-five children in five preschool classrooms and one kindergarten classroom.

For Arlis McLean, vice president for human resources, Fel-Pro's child care programs were a significant factor in her joining the company in 1993. "You cannot put a price on what it means," she says. "It's so wonderful for me to have such peace of mind, knowing that [my son] is well cared for and he is only a few hundred yards away. I can do my job without even worrying about him during the day."

Fel-Pro addresses short-term care needs through an arrangement with Family Care Services of Metropolitan Chicago. If employees have dependents who are ill, Fel-Pro will subsidize the cost of sending trained caregivers to their homes, for up to five days a year, thus allowing employees to maintain their regular work schedules. Fel-Pro also helps employees make appropriate arrangements for their elderly parents through a consulting and referral service run by the Illinois Alliance on Aging.

PASSIONATE SUPPORT FOR EDUCATION

Fel-Pro management sincerely believes that business must do its part in helping Americans improve themselves through education. Going far beyond lip service, the company pays for tuition, tutoring, college counseling, and professional development, among other educational services. These programs not only help employees and their families move up in the world, company managers explain; they also help the company to compete more effectively.

Explains co-chairman Ken Lehman:

> In the old days, a machine operator would punch his press all day long. There was a separate quality department that would grade our products. We had a classic functional organization—supervisors told you what to do, and you did it. Now we're organized in teams, and the teams tell themselves what to do. Everyone in the team is expected to know all the jobs in the team, to have the full range of skills, and everyone is responsible for quality.

Fel-Pro's focus on education dates back to Elliot Lehman's tenure as CEO in the 1960s, when the company instituted a college scholarship program for employees' children. But unlike many companies that offer a limited number of scholarships on the basis of exceptional achievement or need, Fel-Pro made its scholarships available to any employee's child who was accepted at an accredited college or trade school. Scholarships for tuition and supplies are made for as much as $3,300 per year. Satisfactory educational progress is the only further requirement.

In addition to extensive internal training and improvement programs, Fel-Pro offers tuition reimbursement for outside education that advances an employee's professional development. Approved courses of study are 100-percent funded, up to a total of $3,000 per year for undergraduate studies and $6,500 per year for studies leading to a postgraduate degree. A $1,000 bonus is awarded to any Fel-Pro employee upon completion of an advanced degree.

Because she was the child of a Fel-Pro employee, Gloria Lloret's undergraduate education was supported by the company. Then after she joined the company, Fel-Pro supported her graduate work through its tuition reimbursement program.

Now Lloret is a manager in the company's international market-ing division. "The education and the value that I have received from it," says Lloret, "I can pay back to the company probably a hundred times more than they have paid."

Fel-Pro's commitment to education is so comprehensive that it has created a tutoring program to help employees' chil-dren overcome difficulties with elementary and high school course work. A tutor comes to the employee's home three days a week to provide diagnostic testing and individualized instruc-tion. Since many children of Fel-Pro employees are the first in their families to aspire to college, the company has contracted with an outside firm to offer career counseling, curriculum plan-ning, and advice on financing a college education.

To skeptics who scoff that a cost-conscious business could do without offering such generous education benefits, Paul Leh-man has a ready response: "By doing what we do, we're saying, 'This is what society needs and we are part of that society.'"

THE COMMITMENT IS IN THE DETAILS

Fel-Pro's fierce commitment to the well-being of its employees can also be seen in dozens of small but important ways. One stunning example is the unorthodox first shift, which runs from 7:24 A.M. to 3:54 P.M. The reason? Fel-Pro commissioned a study of Skokie-area traffic patterns and found that these times would minimize the length and hassle of its employees' commutes.

This attention to detail can also be seen in the Fel-Pro health plan, which offers flexible options and comprehensive coverage, as well as access to preventive care, vision care, and dental care (including some orthodontia) at low cost. Any out-of-pocket em-ployee health expenses can be paid in pretax dollars through a medical spending plan. To encourage healthy lifestyles, Fel-Pro makes available to all employees an on-site fitness and wellness center.

Expectant parents at Fel-Pro have access to full medical care and more. The health plan includes complete maternity cover-age and well-baby care. For prospective adoptive parents, up to

$5,000 in assistance is available to defray the legal expenses of adoption.

By acknowledging important milestones—both personal and professional—the company reinforces the mutual loyalty and respect that "family" implies. So on holidays and birthdays, Fel-Pro employees receive small gifts from the company—a box of chocolates on Valentine's Day, for instance, and a free meal in the cafeteria on birthdays. Cash bonuses are awarded for weddings, births, anniversaries of employment, and even the start of a summer vacation.

PATERNALISM OR EMPOWERMENT?

When a company becomes so involved in the personal lives of its employees, many observers perceive potential risks. For instance, is the company indulging in paternalism, that is, caring for its workers but at the same time controlling them through these gifts?

Fel-Pro seems to have achieved a balance: an open, participatory culture, with an exceptionally active and committed work force. Fel-Pro managers are smart enough to realize that generous benefits alone do not secure the loyalty of employees. Pay and benefits must be matched by a respectful, participatory work culture. People need to feel that they are being treated fairly on a day-to-day basis.

Fel-Pro's formal commitment to worker participation began in 1952 when Lewis Weinberg launched the Fel-Pro Employee Forum. For the past four decades this monthly forum has given management and employees a common platform for talking about everything from stale peanut butter and banana sandwiches on the work-break cart to the need for productivity and fairness in the workplace.

The rationale behind the Employee Forum, says Paul Lehman, is that "even small problems are important to people. And small problems that are dealt with quickly and in an open way don't become big problems." Each department annually elects a forum delegate to represent it at meetings, where managers present production goals, long-range plans, and financial reports. This helps ensure that all employees stay abreast of the "big picture" of operations at Fel-Pro.

In the same spirit of cooperation, executives maintain an open-door policy and eschew perks that would set them apart from the bulk of Fel-Pro workers. There are no executive cafeterias or reserved parking places, and executives frequently walk the factory floor, consulting with manufacturing team members and line workers.

The depth of trust between employees and management was vividly illustrated in 1961 by the first and only attempt by a major union to organize Fel-Pro workers. Employees rejected the union by an overwhelming majority. Bob O'Keefe, vice president for industrial relations, says, "Fel-Pro has always made an attempt every year to share their success with their employees."

Do Generous Benefits Make for a Productive Work Force?

While any CEO would covet a flexible, creative work force, the question remains: Do generous benefits actually help produce one? It is a subject that has not been well explored or documented—by Fel-Pro or by other manufacturers. Most research on work/life programs has focused on their impact on employee recruitment, turnover, and absenteeism—tangible performance benchmarks that can be clearly linked to a specific benefit program, like day care. Many such studies have found that these programs generally do, in fact, produce substantial benefits for companies.

Such results are certainly seen at Fel-Pro, where there is always a waiting list for job openings, even though the company rarely advertises. Total annual turnover at Fel-Pro is 6 percent, compared to a national average of over 12 percent for companies of comparable size. When these statistics exclude people who retire, move out of state, or become otherwise unavailable to the local work force, the contrast is even more dramatic: 1 percent annual turnover at Fel-Pro versus 9 percent nationwide.

The average cost of recruiting a Fel-Pro production employee is $339, a fraction of the national average of $1,563. For exempt employees, the price tag is $1,864 compared to $8,437 nationwide.

BUT CAN YOU "QUANTIFY" THE RESULTS?

Impressive as these numbers are, Fel-Pro executives believe that some of the most important benefits cannot really be measured. It is the *way* Fel-Pro employees work, they believe, that really gives Fel-Pro a special competitive advantage.

For years, many business leaders regarded Fel-Pro's assertions skeptically because they could not be measured by numbers. To this David Weinberg retorts, "Things like good relationships with your customers are usually not quantifiable. They are attitudinal. You have to just simply have the belief that, having loyal employees, you are going to get a lot more accomplished."

In 1990, however, Fel-Pro had the opportunity to document this faith. A group of University of Chicago researchers asked to study Fel-Pro's work/family programs and their business impact. The researchers wanted to develop new ways of measuring "worker engagement," which is considered central to the success of total quality management.

In particular, the researchers wanted to assess four types of employee engagement: (1) willingness to participate and cooperate; (2) level of effort and attention to work; (3) generation of improvement suggestions; and (4) adaptability and willingness to change. By measuring such things as the number of suggestions made, participation in teams, and support for corporate goals, the researchers devised new quantitative measures of the quality of employees' output, which they called "quality enhancement performance." These indices, in turn, could be correlated with employees' participation or nonparticipation in work/life benefits and support programs. (The 1993 report, by Susan Lambert et al., is entitled *Added Benefits: The Link Between Family-Responsive Policies and Work Performance at Fel-Pro, Incorporated*.)

The University of Chicago study confirmed what Fel-Pro managers had long believed: Work/life benefits help cultivate a

work force that can thrive in today's competitive environment.
Paul Lehman summarizes its results:

> What it showed was that the employees who participate
> most in our benefits also have the best work records. They
> have the fewest disciplinary notices. They have the best
> quality records. They participate the most in voluntary
> teams. They give us the most suggestions for productivity
> and quality improvement.

> But, most importantly, workers also from their own reports
> say that they understand why Fel-Pro has to continue to
> change. They trust us and they want to change along with
> the company. And, in many cases, they provide the leader-
> ship for change. So, for the first time, I think that we have
> been able to document that this kind of business philoso-
> phy, the philosophy we have about people, is really good
> for business.

The efficacy of Fel-Pro's philosophy can also be measured
in its growing market share and international expansion, as well
as in the parade of quality awards and accolades from such
major customers as Cummins Engine, the Ford Motor Company,
General Motors, Harley-Davidson, and Mack Truck. Says Ken
Lehman:

> Ours has been a record of steady growth in terms of market
> penetration, sales, and steady profits. We have done this all
> the old-fashioned way: no heavy leveraging, no fancy fi-
> nancing, no smoke and mirrors. Just increasing our market
> penetration year by year, and treating our employees fairly
> so that they would be our allies.

THE WORKPLACE AS FAMILY

That Fel-Pro's philosophy is premised on a practical two-way
relationship is made clear by an incident David Weinberg recalls:

Somebody once said to me, "Gee, we are so proud of Fel-Pro, because they are so charitable toward their employees." And I stopped that person immediately and I said, "You know, that is really not the case, because being charitable implies that there is somebody who is in need and it is a one-way giving. That is not the case at all. We don't give charity to our employees. We give charity to the community. We have a give and take relationship with our employees where we offer them respect, and we offer them a set of benefits, and in return, they offer us loyalty and hard work and a conscientious effort."

Gary Charlton is one such employee who appreciates Fel-Pro's efforts.

We really put out 100 percent work or more because we know what a wonderful company this is, and what they offer. They really try. I've been here for six and a half years and as of the month of January I'll have perfect attendance for five years. I have never missed a day. I love coming to work. I aim to stay here twenty more years. My goal is to work hard and make Fel-Pro a successful company.

"We expect a lot out of our employees," concludes Paul Lehman, "and our employees expect a lot out of us. And I think, in both cases, our employees deliver for us and I think we deliver for them."

SECTION FIVE

THE REWARDS OF CORPORATE CITIZENSHIP

Introduction by Sol M. Linowitz

Sol M. Linowitz is honorary chairman of The Academy for Educational Development. Mr. Linowitz served as chairman of the board of Xerox from 1960 to 1966, a critical period of product innovation and introduction. In 1966, Mr. Linowitz was appointed U.S. ambassador to the Organization of American States. He was conegotiator of the Panama Canal Treaties from 1977 to 1978, and presidential Middle East Peace Negotiator from 1979 to 1981.

"Why should an industrial company, organized for profit, think it a good and right thing to take a million dollars and more, of that profit, and give it to this community?" asked J. Irwin Miller on the occasion of yet another Cummins Engine Foundation gift to Columbus, Indiana. "Why, instead, isn't Cummins—the largest taxpayer in the county—spending the same energy to try to get its taxes reduced, the cost of education cut, the cost of city government cut, less money spent on streets and utilities and schools?

"The answer," said the legendary former chairman of Cummins Engine Company—profiled in Chapter 21—"is that we would like to see this community come to be not the cheapest community in America, but the very best community of its size in the country."

Cummins, like many other companies large and small, understands the essence of corporate citizenship: that business is not an island unto itself, as the term *private sector* implies, but an institution whose fate is intimately connected with the well-being of many other constituencies.

These bonds of connectedness radiate outward—to the public schools, on which business depends for an educated work force; to the buying public, whose confidence is necessary to any functional marketplace; to local communities, whose stability and support are important to business success; and to the environment, which must be regarded as a scarce capital asset, and not as limitless current income.

The poor and disenfranchised are regarded by some as "economically irrelevant" because they are incapable of being either consumers or employees. Yet the essence of corporate citizenship is realizing that we all have ties that go deeper than our marketplace relations; we have profound human and social bonds. Honoring those bonds, as businesses, is one way we sustain our social ethic, or community life, and, indeed, our own sense of human dignity.

It is tempting for a business to ignore these larger noneconomic bonds of connection and dependence, and instead to define "success" in a narrow, short-term manner. This is the animus behind the American myth of the "self-made man"—and woman: the self-delusion that individuals succeed or fail only through their own efforts.

We are tempted, also, to overvalue the short-term goals of our businesses at the expense of the long-term needs of the commonweal. The immediate costs of pollution controls, for example, seem far more important than their diffuse, speculative future benefits. So, too, other collective investments such as education, the environment, and civic life often seem to be "someone else's business."

Yet the astute manager recognizes this as a snare. "There is no free lunch," as the economists always point out. So it is that the resources of a community are not self-replenishing. They must be constantly tended to by everyone in the community, including business. Section Five showcases the stories of several farsighted, socially minded businesses that have successfully met this challenge.

The profiles include a remarkable restaurateur, Judy Wicks, who has used her business, the White Dog Cafe, to bring diverse people together into a community of civic dialogue and social concern. Her story shows how even a rather commonplace business, a restaurant, can have an enormous catalytic effect on a community while at the same time becoming more competitive. With its combination of excellent meals and service, the White Dog's highly visible social leadership has earned it a loyal following and a distinctive market identity in an extremely competitive industry.

In the "Share to Gain" program launched by GE Plastics, hundreds of employees provided manual labor to renovate YMCAs, homeless shelters, and other nonprofit community facilities. The projects were not simply acts of corporate charity, but a way for the company to forge an esprit de corps among its work force while fostering an ethos of corporate teamwork.

Gail Mayville, an administrative assistant at Ben & Jerry's Homemade, became the driving force behind that company's environmental initiatives in the late 1980s. At a time when recycling was not common, Mayville helped convince management of its environmental necessity and of the significant cost savings it would bring. Her vision and imagination indicate that corporate citizenship is not the domain of CEOs and senior managers alone, but of all employees.

Finally, Section Five tells the remarkable story of Merck & Co.'s wonder drug, Mectizan, which can prevent the feared disease river blindness, which afflicts more than eighteen million people in the Third World. Merck knew that the potential market for the drug would be virtually nil because of the poverty of the people who needed it. Still it decided to spend millions of dollars on research; to sponsor expensive and lengthy clinical trials; and to help create a vast distribution scheme so that an ancient and horrible scourge might be eradicated. The company has not only gained important new knowledge about an important drug compound but has reaped significant goodwill from potential Third World customers and public health authorities.

Like any great achievement, the best acts of corporate citizenship are singular. There is no simple formula. What matters most is the spirit of engagement—the willingness to explore new possibilities, the eagerness to serve the larger community in meaningful ways. The most meaningful results are also personal and internal: the sense of fulfillment and pride that comes with giving freely without expectation of direct returns.

Justice Felix Frankfurter once wrote:

> The ultimate foundation of a free society is the binding tie of cohesive sentiment. Such a sentiment is fostered by all those

agencies of the mind and spirit which may serve to gather up
the traditions of a people, and thereby create that continuity of
a treasured common life which constitutes a civilization.

As these stories demonstrate, American business can do a great deal
to foster "the binding tie of cohesive sentiment" that is so critical to
our future as a nation.

17

Judy Wicks and the White Dog Cafe

TABLE FOR SIX BILLION, PLEASE!

The darkened street outside the Victorian brownstones is filled with a pulsating Latin beat generated by five sweaty, swaying musicians. In the middle of the street, a distinguished-looking gentleman in a blue blazer boogies over a manhole cover with his graying wife, while nearby some twenty-somethings raise their glasses in a toast. Several middle-aged White couples at adjacent tables share a lively dinner conversation with two African-American parents holding their one-year-old infant. Presiding over the spectacle, atop a buffet of black bean casseroles and vegetable taquitos: a roast suckling pig.

It is *Noche Latina*, or Latin Night—yet another multicultural, intergenerational happening in the life and times of the White Dog Cafe. Tucked away on a side street near the University of Pennsylvania campus, the White Dog is more than an acclaimed Philadelphia restaurant. It is a community of customers who thrive on great food, spirited conversation, and community involvement. At the center of it all, the flamboyant impresario who has willed this community into being through her own theatrical imagination and business acumen, is the White Dog's founder and proprietor: Judy Wicks.

If everyone in Casablanca knew Rick, it seems that everyone in Philadelphia knows Judy. This is because, for Wicks, running a restaurant means more than serving up exquisite "new-style" American cooking. It means inviting prominent writers and politicians to give weekly after-dinner lectures . . . lining up talent for her weekly storytelling salon . . . leading customers on tours of "sister restaurants" in various foreign nations and inner-city neighborhoods . . . celebrating the birthdays of Mahatma Gandhi and Martin Luther King, Jr., with special banquets . . . and convening rollerblading parties for post-forty-year-olds followed by a meal at the restaurant.

These events are not just Wicks's idea of a good time, although they are certainly that as well. Wicks's many community-minded programs are a prime reason for the restaurant's great success. In a fiercely competitive industry, the White Dog's distinctive social values have attracted a fiercely loyal clientele and given it a singular market identity. Philadelphia Mayor Ed Rendell, a frequent customer and friend of Wicks, explains, "Going to the White Dog is always new and fresh. It's fun. It's one of those places where you walk in and it's tough not to feel up and alive and happy."

The recipe has wide appeal, attracting Puerto Ricans from North Philadelphia, students from the University City section of town, suburbanites in search of a fun urban experience, attorneys from downtown law firms, and top political figures from around the city and state. When the famous Zagat survey asked diners to select the best Philadelphia restaurants, they ranked the White Dog fourth, surpassed only by much more expensive restaurants. The White Dog, with a typical dinner tab of $30 a person, is a fashionable yet affordable place to have a great meal.

It is a formula reflected in a robust bottom line. In 1995 the restaurant—in conjunction with the adjacent gift shop, The Black Cat, also run by Wicks—had sales of $4 million. Net income was more than $300,000, giving it an 8 percent profit margin in an industry that averages about 3 percent. The 200-seat restaurant served up more than 150,000 satisfying meals in 1995.

"Everyone is always trying to find out, How can my business be different from someone else's? How can my business be unusual?" says Wicks. "Well, don't look too far, because the way that your business can be unusual is by having it reflect yourself. Everybody is different, and if your business actually reflects you as an individual, it's going to be different."

"My business," Wicks confesses, "is who I am."

THE IRREPRESSIBLE JUDY WICKS

And who is Judy Wicks?

A child of the Pittsburgh suburb of Ingomar, Pennsylvania, Wicks graduated from Lake Erie College in 1969 and married her childhood sweetheart. After a stint as VISTA volunteers in an Eskimo village in Alaska, the couple settled down near the University of Pennsylvania and, sensing a market, started an alternative clothing store. Although the store flourished, the marriage did not.

Wicks began waiting tables at a popular French restaurant, La Terrasse, whose hanging plants and chalkboard menus were at the forefront of a 1970s trend. In 1974, Wicks was named vice president and general manager, and within five years she had boosted gross revenues from $300,000 to $1.5 million. Although she had been promised an equity stake in the restaurant, the business later closed, leaving Wicks with "a nothing share of nothing"—and no job.

Undaunted, Wicks opened her own carry-out muffin shop down the street from the failed restaurant, just below her second-story apartment. One day when there was a long line of customers waiting to be served, she moved a table down from her apartment and invited everyone to take a seat. Soon she hired a waitress and started serving hot food cooked on a barbecue in her backyard. Dishes were washed in a sink in the dining room, and the public bathroom was upstairs in her apartment. The next year, with a $75,000 loan from a friend, Wicks finally built a small kitchen with a grill and expanded the restaurant into the adjacent building.

In the mid-1980s, Wicks refinanced her brownstone, built a full kitchen in the basement, obtained a liquor license, and began offering a more sophisticated menu. She transformed the first-floor space into a series of airy, exposed-wood, bare-brick dining nooks with an intimate, country-casual feel, complete with lace curtains, dog figurines, and whimsical canine art. Later, by annexing the space of a third brownstone, Wicks expanded seating capacity at the White Dog to 200. Then, fourth and fifth buildings were connected to the White Dog by an enclosed breezeway, allowing customers to wander to a companion business started by Wicks, The Black Cat Gift Shop, which sells fanciful household items and gifts.

Given the White Dog's quirky origins, it seems fitting that its name traces back to Madame Helena Petrovna Blavatsky, the eccentric nineteenth-century co-founder of the Theosophy religious group and a former occupant of the building. Legend has it that Blavatsky's infected leg was cured after her white dog fell asleep on it. Today the white dog that rules the roost is Emily, a toy poodle that pads along behind Wicks wherever she goes.

BUILDING A BUSINESS BASED ON SHARED VALUES

The sense of celebration and community spirit that pervades the White Dog Cafe is not simply the magic of one woman's theatricality. It is a solid business enterprise. The first priority of the restaurant, Wicks insists, is excellent food and attentive service. Soon the White Dog began attracting the attention of Philadelphia restaurant reviewers, and then national critics. In 1993, Mimi Sheraton of *Condé Nast Traveler* magazine hailed the "quaint charm" and "delightful culinary experimentation" of the White Dog, proclaiming it one of the top fifty restaurants in the country—the only Pennsylvania restaurant cited on her list.

The person responsible for the White Dog's unusual, artfully presented meals is Kevin von Klause, whom Wicks invited to become her chef/partner in 1986. *Gourmet* magazine raved about Klause's "eclectic cooking" and the relaxed atmosphere of the White Dog, calling it "A Declaration of Independence" in a world of starched-shirt *haute cuisine*.

While many restaurateurs would be wary of messing with a proven business formula, Wicks saw her early success as a launching platform for something greater: making the White Dog a special kind of community institution. She wanted to make her restaurant a place where events of the day could be discussed and debated, and where people of diverse persuasions could get to know each other. Wicks began to realize that creating a restaurant/salon/civic forum would not just be immensely satisfying from a personal perspective; it could be a highly attractive business proposition.

What Wicks wanted to create was nothing less than an American institution now in decline, what sociologist Ray Oldenburg calls "a great, good place." Whether it is the corner barber shop or the neighborhood bar, a great, good place is "a meeting place where citizens can gather, put aside the concerns of work and home, and hang out simply for the pleasures of good company and lively conversation." Every great civilization has such places, Oldenburg writes, whether they be French sidewalk cafés, German biergartens, or London pubs. And such places are not incidental to the vitality of a society, he adds: "They are the heart of a community's social vitality, the grassroots of a democracy; without them, the diversity of human contact diminishes and citizens become estranged."

Such was the ambition of the White Dog Cafe as Wicks conceived it: a place that could help break down barriers between people and help build new bridges of people-to-people understanding. The critical tool would be great food and fun—elemental human enjoyments that transcend the boundaries of politics, religion, race, and nationality, which so often separate people.

THE SPIRITED "TABLE TALK" LECTURES

Wicks did not follow a grand blueprint in pursuing this goal. Rather, it was an improvisational faith. As a small-business owner struggling to stay afloat, for example, Wicks was frustrated that she had so little time to keep up with current events. So she began inviting speakers to come speak to breakfast customers before everyone headed off to work. "It was my way of linking our business with the important issues of the day," says Wicks. The talks became so popular that other White Dog customers started complaining because they couldn't attend at breakfast time.

This sparked a business epiphany. Wicks knew that Monday nights are traditionally the slowest times of the week for any restaurant. So why not turn Monday evening into a full house by featuring celebrated guest speakers with dinner? The result: the *Table Talk* series, which features family-style dining, followed by a lecture and a question-and-answer period. Strangers attracted by the same topic get to know each other over dinner, which has special appeal for many singles customers.

The talks themselves are often formidable presentations. Over the years, The Table Talks have featured a stellar array of authors, academics, artists, and political figures talking about everything from neo-Nazism to health care to tax reform. "I think I was more nervous about giving a Table Talk at the White Dog than I was giving a lecture at the Sorbonne," said Dr. Houston A. Baker, Jr., an English professor at the University of Pennsylvania. "You knew that you couldn't just toss it off, because it was going to be a really tough crowd, but a tough crowd because it's extraordinarily diverse and intergenerational."

To promote the Table Talks, Wicks started a quarterly newsletter, *Tales from the White Dog Cafe,* written by Wicks herself and illustrated with her whimsical dog sketches. With a mailing list of more than 15,000 extremely loyal customers, the newsletter is a highly effective tool for building a community of shared values. The restaurant receives dozens of calls a month from people who want to receive the newsletter and, in effect, declare their allegiance to a special sort of urban community. "It's like the old Sears' wish book that used to come when I lived in the hills of West Virginia," exclaims customer Harriette Behringer. "You can't wait to see what you check off."

The newsletter is also a highly effective vehicle for marketing all sorts of special dinner events and street festivals, often based on socially relevant themes. At harvest time each autumn, "The Dance of the Ripe Tomatoes" celebrates organic and humane farming. Local family farmers are feted, and revelers parade around with four-foot-wide tomatoes perched atop long poles. On a more serious note, Gandhi's birthday is an occasion for "a celebration of nonviolent resistance," which in 1994 included a talk by the Dalai Lama's special envoy to the United Nations. Martin Luther King, Jr.'s birthday is cause for another celebratory dinner and a group discussion of his life and influence.

Every fall Wicks hosts a dinner with inmate gardeners at the nearby Graterford State Prison. The White Dog staff prepares a meal using the inmates' organic vegetables, and the prisoners discuss the rehabilitative value of gardening and good nutrition. Each Passover season, a "Freedom Seder" co-hosted by Black and Jewish religious leaders celebrates "the message of renewal and of freedom from tyranny and oppression for all peoples." The list of other White Dog celebrations goes on and on: Bastille Day, the Fourth of July, a Native American Thanksgiving Dinner, a New Year's Day Pajama Party Brunch.

Like the annual *Noche Latina*, the White Dog's many special events put an accent on racial understanding and American diversity. Wicks loves organizing the celebrations simply because they are fun. "A friend of mine once joked that I am such a social person that if there was no one around, I would share a nut with a squirrel," says Wicks with a chuckle. "I love bringing people together." But Wicks also sees multicultural happenings as a great business opportunity. "What's great about the city is its diversity," says Wicks. "That's what we have that the suburbs don't have. I feel that diversity should be a marketable quality."

BUILDING COMMUNITY THROUGH "SISTER RESTAURANTS"

Wicks has gone far beyond street festivals to market the diversity of Philadelphia. With gusto, she has sought to entice a largely White, more affluent and suburban clientele into Philadelphia's inner-city neighborhoods for a good time. Her vehicle: "sister restaurants" she has adopted in several ethnic neighborhoods of the city and nearby Camden, New Jersey.

"She just walked in the front door and said she was from the White Dog Cafe," recalls Daphne Brown. That was how Brown, the owner of Daffodil's, an African-American restaurant in North Philadelphia, was recruited into the sister restaurant program. With Brown's help, Wicks arranged the evening: a play at the nearby Freedom Theater, one of the oldest African-American theaters in the country, followed by dinner at Daffodil's. Several dozen White Dog customers—mostly White—came to the unfamiliar neighborhood, and had a great time. "It's brought new business," reports Brown. "I've got catering jobs. And those customers come back from time to time to eat."

"A lot of what I do is based on what's fun, and not seeing it as a moral issue," explains Wicks. "I personally feel that it's really fun to have events where people who are really different people from each other are having fun together." Wicks, the businesswoman, also sees considerable economic benefit from such "fun" activities as well:

> A lot of times you hear that people in the suburbs are afraid to come to the city. I felt that if we could dispel these fears, that would be good for all of the restaurants in the city, and people would understand what's really great about urban life. To me, it's really important to let the vitality of the city be really strong. That helps all the businesses in the city.

When the local media were sensationalizing the drug-related violence in the Latino section of North Philadelphia and dubbing it "The Badlands," Wicks organized an evening in that neighborhood for her customers. It consisted of a viewing at a Latino art gallery followed by a dinner at a Puerto Rican sister restaurant and dancing at a club. "When the people leave," says Jesse Bermudez, a well-known leader in the neighborhood, "they can't believe they've been in that particular neighborhood. But they have! They now have a different perspective of the community and realize that it's not all of the bad labels that are being placed on it." It is not a one-way street, however. Each year Wicks builds upon these relationships by inviting the Latino community to her *Noche Latina* festival.

EATING WITH THE ENEMY

Taking her good idea to daring new levels, Wicks launched an international sister restaurant program in 1987 to foster people-to-people understanding. The program consists of Wicks leading as many as two dozen customers on tours of various countries that have foreign policy misunderstandings and disputes with the U.S. Government. To date these have included Nicaragua, El Salvador, Vietnam, Thailand, Cuba, and the former Soviet Union (Lithuania). "Sometimes we joke, and call it our

'Eating With the Enemy' program," says Wicks. "It's the idea of *why* is this nation our enemy? Let's try to find out through the process of eating food together, and find out what common ground we may have." Wicks formally calls the program "Table for Six Billion, Please!" to stress the need for everyone in the world "to have a place at the table."

In 1994, Wicks led a group of her customers to Southeast Asia. In Ho Chi Minh City (formerly Saigon), they visited a sister restaurant run by Madame Di, a former South Vietnamese senator who crusades against the city's social problems. At a Bangkok restaurant the visitors learned about Thailand's crippling AIDS epidemic, sex industry, and thousands of orphans. The owner, Mechai Viravaidya, uses his restaurant much as Wicks uses the White Dog—as a platform from which to discuss and help address pressing social problems. The Bangkok restaurant also works with major corporations like Mobil and American Express to "sponsor" rural villages and advise them about economic development.

One of Wicks's goals in the international sister restaurant program is to show how free enterprise can be a force for good:

> In countries that have been burnt by capitalism, where companies have mistreated workers or the environment, we try to show that it's not always like that. Capitalism *can* serve the common good. Business can be a way to meet everyone's needs.

It is a message that had special meaning when Wicks visited her sister restaurant in Lithuania, which was the second private business founded after the former Soviet Union dissolved in 1989.

Another goal is for White Dog customers to bring their stories home to share with others. At special Table Talk lectures travelers share their firsthand accounts and discuss the political and social situation in the particular country they have visited. The visits are not without culinary benefits as well. Chef Kevin von Klause typically exchanges cooking ingredients and dishes with his counterparts, and later incorporates his discoveries into the White Dog's menu.

HELPING CUSTOMERS BECOME ACTIVE CITIZENS

Wicks is only half-joking when she explains, "I use good food to lure innocent customers into social activism." Although she has no interest in becoming a shrill partisan, she does find great satisfaction in introducing her customers to the joys of civic engagement.

For example, when Wicks learned that playgrounds throughout the city no longer had swings—"sending the message to our children that no one cares"—she organized the Philadelphia Swing Project, which raised tens of thousands of dollars to rehabilitate the playgrounds. In 1995, Wicks organized a special cycling event to dramatize how bicyclists can use the train to commute to work. To help promote Philadelphia restaurants, Wicks suggested to then-mayor Goode that the city host an annual day—"The Book and The Cook"—at which famous cookbook authors would come to city restaurants to cook, meet diners, and sell their books. The event is now in its twelfth year.

Wicks has also developed a number of popular annual events that bring attention to the city's problems and successes. At the annual "Child Watch Visitation" tour, customers have breakfast at the White Dog, then visit a school, a public health center, and a shelter or other facility that serves children and families. The idea is to let people learn firsthand about various city services for children.

A similar event is the annual Community Gardens and Wall Mural Tour, in which Wicks leads a busload or two of customers to the renowned inner-city murals and gardens of Philaldelphia. Customers return to the White Dog for lunch and a short talk about the antigraffiti efforts and empowerment strategies of various nonprofit groups. There is a festive spirit to the inner-city tour, as well as a sense of serious civic commitment.

"TAILS": THE STORYTELLING SALON

The many special events that Wicks organizes have nothing to do with "political correctness" and everything to do with getting people to talk more honestly and openly with each other. In yet another creative outlet for this impulse, Wicks created Tails, a storytelling salon, in 1994 to let "underrepresented" people tell their life stories to intimate audiences of about forty people. The guests have included refugees from Croatia, former prison inmates, elderly women who worked in factories in the 1920s and '30s, African-American women from the South, and homeless residents of a local shelter.

"There's a real need for people to really talk to each other in more personal ways about their own lives," Wicks explains. "It's really kind of a magical thing when it happens, because people begin to understand each other in a more intimate way than we usually have opportunity for in our society." Again, Wicks contrived to make her social vision a sustainable business proposition. The storytelling, which happens every Tuesday night, has turned another slow restaurant evening into a popular attraction.

THE BLACK CAT GIFT SHOP

Another vehicle for Wicks's boundless creative energies is the Black Cat Gift Shop, which she founded as a companion business to the White Dog. Several rooms in an adjacent brownstone are bedecked with scores of offbeat gifts that Wicks has gathered from her travels. There are worry dolls from Chiapas, Mexico; velour jesters' caps and goofy caps; bold, contemporary pottery; and an array of White Dog T-shirts designed by Wicks.

A few dozen gifts, which Wicks calls "Whole World Products," manifest some sort of socially responsible purpose. These include wooden boxes made by former street children in Brazil; picture frames made by former teenage prostitutes in Thailand, revenues from which support their shelter; condiments made by a Palestinian/Jewish company committed to peace in the Mideast; and household gifts made by a rural women's cooperative in North Carolina. Each of the Whole World Products is displayed with a small placard explaining its origins and how the product helps some social cause. Wicks considers the products a way to raise the social consciousness of her customers while providing economic support to worthy small enterprises.

In a similar vein, Wicks has reserved a special alcove of the Black Cat for books about socially responsible business practices; books by Max De Pree, Paul Hawken, Tom Chappell, and others are featured. The books complement a quarterly lecture series at the Cafe, "New Visions for Business," which has featured talks on such topics as "Using Business as a Tool for Ecological Change" and "Employing the Disenfranchised—Businesses That Profit."

THE WHITE DOG FAMILY

For all her concern about community outreach, Wicks also lavishes special attention on her work force. The restaurant employs nearly 100 people, and turnover is much lower than industry norms. People love working there so much, goes the joke, that someone has to die in order for a job to open up at the White Dog.

One reason for such low turnover is the restaurant's celebration of people's social values and personal lives. Simply working there makes employees feel connected to important community issues. Three-year veterans (currently more than twenty-five of them) are honored at the annual "Old Dogs Dinner." At the annual "Howl," employees share and celebrate their personal achievements—new babies, volunteer work, art and poetry—while Wicks delivers the "State of the Dog" Address explaining the restaurant's financial and community achievements. Any employee can go on the international sister restaurant tours for half price, a policy that allowed the head busboy to visit Vietnam and Thailand in 1994. It is not surprising, given this solicitude for employees, that *Inc.* magazine saluted the White Dog Cafe in July 1993 as "one of the best small businesses in the country" to work for.

Wicks has also reached out to teenagers to give them a helping hand into the hospitality business. A few years ago, Wicks started the White Dog PUPPY (Promoting Urban Partnerships With Philadelphia Youth) program to mentor young people and to help ease the school-to-work transition. She has also started a nonprofit arm, Urban Retrievers, to help teenagers become involved in community problems and help expand the White Dog's other nonprofit projects. At a monthly "Saturday Rap," teenagers can connect with guest speakers and each other while discussing such disparate topics as human rights, environmental issues, and student videomaking.

USING ONE'S VALUES TO DRIVE A BUSINESS

Conventional wisdom often holds that "social values" and "good business" are locked into an eternal antithesis, always pulling in opposite directions. Wicks has shown quite the opposite to be true: that honoring one's deepest personal values can be the engine of a successful business. It can greatly distinguish a business in a crowded market. It can cultivate a loyal customer base. Striving to achieve one's highest values can be at least as profitable as the "race to the bottom" strategy that many companies pursue.

The numbers bear this out. For the first five years of its existence, the White Dog's revenues doubled each year. Now, after thirteen years, the restaurant continues to grow by 15 percent a year. It has a singular franchise in the Philadelphia restaurant world, and profits that consistently outstrip the industry average.

There is no substitute for an excellent product, Wicks agrees. She takes pride in her restaurant's great food and service. But Wicks believes the values she expresses through her business are equally important to her competitive success:

> The more I get into expressing what I believe in and care about, the more popular we've become. People are very much drawn to that—drawn to the honesty of it, and drawn to the excitement of it. . . . There is nothing more exciting than using your business not only to support yourself, but to add to the common good.

Mayor Rendell, for one, is appreciative: "We've got a good business community here in Philadelphia, but would that we had a thousand businesspeople who had the same social commitment that Judy does."

But why not pursue the common good through a nonprofit, a civic group, or political office? "To me, business is the only effective way to address the problems of our society," says Wicks. "It's the only institution that is large enough and powerful enough to really make a difference in the world." There is little question that Judy Wicks is doing her part.

18

Gail Mayville of Ben & Jerry's Homemade

GOING GREEN AT THE VERMONT ICE CREAM MACHINE

When Chico Lager had the audacity to challenge his employees to bring their values to work, Gail Mayville had the nerve to take him seriously.

The results were a happy convergence of gains for all parties concerned: new levels of collaboration between management and workers, new production efficiencies, and new standards of environmental performance.

Such a story may not seem remarkable when one learns that it occurred at Ben & Jerry's Homemade, Inc., of Waterbury, Vermont. After all, this is the zany company whose entire identity is based on trying to save the rain forest, buy from socially responsible vendors, and pioneer splashy social innovations—all while serving up great ice cream.

But just because Ben & Jerry's has staked out a highly visible social agenda does not exempt it from the messy challenges of management. Indeed, having raised expectations so high, Ben & Jerry's must work especially hard to live up to its own ambitions as well as the expectations of the public and the press.

Even with a sincere commitment to "doing the right thing," organizational change is often confusing and disruptive. In this case, where the chief proponent of change, Gail Mayville, was not even a manager but an administrative assistant, internal change became even more complicated. Yet hardly insuperable.

In a work culture that honors openness and accountability, the initiative of a single employee was taken quite seriously by CEO Chico Lager and co-founders Ben Cohen and Jerry Greenfield. While modest at the outset, the internal reforms soon sparked more ambitious improvements in manufacturing and office practices, making them more efficient and environmentally benign. The commitment in time gave rise to a host of new and more sweeping environmental programs that have yielded tangible business benefits. More important, the company continues to make frank assessments of its environmental progress and prod itself to do better. Notwithstanding occasional potshots, Ben & Jerry's remains a work culture that earnestly tries to live up to its own ideals.

LIKE "WALKING INTO A CARTOON"

Growing up on a small dairy farm in Milton, Vermont, Gail Mayville was raised on "farmer's logic." She learned at a very early age, "You'd better put back what you take from the land, or it's not going to be able to sustain you very long." Everything the family owned was reused, over and over again, until it was unusable—and then it was recycled and used for something else. Although driven primarily by economic necessity, preserving nature was simply a way of life. No one in Mayville's community had thought yet to call their closed-loop system "recycling."

This ethic stayed with Mayville when she went to Champlain College in the early 1970s, and later to a series of jobs at IBM, a child care center, and a television station. After a stint in Boston, Mayville decided to return to Vermont. Having heard that Ben & Jerry's was a great place to work as well as a socially committed company, she applied for a job—and ended up working as administrative assistant to then-president and CEO Fred (Chico) Lager.

When Mayville first stepped into Ben & Jerry's bright and cheery corporate offices in November 1986, she remembers feeling as if she were "walking into a cartoon." Founded in 1978 by lifetime pals Ben Cohen and Jerry Greenfield, the business was based on a $5 Penn State correspondence course on the art of making ice cream. Cohen and Greenfield created twelve all-natural flavors of hand-cranked superpremium quality (high butterfat and low air content) ice cream, and sold it out the front door of an old, converted gas station in Burlington, Vermont.

The two "chubby nerds from New York," as they once described themselves, were shocked by their own success. The business grew rapidly. In 1981, *Time* magazine named Ben & Jerry's the "best ice cream in the world," and sales skyrocketed.

WORK AND PLAY AT BEN & JERRY'S

Since then Ben & Jerry's has become a big business. A publicly owned company, Ben & Jerry's is now the second-largest superpremium ice cream maker in the United States, with annual sales of nearly $155 million in 1995 and a 4 percent annual growth rate. Only Haagen Dazs has greater sales. With three production plants in Vermont, the company now boasts 100 "scoop shops" in the United States, Canada, Western Europe, Israel, and Russia. It employs 760 people worldwide.

It is not surprising that a company of such unconventional birth would grow into an equally unusual organization. Cohen is one of the new breed of entrepreneurs who are determined to pioneer a more human, socially engaged style of management. To enliven the workplace, for example, Cohen started the "Joy Gang" led by a "Minister of Joy," whose mission is to spread joy throughout the workplace with funny stunts, back rubs for employees, and other antics.

Cohen specializes in new flavor development, creating offbeat offerings such as Cherry Garcia, Wavy Gravy, and Chunky Monkey. He is also renowned for a wacky marketing style that blends humor, countercultural sensibilities, and social activism. This can be seen in such products as the nut brittle Rainforest Crunch, some of whose profits were channeled to rain forest preservation, and Peace Pops, which earmarked 1 percent of profits for peace advocacy. Another splashy idea was the company's nationwide search for a CEO in 1994, which invited applicants to write 100-word essays on "Why I Would Be a Great

CEO for Ben & Jerry's." The gambit attracted some 20,000 entries—and lots of media coverage.

The marketing is not simply self-promotion, but a way of popularizing certain business values. Says Chico Lager, "We believe that, given a choice, people will choose to buy products from companies that are socially responsible."

Cohen, now chairperson of the board, recalls that his company's aggressive commitment to social change was propelled by the company's rapid growth. As he told *People* magazine:

> When Jerry and I realized we were no longer ice-cream men but businessmen, our first reaction was to sell. We were afraid that business exploits its workers and the community. We listed the company with a broker and actually had a buyer. We ended up keeping it, but we decided to adapt it so we could feel proud to say we were the businessmen of Ben & Jerry's.

It was at this point that Cohen and Greenfield, acknowledging that they lacked the business background to properly steer such a rapidly growing organization, brought Fred (Chico) Lager on board as president and CEO.

As their work force expanded, Cohen, Greenfield, and Lager made a commitment, very early on, to the welfare and participation of their employees. The company runs child care centers for its employees' children; offers six weeks of maternity leave at full pay; and pays 100 percent of its employees' health insurance, which even covers acupuncture and homeopathic care.

Ben & Jerry's has an equally strong commitment to the communities of Vermont. The company donates a full 7.5 percent of pretax profits to a company foundation, which, under the guidance of Ben & Jerry's employees, distributes the funds to worthy charities. (Nationwide, corporate donations average about 1 percent of pretax profits.) Ben & Jerry's also prefers to buy from local and state businesses, especially Vermont farmers. It even went so far as to boycott milk produced by cows injected with an experimental growth hormone thought to boost milk production.

In an effort to rigorously assess its social performance, Ben & Jerry's hires independent outsiders to conduct "social audits" each year, then publishes the findings in its annual report. The auditors evaluate employee morale, the company's environmental performance, vendor satisfaction, customer attitudes, and community impact, among other factors. It is certainly one of the most probing, extensive public self-evaluations that any company has performed.

BRINGING "FARMER'S LOGIC" TO AN ICE CREAM BUSINESS

Soon after she began as Chico Lager's administrative assistant, Mayville was promoted to office manager and charged with managing the phone and mail systems, office equipment, and office supply purchasing.

While these duties occupied most of her time, Mayville soon learned that the factory was having trouble disposing of its large output of liquid wastes, produced mostly at the beginnings and ends of ice cream runs. Because Ben & Jerry's ice cream is made with lots of butterfat, the waste does not degrade easily.

As demand for Ben & Jerry's ice cream soared, so did wastes. As much as 3 percent of total production ends up as waste. The company creates nearly a gallon of diluted dairy waste for every gallon of ice cream produced, or approximately eight million gallons in 1994.

In 1989 the rapidly growing company was grappling with its waste problems in a serious way. Although it was trying to build new waste pretreatment lagoons, it was encountering delays. Meanwhile the town of Waterbury threatened to shut down operations if the company continued to violate waste discharge limits.

Mayville offered to help. The first option, she realized, was "land application"—dumping the wastes on land with the proper gradient and that was an acceptable distance from bedrock and wells. But since few landowners would accept such a proposal, Mayville came up with the perfect alternative: Feed the waste to pigs.

A few days later, Mayville located a farmer in Stowe who had just sold his cattle herd, and had 350 acres of flat, empty land. But Earl Mayo did not own any pigs, so Mayville offered to buy a few hundred for him, and a deal was struck. When neighbors heard about the plan and became distraught, however, Mayville had to spend several weekends going door to door to allay the neighbors' worries.

It was an ingenious solution that seemed to make everyone happy: Ben & Jerry's, the town of Waterbury, Earl Mayo, and, perhaps most of all, the pigs. "They like all of it except for Mint Oreo," Mayville reports.

Since the early 1990s, Ben & Jerry's has gone on to develop other systems to help reduce its ice cream wastes. One is a Dissolved Air Flotation system, which helps cull out "high-strength" waste before the pretreatment process. Another involves composting dairy wastes, some of which are used in community garden plots and farmlands that have been historically overutilized.

DO WHAT YOU LOVE, THE JOB WILL FOLLOW

Even though Mayville's chief job responsibilities were as an office manager, her brief stint as a corporate environmentalist had quickened her passions. She had found a challenge that engaged her deepest values.

She also began to realize that Ben & Jerry's had only a limited awareness of its environmental impact. "I was beginning to notice and become very conscious of a lot of the waste that I was seeing around the company," Mayville recalls. "Even all those virgin plastic ballpoint pens that are thrown out." It irritated her to see so many resources squandered. And, as the employee charged with ordering office supplies, she was acutely aware of the wasted money as well.

While she had always been proud of her company's management, she was frustrated by its blind spot. "It wasn't that people at Ben & Jerry's were *against* recycling, it just hadn't occurred to them," says Mayville. "I just wanted us to do something of substance internally in managing our own solid waste stream that would match the vision that people have of our company."

But "company environmentalist" was not in Mayville's job description, and she felt uncomfortable pushing her bosses to do more. So she scribbled dozens of her ideas onto scraps of paper over the next two years, and threw them into a file folder. Perhaps they might come in handy someday.

BEN & JERRY'S ANNOUNCES A MISSION STATEMENT

That opportunity arrived unexpectedly in September 1988, when the company's board of directors announced a formal mission statement. "We wanted everybody at the company to understand that the company did not run on the whims of Ben or Jerry, although it sometimes appeared that way," explains Jerry Greenfield, "but that the company is based on values, and that everybody's job is to carry out those values."

In an attempt to articulate more fully how they would balance profitability and social and economic concerns, Ben & Jerry's coined a new concept, "linked prosperity," which emphasizes the interconnection among Ben & Jerry's products, economic well-being, and social factors. While the product and economic missions offer no surprises—quality products, profits, and growth—the distinctive addition is the social mission: "To operate the company in a way that actively recognizes the central role that business plays in the structure of society by initiating innovative ways to improve the quality of life of a broad community: local, national and international."

Lager challenged employees to find ways to help the company meet the "two-part bottom line."

Mayville happily accepted the invitation. Over the next few months, she assembled her scraps of paper, and in January 1989 submitted a lengthy memorandum proposing three major reforms at Ben & Jerry's: a dramatic reduction in the plant's waste, the creation of a consortium to buy recycled paper, and the replacement of plastic packaging on Ben & Jerry's Brownie Bar Twin Packs.

Impressed by her previous resourcefulness, Lager gave

Mayville the go-ahead on the paper recycling, which Mayville proceeded to take as a green light for her entire proposal.

A FLURRY OF INITIATIVES

Mayville's first concern was the huge volume of cardboard being discarded. All of Ben & Jerry's empty ice cream containers, and even some of its ingredients, are sent in cardboard boxes. As it happened, a small group in the production department had already purchased a baler to recycle the boxes. After buying another baler and lining up a paper broker, Ben & Jerry's diverted 520 bales from the landfill in the first year alone, saving $17,500.

To save on white ledger paper, Mayville bought a copy machine with a double-sided copying feature. Employees were told to place used paper in boxes, which were then taken to a printer to be made into scrap-paper pads. Recycling bins were placed throughout the offices.

While recycling efforts are now commonplace, Mayville's initiatives at the time were novel. There were few technical support systems or publications, let alone cultural support, to make recycling easy. To institute recycling at Ben & Jerry's, Mayville had to learn confusing new terminologies and master the arcane recycling processes. She had to learn how to compare prices of the various recycling companies, about their collection requirements, and whether they provided free storage containers.

Reducing the company's plastic waste was Mayville's most difficult, time-consuming challenge. It turned out that each year Ben & Jerry's was sending approximately 50,000 four-and-a-half-gallon buckets to the landfill, at substantial cost. These buckets, which store the egg yolks, banana puree, peanut butter, and other ingredients used to make ice cream, could not be washed out on-site because of local sewage-treatment limitations.

When no recycler could be found for the HDPE (high-density polyethylene) buckets, Mayville found a company, Vermont Republic Industries, that agreed to start its own HDPE operation if Ben & Jerry's would provide a steady stream of buckets. Mayville, in turn, helped the recycler locate an HDPE manufacturer who would buy the "regrind," as it is known.

Creating the infrastructure and logistical arrangements took about a year. But the savings were immediate and significant: $6,500 per year to recycle the plastic, including truck rental, mileage, gas, driver, and refrigeration, versus $30,000 per year to landfill it.

As Mayville's inquisitive eye searched the company's operations for waste, she discovered that Ben & Jerry's Brownie Bars and Peace Pops were an environmentalist's nightmare. At the time, they were sold in a polyethylene wrapper, on a polystyrene tray, surrounded by three layers of bleached paperboard. By contacting paper suppliers, Mayville had the boxes switched to 100 percent recycled paperboard, a change that by itself saved 8 to 9 percent of costs, and the plastic trays changed to 100 percent recycled plastic. Despite her best efforts, however, Mayville found no substitute for the cellophane that served as a vapor barrier.

Because even little bits of waste add up, Mayville changed some of the most seemingly trivial office practices. The plastic pens it orders are now refillable. Legal pads are made of 100-percent recycled newspaper. Annual reports are printed on recycled paper. Production uniforms are delivered without plastic wrapping.

RECYCLING IS NOT ENOUGH: CLOSING THE LOOP

While the early recycling efforts were important, Mayville's ambition was to "close the loop" to ensure that the waste products were actually reused. She explains:

> If you're going to recycle and put all this secondary material on the market, you don't want it to just end up in somebody's warehouse. You want it to actually be made into something new again, something that's useful . . . and to have a market for that secondary material.

To help kick-start that market, Mayville decided to exploit Ben & Jerry's purchasing power. She quickly found, however, that the only way she could buy recycled paper at a price comparable to virgin paper would be to buy an entire truckload, and to ship it from quite a distance—an unaffordable proposition.

Undeterred, Mayville contacted every small business, non-profit organization, and state agency in the area, taking orders for recycled paper. Ream by ream, Mayville amassed enough orders to fill a truck of 100 percent unbleached post-consumer-use recycled paper, for the same price they had been paying for bleached virgin.

The real satisfaction came when a recycled paper distributor got wind of the "new" demand in the Waterbury area, and set up shop. Now all the members of the coalition can buy recycled paper locally, in small volumes, and at a low price.

Mayville showed the same resourcefulness in buying recycled computer paper, which was then three times more expensive than virgin paper. She struck a creative deal with a Canadian company: Ben & Jerry's would spend 5 percent of its computer paper budget at the firm and pay the premium price over virgin paper, if it would supply it with post-consumer-use recycled paper. Then, as the manufacturer's customer base grew and prices fell, Ben & Jerry's would increase its order accordingly. When prices for recycled paper became comparable to those for virgin, Ben & Jerry's switched over completely to recycled paper.

THE TRIUMPHS AND THE RESENTMENTS

"I was really inspired by Gail's suggestions," recalls Greenfield, "not only because of her incredible knowledge, but [because of] the passion she brought to what she was doing." CEO Lager gave her plenty of room to expand her expertise and influence.

Soon the Association of Vermont Recyclers, impressed by Mayville's expertise and drive, invited her to join its board. She began receiving invitations to serve on various environmental panels, to speak to employees at other companies, and even to lecture to students majoring in environmental studies at several universities and to a special environmental delegation of the United Nations.

While Mayville was overjoyed at her growing national prominence, her colleagues back at Ben & Jerry's were not necessarily so excited. Some were resentful. As the company's resident expert, Mayville could readily explain the new policies and their environmental significance, but she was slow to enlist the support of fellow employees. "In looking back," says Mayville, "I can see that I probably didn't approach this in just the right way. . . . You can't set up an environmental program for a company if you don't understand what everyone else's needs are."

So Mayville cut back on speaking engagements and tried to rekindle her personal interactions at work. She recalls Lager's sobering advice at the time: "Until you learn to work effectively through other people, you're only going to be able to accomplish what you yourself can do."

Stepping back from her solo mission to make Ben & Jerry's a green machine, Mayville suddenly realized, "There are other people in the company who have expressed an interest in working with different environmental projects internally. Why not start a 'Green Team'?"

THE BEN & JERRY'S GREEN TEAM

In 1990, Mayville proposed a new job description for herself, with the title "Environmental Program Development Manager." Except for the length of the title, Lager was happy to sanction her new role.

Realizing that she needed to enlist broader support, Mayville invited anyone in the company to join a special task force to research, develop, and implement new environmental programs. She called it The Green Team. With seventeen volunteers and formal recognition by senior management, the team's first priority was to increase the amount of in-house recycling and to educate employees.

The Green Team also launched some local recycling projects. Every January, Ben & Jerry's, in cooperation with a local utility, sponsor the "Merry Mulching" project so that people can get their old Christmas trees turned into wood chips instead of dumped in the landfill. Ben & Jerry's also sponsors a companywide "Green Flea Market" as a benefit for a federation of environmental groups.

Blessed with a supportive management, Mayville and her enthusiasm have been catalysts for other environmental changes at the company. Attention was now focused on the cost savings and environmental impact of waste and the cost savings of avoiding waste. When Randy Yantz, a manufacturing employee, became a kind of "energy czar" for the company, he retrofitted the entire plant to make it more energy-efficient. He switched to more efficient lighting; recovered more waste water and heat; and purchased more efficient compressors and motors.

BIG OAKS FROM LITTLE ACORNS GROW

From the vantage point of the late 1990s, the environmental reforms instigated by Gail Mayville may seem prosaic, so rapid is the pace of change. Since Earth Day 1990, recycling has become almost routine in many businesses, and environmental management is now a distinct specialty within companies. Yet for their time, and in a fairly small company, Mayville's initiatives were quite extraordinary, and required considerable research, innovation, and imagination.

Although Mayville left the company in 1992 to become a consultant, she proved to be a critical catalyst in expanding Ben & Jerry's long-term environmental commitment. One of the company's first major acts was to commission a comprehensive environmental and energy assessment. While lauding the company's recycling, waste, and general environmental programs, the report found that the company "lacks a unifying environmental mission or vision."

Since then, Ben & Jerry's has launched a companywide plan to reduce waste, energy, and emissions. It also hired a full-time director of natural resources management, Andrea Asch, to develop new programs and coordinate existing ones. The company's 1995 plans were to reduce solid waste by 30 percent and dairy waste by 20 percent.

Whatever it environmental shortcomings, Ben & Jerry's has not sought to conceal them. In its 1994 annual report the company published a frank, detailed critique of its environmental performance, citing specific quantities of waste (64 million pounds of dairy waste) and the overall impact on landfills (15,550 cubic yards of packaging).

Nor has the company been afraid to broach new environmental issues such as the implications of sourcing sugar, chocolate, and coffee from Third World countries. Frequently, the growing of these cash crops displaces indigenous peoples, exhausts the soil, and requires more synthetic fertilizers and pesticides.

In his 1994 audit of Ben & Jerry's social performance, Paul Hawken, the entrepreneur and business commentator, reflected:

> When a company is as different as Ben & Jerry's, the larger society tends to be both fascinated and impressed. But there is also a subconscious desire to see it fail at being different. The reasons for this are complex, but basically if a company like Ben & Jerry's can succeed in its direct and outspoken effort to help humankind through "caring capitalism," it questions many old assumptions about the real task of business.

Andrea Asch, for her part, says:

> If there's something to be learned from us, it's that we're not through learning. If there's something other companies should realize from our example, it's that their possibilities for being profitable and environmentally responsible at the same time are as unlimited as their willingness to explore them.

It helps, as well, to encourage passionate employees like Gail Mayville to enact their values at work.

19

GE Plastics' "Share to Gain" Program

BUILDING CORPORATE LOYALTY WHILE REBUILDING THE COMMUNITY

Team building has long been an important concept with corporate management. Good teamwork, the experts say, breeds new ideas, keeps morale high, improves quality, and ultimately increases profits. Although teamwork was historically tackled through office parties and sports outings, companies today are exploring a wide range of experimental vehicles to build teamwork—everything from wilderness expeditions to rope-climbing. The common goal is to get employees to know each other better and to work together enthusiastically toward a shared goal.

In the late 1980s, GE Plastics, a division of the General Electric Company, came up with a simple yet powerful innovation for team building. Management hypothesized, and later proved, that GE Plastics could build team spirit more effectively by putting its employees to work helping the community. At the time, GE Plastics needed good teamwork more than ever. The division had recently acquired an old rival, Borg-Warner Chemicals, creating the formidable challenge of integrating two dissimilar work cultures.

In the past, GE Plastics had its employees participate in contrived sporting events, silly group stunts, and golfing competitions. But Joel Hutt, manager of marketing communications and part of the team charged with organizing GE's corporate meetings, wondered whether there were more effective ways to build teamwork.

Hutt's questioning sparked the creation of "Share to Gain," a new model that provides significant, lasting benefits to the community while introducing employees to the satisfactions of community service. At the same time, the program binds employees together more readily perhaps than any other type of team-building event.

TURNING RIVALS INTO TEAMMATES

General Electric Company, the sixth largest corporation in the world, might not seem a fertile ground for innovative approaches to team building. Team building has long had a prominence in GE activities, however, perhaps because Jack Welch, GE's chief executive since 1981, is a devout worshiper of productivity. He has streamlined GE with an all-out attack on excessive bureaucracy, superfluous meetings and memos, and unnecessary jobs. His other strategy to increase productivity has focused on creating a genuine sense of team spirit and equality among GE employees. The internal environment that has resulted at General Electric is a seemingly contradictory combination of teamwork and competition. Yet it succeeds. GE Plastics' division meetings in the 1980s featured many team-building activities—rowing events, donkey races, wilderness experiences.

Headquartered in Pittsfield, Massachusetts, GE Plastics is a global leader in engineering plastics. The $6 billion division was created in 1928, and in 1996 employed 13,000 people. Since the introduction of engineering plastics, GE Plastics has brought scores of innovations to the market, using basic resin chemistries to replace glass and metal in manufactured products. The high-performance, lightweight replacements can be found in everything from impact-resistant bumper systems to computer components.

Each year, GE Plastics holds meetings for its four main divisions: sales, marketing, manufacturing, and technical support. Historically, these winter get-togethers, usually in a warm climate, were anything but relaxing. Long, grueling days were filled with educational seminars, sessions about new manufacturing techniques, messages from management, and team-building activities.

Planning the team-building event for the 1988 annual division meetings, Joel Hutt devised a new team-building idea that fulfilled the company's fundamental needs while dramatizing the technology side of the business: a desert construction challenge.

One morning, following days of intense meetings, 380 unwitting GE sales employees—men and women, vice presidents and new hires from all parts of the country—were hauled to the desert, randomly divided into thirty-one teams, given the necessary materials, and instructed to design and build houses. Cooperation and teamwork were essential in that each group would be required to sleep in its house that evening, and the desert nights were chilly.

The exercise was an immediate success. Buses arrived the following morning to find the GE employees tired and cold, yet excited and proud of what they had accomplished together in such a short time. Just as the buses pulled away, a crew arrived to clean up the construction materials.

"Watching the structures pulled to the ground made a real impression on me," recalls Hutt. "It was clear a group with that much creativity and energy could do just about anything. I remember thinking it was a shame to waste all that effort."

CAN THESE TWO CORPORATE CULTURES BE MERGED?

The need for team building took on a new urgency in June 1988 when GE announced its intention to purchase Borg-Warner Chemicals, a billion-dollar division of the Borg-Warner Corporation, based in Parkersville, West Virginia. The two divisions had been competitors for years, both producing high-performance engineered plastics.

But Borg-Warner and GE Plastics had very different corporate cultures. According to Bob Hess, GE Plastics' manager of customer communications and a former Borg-Warner employee,

Borg-Warner had a much more paternalistic atmosphere than GE, with older employees who tended to stay put. "Family-like," says Hess. "Everybody knew everybody." GE Plastics, by contrast, was described as fostering a more youthful and aggressive environment. "A much tougher company," was the way Hess and Borg-Warner colleagues had thought of GE before the integration, "maybe a little colder."

Still, the two work forces were complementary: Borg-Warner boasted a successful sales force, whereas GE Plastics' strength lay in its aggressive marketing group. Acquiring Borg-Warner gave GE Plastics a real boost in technical and manufacturing strength, new products, and domestic and offshore marketing facilities.

Morale, however, took a dive after the purchase of Borg-Warner was approved by the Federal Trade Commission in September 1988. During an agonizing "weeding out" period, GE management pondered which Borg-Warner employees would make the move from Parkersville to Pittsfield, and which would lose their jobs. Some Borg-Warner employees who had been invited to join GE were still undecided; other employees visited Massachusetts to "test the waters" while their families remained in West Virginia. When all was said and done, 5,000 wary Borg-Warner employees remained to join and assimilate with a GE Plastics force of 9,000. (Through attrition and minor layoffs, the work force has since shrunk by 1,000.)

GE Plastics managers knew that the annual meetings, set to begin in January in San Diego, would be a critical opportunity for integrating the two discordant work cultures. Realizing that anxiety would be at record highs, Joel Hutt wondered how GE Plastics could cultivate trust and loyalty among former Borg-Warner Chemical employees and "rerecruit" its own existing employees. Above all, how could they help the two work forces become a single team?

The previous year's desert exercise made it clear to Hutt what was lacking—a team-building experience that would make a lasting impression on the participants while serving some larger, more elevated purpose. This revelation led Hutt to ask himself, "Instead of playing golf or going fishing or sailing, why not take the tremendous energy and creativity of four or five hundred people and do something constructive, with enduring value—something to help other people?" Making something last: That was the spark for "Share to Gain."

Such a change from the previous team-building activities needed upper management's approval, so Hutt took the concept to senior vice president Glen Hiner. The need to integrate Borg-Warner employees into the GE culture was no secret, and Hiner's team was eager for suggestions. Hiner and other top managers were so enthusiastic that Hutt calls it the "easiest sell of my life."

NEXT: A LOGISTICAL NIGHTMARE

With the go-ahead from senior management, a four-month planning session ensued. It was decided that between January and April of 1989, GE Plastics employees would renovate five non-profit facilities—one by each of the four main divisions that would meet in San Diego, and one by another sales group that would be attending. Building renovations would be a particularly apt team-building project because participants could use many of the company's own products.

Ideally, GE Plastics wanted to renovate dilapidated facilities that were open to and served the entire community. After considering twenty different possibilities, the planning committee chose five: the Ira C. Copley Family YMCA near downtown San Diego; the Armed Forces YMCA, an antiquated facility catering to young enlisted personnel; the YMCA Surf Camp, an overnight beach site for YMCA's youth groups; the St. Vincent de Paul/Joan Kroc Homeless Shelter, a facility providing shelter for over 400 homeless people; and, finally, the William J. Oakes Boys' & Girls' Club, a safe haven for children of a dangerous San Diego neighborhood.

Working out the details for each site consumed the next several months for Hutt's five-person planning team. A local general contractor was hired to compile a detailed list of what each facility needed. Project architects were retained in San Diego to examine the sites, provide color schemes, select tile and carpet, and provide documentation and blueprints indicating the precise requirements for each GE Plastics group.

To keep the Pittsfield headquarters informed about renovation planning, Hutt's team appointed two Pittsfield employees to act as liaisons for each renovation project. A GE Plastics technician was chosen as the engineering leader to make sure all work was progressing according to schedule, and at reasonable cost. Project leaders were chosen from the marketing communications department to be in charge of all nonconstruction components: transportation, team selection, rules, material layout, catering tents, sound system, press inquiries, community relations, photography, and emergency considerations.

GE Plastics provided many of its own products, then purchased locally most of the other tools and supplies needed. Finally, planners worked with the host agencies to see what equipment could be borrowed from local sources. The city of San Diego and the local electric company were generous with ladders, wheelbarrows, shovels, and other tools.

Back in Pittsfield, planners were busy dividing participants into groups, determining who was best suited to the various tasks, based on their skill levels and possible limitations. Team-building activities traditionally remain a secret until the evening before the event, so an employee survey with disguised questions gave planners a better idea of people's talents and weaknesses at various manual labor tasks. Although skilled participants would have to be assigned the more challenging tasks, planners were careful not to put all the engineers or any other group of specialists together. The idea was to meet new people from other locations and, above all, to mix former Borg-Warner people with GE employees.

On the day before the first scheduled renovation, Joel Hutt inspected the site of the Copley Family YMCA. For two months, the facility had been prepped: Dead shrubbery was pulled, swimming pool windows were removed, tile, paint, tools, and scaffolding were assembled, lumber was precut, empty dumpsters were put in place, and a cement mixer stood waiting. The entire project site was clearly marked, awaiting the arrival of the GE army.

THE "TEE-UP"

The second night of the conference, Hutt took the stage before a marketing force of 470 at the San Diego resort. The days of golf tournaments and other events were over, Hutt announced, and the room filled with disappointed groans. But the crowd fell silent when Hutt asked, "What if we took all the energy in this room and did something constructive, something that has enduring value? I'd like to show you a different video," he said, queuing up a short film of the run-down Copley Family YMCA.

Located in a low-income neighborhood riddled with gangs and drugs, the facility is an alternative to the streets for kids. But cutbacks made in the 1970s forced maintenance to be delayed and vandalism ignored. The building and grounds had fallen into serious disrepair. Windows were broken, graffiti covered the walls, the yard was overgrown with weeds, and the interior was a disaster.

"The director of this Y says fixing this place up will cost $500,000 and take years, if it can be done at all," Hutt told the GE employees. "Well, I'm here tonight to tell you it's not going to take years. This GE army is going to attack this place. We're going to do it in eight hours, and we're going to do it tomorrow!"

Hutt was a cheerleader with a challenge, and the idea was infectious. He told the group that they shared the power of the GE Plastics team, and that they alone could renovate this building in one day. Enthusiasm was immediate and the marketing employees cheered from their seats.

Sent outside to a gigantic tent, the force was divided into thirty preselected teams, each containing members ranging from entry-level marketing employees to senior management and a deliberate mix of former Borg-Warner and veteran GE Plastics workers. Hutt asked the groups to choose team names, mottoes, and logos, and then to elect project leaders and officers to be in charge of safety, materials procurement, logistics, specialty skills, quality control, and graphic arts. The only condition: No GE executive or manager could play any leadership role.

Each team received a specific project along with a detailed description of the assignment, photographs, and a list of the materials needed. Dinner, served family-style, provided an opportunity to get to know new teammates, start planning, and develop a sense of shared purpose.

After dinner, teams dived into intense logistical planning. Those elected to be specialty skills officers and safety managers met with contractors for training sessions; the "graphic arts managers" saw that every participant's coveralls were imprinted with the team motto. The rest of the team examined blueprints, assigned tasks, and devised work schedules.

THE TWELVE-HOUR MIRACLE

The GE work force, traveling from its plush resort to the Copley Family YMCA the next morning, entered a very different world. As force members piled off the buses, the teams went eagerly and methodically to their first tasks. Assembly lines formed, tattered stained carpet was quickly pulled from the floor, and old lockers were removed.

All day, top-forty tunes and reggae music blasted throughout the building, interrupted only by occasional announcements, progress evaluations, and safety reminders. It was a motley crew of vice presidents and marketing reps, former Borg-Warner and GE Plastics veterans alike, that scraped and primed the decaying ceilings and walls; laid tile; prepared window frames for new panels; built a retaining wall; fixed basketball backstops; replaced an irrigation system; and, after leveling and seeding the ground, rebuilt a soccer field.

Nearly every window in the building was replaced with GE impact-resistant LEXAN® plastic panes. The grounds were landscaped, and one team applied the thirty-four paint colors necessary to restore a twenty-year-old mural that had covered a large two-story outer wall.

The teams had arrived prepared to compete, but as the day wore on, participants noticed that this team-building experience was different from previous ones. This time, they wanted *all* the teams to win. Some teams finished before others, but no one gloated over "winning." Instead, they picked up a slower team's paintbrush or plant and helped complete that project.

Midafternoon, a special guest appeared. Greg Louganis, the Olympic gold-medal-winning diver, had learned to swim in the Copley YMCA pool as a child. He came by to let GE Plastics know what its chosen team-building activity meant to the community.

Teams worked beyond the eight-hour schedule, until nearly eight o'clock that evening, barely breaking for submarine sandwiches and sodas at lunch. By day's end, the GE Plastics marketing force had laid 11,000 square feet of tile and 2,200 square feet of carpeting, polished off 550 gallons of paint, and planted 1,000 flowers, trees, bushes, and shrubs. It had spread two truckloads of topsoil, strewn 300 pounds of grass seed, and poured 21 cubic yards of concrete.

At day's end, participants felt exhilarated and proud of their accomplishments. In twelve hours, they had successfully completed 99 percent of what the Copley YMCA needed (professional construction workers were retained by GE to tie up loose ends the following day). As the newly acquainted GE and Borg-Warner workers drove off to celebrate at a nearby bowling alley, the "new" YMCA was hardly recognizable.

The GE Plastics marketing group set a tough precedent for the four other GE divisions. And that is exactly how Joel Hutt pitched the concept: "If marketing can do it, so can you!" he challenged the other teams.

That same month, two GE Plastics sales groups, 143- and 300-strong, respectively, completely overhauled the YMCA Camp Surf facility and the St. Vincent de Paul/Joan Kroc shelter for the homeless. Later in April, 600 manufacturing employees renovated the William J. Oakes Boys' and Girls' Club. Finally, in May, GE Plastics' 400-member technology division refurbished the huge, sixty-five-year-old, five story Armed Services YMCA.

Five single days, spread over nearly five months, were all it took for just *one* company's divisions to transform a community's public service facilities. In only five days, almost 2,000 people worked more than 18,000 man-hours, spread 3,200 gallons of paint, installed 2,000 windows, laid 40,000 square feet of vinyl and carpet, refurbished over 200 rooms, and planted thousands and thousands of bushes, plants, trees, and shrubs.

THE STUNNING RESULTS FOR GE PLASTICS AND SAN DIEGO

While the effects on the San Diego community are lasting, it was the impact on GE Plastics employees that was most phenomenal. The feelings of camaraderie and accomplishment experienced by participants were more than Hutt and his team of planners could have hoped for.

Ron Pound, a consultant who has worked with GE on numerous acquisitions, claims that the San Diego projects were the turning point in the integration of GE Plastics and Borg-Warner Chemicals. Prior to the meetings, many managers from Borg-Warner still considered GE Plastics to be "the competition." After a day of pounding nails and painting walls, they had shed their rivalries to contribute to a higher cause—and become teammates.

Pound reports that before their "Share to Gain" experiences, many Borg-Warner employees had remained unsure whether they really wanted to be a part of GE Plastics. Like Bob Hess, these employees returned from San Diego and told their families to pack up, they were going to Pittsfield.

"We were dirty, tired, grubby and so proud to be part of the whole project," said one member of the manufacturing department after completing the Boys' & Girls' Club renovation. "As a former Borg-Warner employee," said Bob Hess, "any questions I had about if this is the kind of company I want to work for . . . those questions were gone, absolutely. For us to be able to pull this off and to want to do this really made all the difference."

Ed Koscher, vice president and general manager of GE Plastics, explained in an interview with *Successful Meetings* magazine that when the project was finally completed, "the people were bound together. No longer were people thought of as Borg-Warner or GE people. They were all GE people."

Needless to say, San Diego's five nonprofit groups were thrilled as well. "It's like they were sent from heaven, an answer to our prayers," Arthur W. Curry, director of the Boys' & Girls' Club, told a Springfied, Massachusetts, *Union News* reporter.

"[It] tells me there are people in big corporations who care . . . it humanized GE, and that's a hell of a statement." Copley Y's executive director, Steve Rowe, claims the renovation was "a tremendous boost for the operation and helped boost membership in the facility by one-quarter. We had people coming back who had left because the place was such a mess."

Remarkably, the renovations cost GE Plastics no more than one of their traditional team-building activities. Each of the larger San Diego projects cost approximately $100,000, about the same as sending three or four hundred employees to a local country club for a day on the golf course, meals, and entertainment.

THE CONCEPT SPREADS

Shortly after the first "Share to Gain" project, Hutt began receiving calls from others within GE. Despite a decision to eschew publicity, word of their success had spread quickly in San Diego, and CEO Jack Welch was endorsing the concept wholeheartedly.

Suddenly, outsiders wanted to know how they could do similar projects. Bob Hess, who had been in charge of the St. Vincent de Paul project, was assigned the task of creating a how-to booklet and promotional video, detailing the steps involved, the precautions to take, and the logistical planning needed.

Soon, team-building projects cropped up all over the country. One of the largest was carried out by the National Broadcasting Company (NBC), a division of GE, at a management retreat in Miami. After a day of business meetings, 160 executives rolled up their sleeves and, with President Robert Wright in the lead, completely refurbished a run-down day care center in the nearby neighborhood of Coconut Grove.

Six months later, one of GE's customers, Skyline Displays, a manufacturer of portable trade show displays and graphics, donated 500 people for a day and $60,000 in materials to the construction of an 11,000-square-foot playground, better known to the kids of Burnsville, Minnesota, as "Skyland."

Back within the confines of General Electric there exists a volunteer organization, the "Elfun Society," whose interest in community renovations has mushroomed since GE Plastics introduced "Share to Gain." In November 1989, the Pittsfield chapter took two consecutive weekends to completely transform what was a run-down century-old Victorian rest home into an attractive shelter for the homeless. "Share to Gain" projects quickly became an annual event for every Elfun Society around the world.

In 1990, GE Plastics added a new twist to the concept. The division renovated a run-down family counseling building in a poor area of Sacramento, California, to demonstrate to skeptical GE clients the quality of the "Nailite roof," a plastic alternative to cedar shake roof shingles. This time, GE combined a marketing objective with community service goals.

By 1995, the "Share to Gain" concept had gone global after hundreds of employees at GE Plastics in Europe renovated a weekend retreat for impoverished children in Spain.

To many, the concept is a modern variation on the barn raisings of early America. When a big project needed to be tackled, everyone pitched in their manual labor to get it done. In the process they built lasting relationships and a sense of community. So many have followed GE Plastics' lead because they know that the "Share to Gain" approach to team building works. Resorts are luxurious. Games can be fun. Wilderness adventures are an exciting challenge. But nothing beats the pride and the satisfaction experienced by a team that leaves behind something of lasting value. Nothing binds as tight as the drive toward a common goal, especially when that goal is helping others.

"We didn't invent this concept," Joel Hutt is quick to note. "People are doing projects to help people all the time. What we did is apply it to the business meeting."

20

Merck & Co.

QUANDARIES IN DEVELOPING A WONDER DRUG FOR THE THIRD WORLD

Along a dusty footpath of the West African savanna, a blind man in a flowing tunic is led fitfully forward by a young boy. Elsewhere in the village, blind men and women sit under large trees all day, some picking peanuts off plants, others idle. Then there are the other blind residents who have no family or relatives, who, villagers say, are "finished," a fate considered worse than death.

Such scenes are common in thousands of tiny settlements throughout Africa and in parts of the Middle East and Latin America. The cause of the blindness: a parasitic worm carried by tiny black flies that breed along fast-moving rivers. When the flies bite humans, which occurs thousands of times a day, the larvae of a parasitic worm, *Onchocerca volvulus*, can be passed along.

It is the beginning of a nasty, insidious disease widely known as river blindness. As the worms grow to more than two feet in length, they cause grotesque but relatively innocuous hanging nodules in the skin. People develop a hideous, leathery "crocodile skin." The real harm begins when the adult worms reproduce, releasing millions of microscopic offspring, known as microfilariae, which swarm through body tissue. A terrible itching results, leading some victims to commit suicide. After several months the microfilariae cause lesions and depigmentation of the skin. Eventually they invade the eye, causing blindness.

The World Health Organization (WHO) estimates that some 340,000 people are blind because of onchocerciasis—"oncho"— and that a million or more suffer from partial blindness. Worldwide, some eighteen million people are infected with the parasite, although half of them have no serious symptoms. An estimated eighty-five million people are at risk of infection. In some villages close to fly-breeding sites, nearly all residents are infected and a majority of those over age 45 have gone blind. Young children frequently consider severe itching, skin infections, and blindness to be a normal part of growing up.

Now, for the first time in recorded history, there is hope for preventing onchocerciasis. In 1987, after nearly a decade of work, scientists at Merck & Co. demonstrated the safety and effectiveness of a new drug, Mectizan. Derived from ivermectin, an antibiotic compound discovered by Merck researchers in 1975, Mectizan is a wonder drug truly deserving of the term. The drug is so effective it can be taken, in pill form, as infrequently as once a year. It is so safe that it can be administered with confidence to large numbers of people who do not receive regular medical care.

THE DILEMMAS POSED BY A WONDER DRUG

The discovery and development of Mectizan may well rank as one of the boldest public health triumphs of the century. But it also presented Merck scientists and executives with a set of rather extraordinary dilemmas. How could a profit-making enterprise justify the development of a drug that its potential customers could not conceivably afford? Even with more than eighteen million potential customers, few of them could afford to pay even pennies for one pill (the annual dose) of Mectizan. As for their governments, many of them are too embattled with famines, civil wars, and other crises to address a chronic health problem which seems, in any case, to be inescapable.

Aside from the payment issue, Merck faced other knotty problems. How could the company distribute the drug to villages that were far beyond the reach of pharmacies, doctors, and telephones and sometimes not even accessible by dirt roads? And how could the company help ensure that the drug would be safely used and that unforeseen side effects would be identified and treated?

Faced with many quandaries—moral, practical, and financial—Merck executives set new precedents for the drug industry by making an ambitious commitment to curb, if not eradicate, a dreaded Third World disease. They applied the company's huge R&D resources to addressing a problem with little foreseeable profit potential. Yet paradoxically, their social leadership proved not only feasible but beneficial to the long-term health of the company.

MERCK'S DISTINCTIVE CORPORATE CULTURE

Any inquiry into why Merck behaved the way it did must begin with an examination of Merck's distinctive corporate culture. The company is renowned for its unswerving commitment to basic research, its excellent management team, and its long-term perspective. With an R&D budget of $1.5 billion in 1996, Merck is a veritable engine of new blockbuster drugs, such as the cholesterol-lowering Mevacor, the antihypertensive Vasotec, a new asthma treatment, and the first chicken pox vaccine ever. With sixteen products earning more than $100 million in annual sales apiece, Merck far outstrips any of its rivals in pharmaceutical innovation.

It is not surprising that for seven straight years, 1986 through 1992, Merck was voted the "most admired" company in *Fortune* magazine's annual Corporate Reputations Survey. Merck's compounded annual profits from 1986 to 1992 exceeded 24 percent. *Business Week* lauded Merck as "The Miracle Company" in a cover story, saluting its "excellence in the lab and executive suite." With 1995 sales of $16.7 billion and a net income of $3.3 billion, Merck is the nation's largest drug company.

In its pursuit of financial success, however, Merck has not lost sight of its social obligations. "Merck has a long legacy of social responsibility, derived from a sense of how their business impacts directly on public health," according to *Everybody's Business*, an almanac on the social performance of major corporations. Merck has shared its early research findings on the HIV virus with other companies, and has shown sensitivity to the work/family problems of its employees. Unlike some drug companies, Merck is virtually never criticized for inferior research or failures to disclose harmful side effects.

ROY VAGELOS FACES AN INTRIGUING CHOICE

If there is one person who most embodies Merck's straight-shooting style and long-term vision, it is Dr. P. Roy Vagelos, the legendary chairman and CEO of Merck from 1985 to 1994. (Vagelos retired from Merck and became chairman of Regeneron Pharmaceuticals Inc., a small biotechnology firm, in 1995.) A physician and biochemist, Vagelos first joined Merck in 1976 to run its research labs. Later, as Merck's top executive, Vagelos was "one of the few CEOs in his industry with a grassroots understanding of scientific discovery," observed one business reporter.

As fate had it, Vagelos was head of the Merck research labs in December 1978 when he received a memorandum from a senior researcher in parasitology, Dr. William C. Campbell, that made a highly intriguing suggestion—that a new antiparasitic compound under investigation for use in animals—ivermectin—just might be able to prevent the blindness associated with onchocerciasis.

The discovery had its origins in a scoop of soil dug up at a golf course near Ito, Japan. Merck researchers were startled to detect strong antiparasitic activity in the soil. Even more exciting, the compound eventually isolated—ivermectin—proved to have an astonishing potency and effectiveness against an unusually wide range of parasites in cattle, swine, horses and other animals.

Merck decided to develop the substance for the animal health market, and by 1981 the first ivermectin-based animal drug, Ivomec, was introduced to the market. By the end of the 1980s, Ivomec had become the single best-selling animal health product in the world, propelling the company's animal health and crop protection division to more than $1 billion in sales.

In the late 1970s, as clinical testing of ivermectin was progressing, Dr. Campbell discovered that ivermectin, when tested in horses, was effective against the microfilariae of an exotic, fairly unimportant gastrointestinal parasite, *Onchocerca cervicalis*. This particular worm, while harmless in horses, had characteristics similar to the insidious human parasite that causes river blindness, *Onchocerca volvulus*.

Dr. Campbell wondered: Could ivermectin be modified to work against the human parasite? Could a safe, effective drug for river blindness be developed?

MERCK DECIDES TO DEVELOP MECTIZAN

For Drs. Vagelos and Campbell, of course, it was an irresistible possibility. "Emotionally, you become very involved in what you can accomplish, as a research group and as a company," Dr. Vagelos explains. "And so we could hardly wait to start these experiments."

Yet Dr. Vagelos and his associates immediately realized that a successful onchocerciasis drug would not generate much revenue for Merck. This was not a happy prospect because the process of developing new drug compounds is long, laborious, and fraught with uncertainty. It is also expensive. The Pharmaceutical Manufacturers Association calculates that the average cost of bringing a new drug compound "from the lab to the shelf" is $359 million. The problem with ivermectin was not that the potential customer base was too small, as with "orphan drugs" for rare diseases, but that the potential users were too impoverished to pay for the drug.

Thus, Merck faced a wrenching moral dilemma: Should a

potentially useful drug compound be developed even though the economic rewards—or even the recovery of basic costs—might never materialize?

"We had never undertaken the development of a drug that was going to be broadly used, such as 18 million patients, with the idea that we were not going to make money," Dr. Vagelos explains. In general, Merck discontinues the development of drugs that are expected to earn $20 million or less a year, he says. Certainly no one expected Mectizan to generate a fraction of that sum.

"On the other hand," Vagelos notes, "the company is so large and the laboratories so prolific, that one can never guess what is going to come out." Further investigation of ivermectin, however problematic, could end up yielding useful knowledge. And the researchers were exceedingly eager to forge ahead, both for scientific and humanitarian reasons. Failing to move ahead could inflict a serious blow to the morale of researchers, arguably the most critical employees in the firm.

Vagelos decided to proceed with further preclinical research, if only to expand Merck's knowledge of ivermectin. By 1980 the compound had been sufficiently studied in the lab, and synthesized, which led to another crossroads: Should Merck take the next momentous step of proceeding with human clinical trials?

THE PERILS OF UNDERMINING ONE'S OWN LUCRATIVE MARKET

Moving ahead would entail some serious new risks. If ivermectin proved to have any adverse health effects on humans, this could taint its reputation as a veterinary drug and potentially undermine its sales, which were then estimated at several hundred million dollars. And, in fact, early tests on certain mammals such as collies produced some disastrous effects, says Dr. Brian Duke, then a research scientist with the World Health Organization. Since the cross-species effectiveness of antiparasitic drugs is unpredictable, "there was always a worry that some race or subsection of the human population" might be adversely affected.

Unsettling new questions might arise if the drug caused isolated instances of harm in humans, or if it were used improperly in Third World settings. There were other worries as well: Could the drug harm certain animals in ways not yet discovered? Could drug residues turn up in meat eaten by humans? Would any human version of ivermectin distributed to the Third World be diverted into the black market, thereby undercutting sales of the veterinary drug?

As it turned out, all these concerns were unwarranted. But at the outset of research, Dr. Bruce M. Greene, a prominent university scientist associated with the development of Mectizan, recalls, there was "a lot of turmoil in the company [in the early 1980s] about whether we should expose this fabulous commercial product to the risk of human usage"—a worry echoed by other scientists and a top WHO official, and reported by *The Wall Street Journal* in 1992. Dr. Vagelos conceded in a 1991 interview that there had been some debate within Merck about these concerns, but added, "It was limited. I squelched it."

THE COMPLICATED CHALLENGES OF HUMAN CLINICAL TRIALS

In the end, Merck took the chance and decided to conduct clinical trials. In January 1980 the Merck Research Management Council agreed to move forward with human clinical trials, in cooperation with the WHO. The baton now passed to Dr. Mohammed A. Aziz, senior director of clinical research at Merck, a tropical disease expert and native of the region now called Bangladesh. A quiet, polite man of steely determination, Aziz is widely credited with championing Mectizan within Merck and shepherding it past numerous scientific and corporate obstacles.

Aziz immediately encountered a fresh set of dilemmas in determining the human safety and efficacy of ivermectin. Clinical trials require close medical oversight of test subjects and the rigorous collection of data. Yet river blindness victims rarely live within hailing distance of modern medical facilities. Realizing it would need help, Merck turned to the World Health Organization, the Geneva-based consortium of 189 member nations, "to determine the most appropriate approach to the problem—from the medical, political and commercial points of view."

It was a logical partnership. Merck had a compound that might treat river blindness; WHO had access to a global network of government health officials and scientists who could help run clinical trials. The first human tests of ivermectin began at the University of Dakar, Senegal, in February 1981. Merck supplied the drug, grants-in-aid for the studies, and the resources to apply for regulatory approval. WHO provided scientists and research facilities.

Despite their shared interests, the initial collaboration between Merck and WHO was rocky. WHO was already deeply committed to a $26-million-a-year program to eliminate black flies through aerial larvacide spraying—a program that by 1995 had reduced the number of infected people in targeted areas from 1.5 million to practically nil. WHO officials feared that this program might be jeopardized if ivermectin really worked, according to Dr. Vagelos in 1991. "The only way we could get them to collaborate with us was to tell them that we would continue to support their vector control program," he said.

WHO scientists also questioned the medical promise of ivermectin, suspecting that it would have unacceptable side effects and require close medical supervision. Furthermore, WHO scientists believed that any new drug for river blindness must attack the adult parasite, not the microfilariae offspring, if new generations of microfilariae were to be conclusively eradicated.

Notwithstanding periodic clashes of scientific judgment and institutional cultures, a working collaboration evolved over time. By the end of 1981, the early results appeared encouraging: There were no adverse reactions, and a single, extremely small dose of ivermectin dramatically reduced microfilariae counts. A second study conducted in Paris confirmed the Dakar results.

But the skeptics remained. One highly respected scientist at the University of Geneva and former WHO official, André Rougemont, wrote a stinging letter to *Lancet*, the prestigious British medical journal, in November 1982, accusing Aziz et al. of being "over optimistic." He charged that ivermectin "brings

no really new or interesting feature to the treatment of onchocerciasis."

Prodded by such a bold public attack, Dr. Aziz redoubled
his efforts to prove that ivermectin was indeed superior to the
existing drug of choice, known as DEC. With the help of Drs.
Bruce Greene, Hugh Taylor, and other university scientists, he
ran a second set of tests in 1983 and 1984 that confirmed the
promise of ivermectin. Yet another set of trials in 1985 in Ghana
and Liberia succeeded in establishing the optimum dosage level
and further confirming the drug's safety.

In 1987, nearly seven years after Merck executives had authorized the first clinical trials, the company submitted its data
to the French Directorate of Pharmacy and Drugs, whose judgments are widely accepted by Francophone African nations.
Final approval came in October 1987.

It was a buoyant time at Merck, yet also a critical turning
point. Less than two months after the last regulatory hurdle had
been cleared, Dr. Aziz died at age 58 of cancer. And Merck,
which had spent nearly a decade developing ivermectin, could
not simply bask in the glory of its triumph. Its achievement
would be of little consequence unless it could surmount another
daunting challenge: delivering the new wonder drug to the people who needed it.

THE DECISION TO SUPPLY MECTIZAN AT NO COST

Merck knew that some unorthodox plan to distribute Mectizan
would be needed. Early marketing studies confirmed what
many had suspected: No conventional market for the drug was
likely to materialize. The customers were too poor; they lived in
utterly isolated locations; and they had no access to pharmacies
or routine medical care.

From this point on, according to Dr. Vagelos, Merck moved
forward with a blind faith that some third party, at some point
in the future, would step forward with funding. The anticipated
funders included foundations, international health or development organizations, Third World governments, and—perhaps

the most likely source of all, because of its extensive international outreach—the U.S. government.

The distribution program that Merck envisioned would require an initial commitment of only $2 million a year, eventually growing to a sum of $20 million a year, a pittance by any reasonable standard. It would be hard to imagine a more cost-effective way for the United States to cultivate the goodwill of Third World nations. Yet Dr. Vagelos's visits with top officials in the Reagan White House, State Department, and U.S. Agency for International Development proved futile.

A series of visits to other potential funders—the World Health Organization, African health ministries, foundations, and others—also proved to be of no avail. Merck even called upon rainmaker Henry Kissinger, who sits on one of the company's advisory boards. Again, no luck.

At this point, an impertinent, offhand suggestion made several years earlier may have resurfaced at Merck headquarters. In 1983 or 1984, Dr. Brian Duke had made a provocative suggestion—with no authorization from WHO—that Merck ought simply to donate Mectizan outright. *Just give the drug away!* To his chagrin, Duke saw his casual remark to a reporter turn up in print in *South*, a Third World business magazine. The suggestion did not go over well at Merck headquarters, which regarded the idea as terribly premature, if not downright ludicrous.

When the search for third-party funding failed, however, Dr. Duke's suggestion began to sound much more plausible, and even attractive. The idea of a drug company donating an unlimited supply of a breakthrough drug to millions of people was, of course, unprecedented.

As senior executives debated the issue internally and consulted with peers in the drug industry, they wondered: Would this set a "bad precedent"—by inspiring an expectation that future drugs for Third World diseases should also be donated, which could itself discourage companies from even investigating such drugs? Would Merck face intolerable legal liability if some Mectizan recipients suffered adverse reactions? Would the sheer cost of manufacturing untold millions of doses of Mectizan prove prohibitive?

In the end, Dr. Vagelos and the top Merck management

were willing to brave these uncertainties. At a press conference held in Washington and Paris on October 21, 1987, Merck and Co. announced it would supply Mectizan to everyone who needed it, indefinitely, and at no charge. President Jimmy Carter, who would later coordinate a twelve-year program for distributing Mectizan, launched in 1996, estimated that the donation was worth $250 million.

ANATOMY OF A DIFFICULT DECISION

One factor that helped Merck come to its decision was the astonishing success of ivermectin, which had become the largest selling animal drug in the world. Jerry Jackson, a senior vice president of marketing, told *The Wall Street Journal*, "Merck can easily afford this." Another influential factor was probably the goodwill to be gained from a donation. Unable to negotiate a price for selling the drug to WHO—Merck wanted $1 per dose; WHO, 10 cents—Merck decided to reap its rewards through positive publicity and goodwill among Third World nations and WHO.

As for the "bad precedent," Merck officials now admit that the Mectizan donation does not appear to have discouraged research into Third World diseases, which was quite limited in any case. Indeed, the Mectizan precedent may have subtly made drug company executives more open-minded about innovative collaborations, reports Dr. Colin Ginger of the WHO Onchocerciasis Chemotherapy Project. After the Mectizan donation, Ginger says that Ciba-Geigy, the Geneva drug company, agreed to perform preclinical tests on promising compounds if WHO would perform the animal and human tests. The agreement, a generous improvement over a prior one, saved Dr. Ginger's research program about $2 million.

If anything, the Mectizan donation has elicited great admiration from other companies and the sincerest form of flattery: imitation. In an effort to kill the guinea worm, a parasite spread through contaminated drinking water, American Cyanamid donated millions of dollars' worth of Abate, a larvacide, to developing nations. For the same purpose, DuPont has donated several hundred thousand square yards of nylon, which can be easily used to filter drinking water to remove guinea worms.

A Merck spokesman is quick to point out that Mectizan is a very special case. Here was a drug of almost miraculous safety and efficacy that could be taken only once a year in tablet form, with minimal medical oversight, and it was derived from one of the most lucrative animal drugs ever developed. These peculiar circumstances, the spokesman stressed, enabled Merck to make an open-ended, long-term donation.

GETTING MECTIZAN TO THE PEOPLE

Merck realized that some novel distribution system would have to be established if Mectizan were going to have any value. It also realized that such a challenge was well beyond its capabilities. But then, who would run the system? And how would it operate? Simply getting to some villages in the West African bush requires several days of travel over marginal dirt roads; still other villages are accessible only by footpaths. There are no pharmacies, doctors, or conventional systems of commerce.

Dr. Vagelos and his colleagues came up with a creative solution—the Mectizan Expert Committee, a panel composed of six internationally respected scientists that issued guidelines and procedures for the responsible distribution of Mectizan. This independent authority would help ensure that adverse drug reactions would be identified, medical records kept, and distribution schemes reviewed for logistical feasibility and long-term viability. It also helped nongovernmental organizations to bypass the Byzantine politics of WHO and individual nations, and hasten distribution of Mectizan.

By 1995 more than six million people in twenty-one countries had received at least one dose of Mectizan, and many others were receiving annual doses. Because the drug not only halts the chronic worsening of the disease but quickly stops any itching, African villagers have come to clamor for it. At one mass treatment, in a village in Togo, a huge crowd of people were roaming nearby clamoring to be treated as well. It turned out that the people had traveled from a village ten kilometers away over a dirt road built expressly for the purpose of getting Mectizan. They had walked through the night to arrive in time.

Mectizan distribution received a big boost in 1996, when the World Health Organization and World Bank announced an ambitious twelve-year international project, the African Programme for Onchocerciasis Control. Coordinated by the Carter Center in Atlanta, founded by former President Jimmy Carter, the $124-million effort plans to bring together African governments, bilateral donors, and nongovernmental development organizations. Its goal is to control and eventually wipe out river blindness in Africa, focusing on fifteen million people in sixteen participating nations.

When Dr. Campbell journeyed to Africa to witness some of the first community distributions of the drug he had pioneered, he recalls the joy and relief of people: "I remember one village chief saying something in his native dialect, which was then translated into French. Each time it was translated, there was a little laughter. Finally, it was translated into English. And what the chief was saying to me was, 'This is great! Now go back and find the cause of death and put it in a box, and put a lid on it!' "

ALWAYS KEEPING THE LONG TERM IN MIND

Skeptics have asked Dr. Vagelos and other Merck officials why the company has endured the costs, aggravation, and complexities of developing and promoting Mectizan. At this, Dr. Vagelos turns reflective.

"When I first went to Japan [in the mid-1970s]," he recalls, "I was told by Japanese businesspeople that it was Merck that brought streptomycin to Japan after World War II, to eliminate tuberculosis which was eating up their society. We did that . We didn't make any money. But it's no accident that Merck is the largest American pharmaceutical company in Japan today." The long-term consequences of acts of goodwill are not always clear, he says, but "somehow I think they always pay off."

The same rationale lies behind the decision by Merck in 1986 to sell a sophisticated vaccine-manufacturing technology to the Chinese. The recombinant hepatitis B vaccine will help

China prevent liver cancer, the second-largest cause of death among adult males in China. After intense negotiations, Merck consented to sell the technology, which will allow the Chinese to vaccinate all newborns now and forever, for a mere $7 million. The sale amounts to a giveaway. But Vagelos believes that in thirty or forty years, when China may have joined the rest of the world marketplace, "the Chinese will remember that it was the Merck vaccine that saved all those kids."

Will Mectizan have such a long-term payoff for Merck? No one knows. For now, the company is proud that one of the offshoots of its fertile research laboratories can prevent a horrible, ancient disease from afflicting millions of people.

SECTION SIX

REMARKABLE BUSINESS LIVES

Introduction by Henry B. Schacht

Henry B. Schacht is chairman and chief executive officer of Lucent Technologies, AT&T's spinoff of its communications and technology divisions. He was previously chairman and chief executive officer of Cummins Engine Company. Mr. Schacht joined Cummins in 1964 as vice president for finance. He became president of the company in 1969, chief executive officer in 1973, and chairman in 1977, retiring in 1996. Mr. Schacht is also chairman of the board of trustees of the Ford Foundation.

"There is properly no history, only biography," said Ralph Waldo Emerson. It is an insight of special relevance for students of American business, who may be tempted to regard the life of the market as a world of large, impersonal forces. In fact, as the chapters of Section Six vividly show, the individual in business still matters, profoundly so.

The quality of character that a business manager brings to his or her work; the long-term vision pursued; the moral thoughtfulness applied to complex dilemmas; the social values that are honored through action—these capacities belong to each of us, and cannot be ascribed to impersonal market forces.

This is the value of biography. By exploring the long sweep of a single person's career, it becomes easier to identify recurrent patterns of character and values. Specific decisions can more readily be connected to their actual impact for entire companies, communities, and the nation. Through biography, the consequences of a life become palpable.

It is in this spirit that Section Six offers the profiles of some extraordinary business leaders and one remarkable company. The point is to show how some exceptional individuals—by dint of character and business acumen, moral values and personal courage—not only transformed their industries but significantly influenced American life. Their lives are monuments to the great things that public-spirited management can achieve.

J. Irwin Miller, founder of Cummins Engine Company, offers one of the most striking examples of what a values-driven executive can achieve. The vigor of Cummins Engine, the vitality of Columbus, Indiana, and the forward progress of numerous social concerns have been nourished by Miller over the course of six decades. His greatest achievement may have been to vividly demonstrate why business needs leaders of perspective, personal courage, and human empathy.

James Rouse, too, was one of those rare business leaders whose visions have changed our culture. Rouse started by reimagining the landscape of cities and suburbs, and in particular the meaning of community. By creating the indoor shopping mall in the 1950s, Rouse invented a new kind of Main Street and community institution. In building Columbia, Maryland, he showed how urban planning could respect people and honor their diversity. Through more than a dozen "festival marketplaces," he offered up a more hopeful vision of what cities could be. Then, after retiring, he devoted his time to pioneering new strategies for housing the very poor and homeless.

In the broadcasting industry, Frank Stanton also showed the crucial value of a long-term perspective. Not only did Stanton transform an obscure chain of radio affiliates into a great television network—while, along the way, helping introduce the long-playing record and color television; he also showed impeccable taste in the talent he assembled, the shows he aired, the open style of management he favored, and even in the design and construction of "Black Rock," the CBS headquarters building. Most important, Frank Stanton brought absolute integrity to CBS. This proved indispensable when Edward R. Murrow made his historic broadcast exposing Senator Joseph McCarthy; when President Johnson attacked CBS for its coverage of the Vietnam War; and when Congress sought to subpoena the outtakes of a CBS documentary, "The Selling of the Pentagon."

In the annals of business history, few families have shown greater distinction as innovative, humane, socially committed managers than the Haas family of Levi Strauss & Co. Their achievements can be seen in the company's courageous leadership in fighting AIDS; in its early support for civil rights and its ongoing commitment to workplace diversity; and in its development of stringent sourcing guidelines for its foreign vendors. What is most instructive about the Haas family is the ways in which their values have made them more astute, sophisticated managers and helped them to better adapt to the rigors of global competition.

Finally, this section profiles one of the great business enterprises of our time, the Xerox Corporation, a company of singular values, leadership, and social vision. The company's ethos was launched by Joseph C. Wilson, the company's founder and visionary, who showed an eagerness to take bold risks over the long term; the desire to combine the forces of technology with humanistic ideals; a frank engagement with the social problems that beset our nation; and, even in times of adversity, a steely optimism about the future. After Wilson, this spirit was kept alive—in far different yet equally tumultuous times—by three other extraordinary Xerox chairmen: C. Peter McColough, David Kearns, and Paul Allaire.

All these business managers, each in his time, encountered controversy and resistance to the visions they sought to actualize. The paths they blazed were by no means easy or obvious; in fact, their choices were fraught with great complexities and risks. It is that spirit of business enterprise—and the unleashing of the moral imagination in the marketplace—that the following chapters seek to capture. The stories are a source of both instruction and inspiriation for businesspeople today.

21

J. Irwin Miller

THE REWARDS OF SERVANT-LEADERSHIP

How many unsuspecting travelers have taken Route 31 across the flat Indiana prairie, passing the usual jumble of gas stations, motels, and commercial clutter, only to stumble upon the unlikely spectacle of the town of Columbus?

It is as if the giants of twentieth-century architecture had decided, in a burst of whimsy, to descend upon a little-known town in southern Indiana—population 37,000—to bestow some of their greatest artistic treasures. There is the graceful 192-foot spire of the North Christian Church, designed by the renowned Eero Saarinen, an elementary school by Edward Larrabee Barnes, a public library by I. M. Pei, a manufacturing plant by Harry Weese, and the Cummins Engine Company's headquarters by Kevin Roche and John Dinkeloo. Even the town jail has an artistic intelligence that belies its grim function.

What can account for such a town? How did such a wildly improbable, wonderful vision become real?

A MAN OF FIERCE INTELLIGENCE AND REFINEMENT

One quickly learns that a great many roads in the town of Columbus lead to the office of Joseph Irwin Miller. Within the business world, Miller is best known for transforming a troubled family-owned diesel engine company of sixty employees into a global colossus that controls more than half the North American diesel truck market and employs about 24,300. Cummins Engine Company had assets of more than $3.1 billion and sales of $5.2 billion in 1995.

As general manager (1934–1944), president (1945–1951), and board chairman (1951–1977) of Cummins, Miller not only stayed one step ahead of the competition, he pioneered progressive labor relations, nondiscriminatory employment practices, and environmental protection in the engine business, among other social innovations.

With a commanding 6-foot-2-inch frame, a shock of white hair, and piercing gray eyes, Miller radiates a quiet self-assurance and wisdom. He studied classical philosophy at Yale and Balliol College, Oxford, and is a self-taught expert on architecture, theology, and sacred music. This is a man of fierce intelligence and refinement, a man who reads the New Testament in Greek, and plays his Stradivarius violin—his "fiddle"—for the sheer pleasure of it.

Yet Miller is no dilettante or aesthete. A former member of the boards of AT&T, Chemical Bank, Equitable Life Assurance, the Museum of Modern Art, the Ford Foundation, and the Yale Corporation, among others, Miller is a can-do pragmatist, that rare individual who combines the savoir faire of a sophisticated businessman with the expansive humanism of an artist.

THE VISION OF THE FAMILY CHAUFFEUR

The Cummins Engine Company had its unlikely start in 1919 when chauffeur Clessie L. Cummins asked his boss, Indiana industrialist Will G. Irwin, to invest in a new company that would try to improve the diesel engine, then considered inferior to cheaper, more reliable gasoline engines. Irwin, whose family had made a fortune in banking, toll roads, starch, and grocery stores during the late 1800s, eventually invested $2.5 million in Cummins's business, convinced it would eventually be a contender.

Eleven years after its launch, Cummins Engine Company was still swimming in red ink when Clessie hit upon the idea of driving a diesel-powered car from Indiana to New York on $1.38 worth of fuel. The world began to sit up and take notice; perhaps there was a future for diesels. It would also be the improbable future for the learned, cosmopolitan J. Irwin Miller—Will G.'s nephew—upon his return from Oxford in 1933. After a stint bagging potatoes at his family's grocery store chain in California, Miller started his career at Cummins the next year as vice president and general manager.

In 1936, Cummins Engine Company had its first profitable year ever, seventeen years after its founding. Miller's strategy for building the business focused on three goals: improving the technology, improving production quality, and cutting costs. Fortunately, Cummins and his engineers had finally designed a good, reliable engine, and the Great Depression of the 1930s attracted more customers to the economical diesels. Meanwhile, Miller's introduction of modern production equipment helped boost quality and reduce costs, while a daily inventory-reporting system helped trim working capital.

Business really took off in World War II when the military placed orders for thousands of diesel-powered vehicles, especially for the Red Ball Express. In the civilian market, diesel engines also grew in popularity as engineering advances allowed higher horsepowers and finer design tolerances. By 1945, Cummins had more than doubled in size to 1,700 employees, and business was at full throttle. To help finance expansion, Miller took the company public in 1947.

CUMMINS'S UNORTHODOX SALES STRATEGY

Despite the robust market, Cummins, as an independent engine maker, faced a particularly vexing problem: how to sell engines to truck manufacturers who already made their own engines.

The strategy developed by Miller was to woo the end users of heavy-duty trucks—fleet operators, truck drivers, and mechanics. Miller's challenge was to persuade these "secondary clients," a previousy untapped market, to specifically request Cummins engines when buying a new truck. But the only way for this strategy to succeed over the long term was to be extremely responsive to these customers and to build more reliable, durable, and cost-efficient engines than those installed by truck manufacturers such as Mack, White, General Motors, and Detroit Diesel. In light of the great expense of building diesel engines and their relatively modest sales volume, this was a formidable business proposition.

The key to developing a niche in this forbidding market was a strong distribution and parts business. Throughout the 1940s and 1950s, Cummins set up several dozen regional distributors that not only sold Cummins engines but also serviced them and sold replacement parts. This enabled Cummins to stay close to its clients and to remain responsive to a changing marketplace.

Cummins slowly gained market share and built a reputation for excellence. When the U.S. trucking fleet converted from gasoline to diesel engines following the war, Cummins garnered a huge boost in sales. At the same time, overseas markets began to emerge, in part because so many Cummins-powered vehicles used during the war remained abroad. Manufacturing facilities were established abroad in 1956, in Scotland, followed by plants in Japan, China, Brazil, Mexico, and India, and parts distribution centers in Germany, France, Australia, Taiwan, and Singapore. By 1995, Cummins products were being sold in 110 countries.

GETTING THE UNSUSPECTED BEST OUT OF PEOPLE

J. Irwin Miller realized early on that while a good product and an ingenious marketplace strategy could take the company far, its long-term success would depend on its people. As he explains:

> A leadership that is concentrated on the ideas of one person is very limited. Genuine leadership involves getting all the wisdom that is available in a group, and helping that group come to a better decision than any one of its members would have been able to achieve himself. The servant-leader is the person who gets the unsuspected best out of his group of people.

With this philosophy in mind, Miller set about building a singular corporate culture. Factories were never allowed to have more than 5,000 employees for fear that larger entities would erode the sense of shared purpose and clear lines of accountability. Workers with complaints found that Miller's door was always open to them.

The Cummins tradition of open, humane management was instigated by Miller at the very start, under highly stressful circumstances. In 1936, union organizers with the Congress of Industrial Organizations (CIO) arrived in Columbus with the aim of organizing the town. Even though the Wagner Act, which set forth rules for union organizing and labor relations, had been enacted a year earlier, many labor disputes remained tumultuous and violent during this period. *Fortune* magazine recounted Miller's role:

> When his fellow industrialists called a clandestine Chamber of Commerce meeting to plan the arming of squads of vigilantes, Miller spoke out against the opinion of older men who he respected. "We don't feel right fighting our own people," he said. His stand was considered by some businessmen to be a shocking sellout. But it broke the solid management front—and probably saved Columbus from the kind of strife that left scars on many another industrial town in the Midwest.

Cummins workers in Columbus decided not to join the CIO, but later formed their own union local, the Diesel Workers Union, which repeatedly declined to affiliate with any of the major international unions. Although Miller and his executives have had disputes with their union—some quite rancorous and involving strikes—they never tried to influence their workers' choice of union representation or to undermine the union.

"I wouldn't know how to run a big company without a strong union," Miller confesses. "The unions are management's mirror. They tell you things your own people won't admit." This is such a conviction that Miller once declined to join the state Chamber of Commerce because of its support for a "right-to-work" antiunion bill pending in the Indiana legislature.

At the core of Miller's management style is "the life-long cultivation of the capacity to feel." He asks:

> Does it seem odd that painting and poetry and music and suffering people and great causes and dedication to religion are essential to the making of an effective organization man? Well they are, for without them he is a half-man, half-happy, half-bored, half-effective, killing the time of which at the end he learns there was so very little after all.

Miller's genius has been to show that servant-leadership "is not do-good stuff for the sake of do-good. This is the way you make money," he insists.

By the 1960s, *Fortune* magazine described Cummins as "a tight-knit company where everybody knows what the other person is doing, even in research, and nobody runs a truculent little principality. Miller's top echelons are populated by relaxed but lively men who seem to be learning all the time, just like the boss."

Miller's conviction that executives ought to be well-rounded people, and not simply specialists, is one reason Cummins pioneered the recruiting of liberal arts graduates from Ivy League institutions in the 1950s and 1960s. Sophisticated, well educated, and progressive, these executives thrived in Cummins's open, collegial atmosphere.

One of Miller's most promising young recruits was Henry B. Schacht, a Yale graduate who was appointed Cummins president at age 34, in 1969. Schacht spent thirty years at Cummins, stepping down as chairman in 1995. A year later he became chairman and chief executive officer designate of Lucent Technologies, AT&T's new $20-billion communications systems and technology company.

CUMMINS BOLDLY CONFRONTS FOREIGN COMPETITION

By the 1970s, Miller's tough-minded idealism had helped build the Cummins Engine Company into a potent global competitor. It controlled 55 percent of the diesel engine market for North

American trucks, and it continued to be technologically innovative and highly profitable. When Miller stepped down as chairman of Cummins in 1977, to become chairman of the executive committee, Cummins had enjoyed forty-one straight years of profits. Return on stockholders' equity had been 12 percent or better in all but seven of the preceding thirty years.

But serious competition was on the horizon. In the 1970s several European and Japanese companies introduced high-quality diesel engines that were priced 25 percent below Cummins engines. At the same time, Wall Street began to accelerate its demands for short-term financial returns, putting new pressures on a business that has always required patient capital to develop better technologies.

Realizing that Cummins needed to respond boldly, Chairman Henry Schacht instituted a series of sweeping structural reforms in the early 1980s. More than $1 billion was spent on new plant and equipment. Some 3,400 of 13,000 engine jobs were eliminated. New production techniques such as just-in-time inventory and flexible work teams were instituted. And engine prices were slashed by 20 to 40 percent to help Cummins retain market share. The top-to-bottom restructuring to meet foreign competition, *Business Week* declared in 1988, "has required extraordinary courage."

In 1989, when foreign investors seemed intent on an unfriendly takeover, Miller and his sister, Clementine Tangeman, decided to preempt a possible raid by buying the hostile shares for $72 million—a $5-million premium over the prevailing stock price. "We ate the premium," says Miller's son, Will. "It was not a very '80s thing to do." It appears, instead, to have been the sort of shrewd, long-term investment that is the family trademark. By 1993, business magazines were hailing Cummins's comeback with headlines like "A Long-Term Bet Pays Off at Last" and "A CEO [Schacht] Who Kept His Eyes on the Horizon."

A year later, Cummins announced that three tractor makers—the Ford Motor Company, Tenneco Inc., and Kubota Ltd. of Japan—would provide $250 million in new equity capital and own 27 percent of Cummins stock. The move was seen as a way to lower Cummins's large debt, protect it against any future unfriendly takeovers, create strategic alliances with key industrial partners, and give it greater freedom to implement its long-term revitalization strategy.

THE BUSINESS EXECUTIVE AS COMMUNITY LEADER

From the outset, Miller has regarded his community as one of the most vital ingredients in Cummins's success. Miller stresses that he has always aimed "to facilitate, not to dominate" Columbus. He has studiously avoided any hint of paternalism, insisting that the town make its own democratic choices and develop its own independent leadership.

The notion that business should serve larger public needs was evident in Miller's stewardship of the Irwin Union Bank and Trust following the deaths of his uncle Will and his father in 1944 and 1947, respectively. Miller instituted a regional credit card system and began advertising the bank's services—two novel ideas at the time—and aggressively made loans to churches and other community institutions. Soon the Irwin Union Bank was the fastest-growing bank in the state.

Irwin Union Bank and Trust did not simply sponsor the local orchestra or museum. In the 1970s the bank's foundation financed a two-year study of jails in the five counties surrounding Columbus, with an eye toward recommending reforms. On another occasion, to help the local Community Action Project, the bank actually helped start a credit union. If images of Jimmy Stewart in *It's a Wonderful Life* come to mind, it is because Miller ran his bank with an appreciation of people and their needs. As Miller put it, "The old-time bankers, the best bankers, will always say to you, 'Anytime I've bet on the collateral I've lost; and anytime I've bet on the person, I've won.' " Miller likes to bet on people.

An extreme example of this was when one of his bank tellers was imprisoned for embezzling $112,000. Miller told the parole board that he would provide a job for the man when he was freed—and arranged for the ex-teller to become a stock clerk at Cummins.

By such acts Miller is not simply indulging his seemingly unquenchable need to do good. He realizes that a strong, civic-

minded community will return the favor and provide a supportive business climate. The town's young people will be inclined
to stay rather than migrate elsewhere. It is one of the reasons
that since the 1950s Cummins has given 5 percent of its pretax
U.S. income to charitable causes.

When the Cummins Engine Foundation paid for the construction of a world-class public golf course in 1964, Miller suc-
cinctly explained the rationale:

> Why should an industrial company, organized for profit,
> think it a good and right thing to take a million dollars and
> more, of that profit, and give it to this community in the
> form of this golf course and club house? Why, instead, isn't
> Cummins—the largest taxpayer in the county—spending
> the same energy to try to get its taxes reduced, the cost of
> education cut, the cost of city government cut, less money
> spent on streets and utilities and schools?
>
> The answer is that we would like to see this community
> come to be not the cheapest community in America, but the
> very best community of its size in the country. . . . Cummins
> is not for cheap education, or inadequate, poorly paid gov-
> ernment, or second-rate facilities or low taxes just for the
> sake of low taxes. Our concern is to help get the most for
> our dollar, to help build this community into the best in the
> nation. And we are happy to pay our share, whether in
> work, or in taxes, or in gifts like this one.

In his personal life, too, Miller has shown the same sort of
community commitment. He gives away 30 percent of his personal income, the maximum allowable deduction under IRS
rules. In the 1960s, Miller petitioned the courts to allow him to
give away 30 percent of the income generated by his two eldest
children's trusts. Through the Irwin Sweeney Miller Foundation
headed by his sister, Clementine M. Tangeman, Miller has directed millions of dollars to programs that help abused women
and children, troubled teenagers, and prisoners.

THE BUILDING OF A MIDWEST JEWEL

Columbus did not become the architectural jewel of the Midwest
through some grand design. It grew slowly, simply, and prag-

matically from the response to a rather mundane problem—the need for a new school. When the cash-strapped town needed a new public school in the mid-1950s to accommodate the postwar baby boom, city officials planned a conventional-looking facility using prefabricated materials.

Miller considered this a mistake. "I just think it's very expensive to be mediocre in this world," Miller told *Architecture* magazine in the 1960s. Quality is not only cost-effective over time, Miller insists, it is elevating to the human spirit and to the sense of community. With his eye on future generations, Miller proposed that the Cummins Engine Foundation pay for the architectural design of the new school, while the school board would retain full control over all design and construction.

And so it was that the celebrated Harry Weese designed Columbus's new elementary school, completed in 1957. As the need for new city buildings arose, the Cummins Engine Foundation made similar arrangements.

Soon the town of Columbus had assembled a rich collection of contemporary architecture for its most utilitarian public services—a recreation center, fire station, city hall, public library, and high school, among other structures. By the mid-1960s the nation's top architects considered it a special honor to be chosen to design a public building in Columbus. The proliferation of beautiful city buildings inspired churches, the telephone company, private developers, and others to design their own distinctive buildings.

Within its scant 17.4 square miles, Columbus now has more than fifty public and private buildings by world-renowned designers, making it the most concentrated collection of contemporary architecture in the world. More than 50,000 visitors visit the town each year, largely because of the architecture, bringing in revenues and providing jobs to Columbus residents. Ranked according to the number of buildings by notable architects it has, Columbus is fourth in the nation, behind New York City, Chicago, and Los Angeles. (Washington, D.C., ranks fifth.) All this was achieved with relatively modest leverage from the Cummins Engine Foundation: $12 million by the end of 1995.

The town's unique public architecture has enhanced civic pride, not to mention tourism, while helping Cummins Engine attract top talent to a modest midwestern region such people might otherwise pass by. But it has also served a more basic human need, mused architectural writer Michael Sorkin—the impulse to make one's hometown "the site of the riches most basic to his life. The architecture announces them. In speech after speech that he has given, Miller quotes a line remembered from Euripides: 'Where the good things are, there is home.' "

MILLER ON THE NATIONAL STAGE

In 1967, *Esquire* went in search of the ideal Republican candidate to challenge Lyndon Johnson. "Is it too late for a man of honesty, high purpose and intelligence to be elected President of the United States in 1968?" asked reporter Steven V. Roberts. "Does such a man exist?"

After rejecting a dozen prominent Republicans who might fit the bill, Roberts found a resounding answer to his question in the person of J. Irwin Miller. The cover of the magazine's October 1967 issue brashly proclaimed, "This man ought to be the next President of the United States."

"Dad was embarrassed by that piece," laughs Will Miller, J. Irwin's son. "He had never sought nor received much public attention until then." Given the realities of politics, the would-be movement to draft Miller never got off the ground, and Miller did nothing to fuel it.

Miller's most controversial foray onto the national stage came when thirty-three Christian denominations representing forty million Americans elected him to be the first lay president of the National Council of Churches (NCC) in 1960. Miller was to play a key role in mobilizing the churches to tackle racial inequality and poverty and to sponsor the training of "freedom riders" in the South. He also helped Martin Luther King, Jr., organize his famous March on Washington in August 1963, and helped Presidents Kennedy and Johnson marshal support for civil rights bills.

None of these actions was easy or noncontroversial in the highly charged climate of the times. Large segments of the public and of Christian denominations, particularly in the South, strenuously objected to the NCC's activism. Many business-people insisted that their rights as property owners should supersede anyone's civil rights. And Miller earned two key distinctions: praise from Martin Luther King, Jr., that Miller was "the most progressive businessman in America," and inclusion on Richard Nixon's infamous "Enemies List."

Leaving the NCC in 1963, Miller was invigorated and powerfully influenced by the civil rights movement. Cummins, the first company in its area to hire African-Americans for non-janitorial jobs, stepped up its efforts to recruit, train, and advance African-American employees. When a neighborhood in Columbus tried to prevent a recently hired Black Cummins executive from buying a home there, Miller publicly fought for a city ordinance prohibiting such racial discrimination. Between 1965 and 1973, Miller managed to recruit about a hundred African-American managers and trainees to come to work at Cummins. He was so successful that when Jimmy Carter took office in 1977, Cummins lost some of its most talented executives to the new administration.

A WILLINGNESS TO BE A PARIAH
ON MATTERS OF PRINCIPLE

When activists began plans for the first Earth Day on April 22, 1970, and Ralph Nader blasted business for failing to control air pollution, most industrialists began to hunker down for a long, pitched battle to stave off reforms.

J. Irwin Miller, however, saw a different future. At his urging, Cummins vice president Richard B. Stoner delivered a bracing, unwelcome message to the January 1970 conference of the Transportation Association of America. Stoner warned his colleagues:

> Our industry is either going to fulfill its moral obligation to lead the way in minimizing the threat of air, water, waste and noise pollution in this decade, or the people, led by our youth, will force the government to enact legislation which requires us to do the job we will not do ourselves. . . . Stop-

ping pollution is the number one technological challenge to
the transportation industry in this decade.

Miller remembers, "We supported the Clean Air Act because the problems of smog in the major urban areas obviously
were going to be very dangerous in the future." Cummins defied
its industry and met with top congressional leaders and staff,
trying to find a reasonable, good-faith solution to an undeniable
problem.

According to Stoner, the Diesel Engine Manufacturers Association took the position that there should be no exchange of
any information with the federal government, to the extent that
that was possible. "It was just a stonewalling deal," Stoner recalls, still indignant at the thought. "That wasn't going to fly
here [at Cummins]." In the end, Cummins was largely responsible for drafting Section 204 of the Clean Air Act, which set forth
a process for reducing emissions from heavy-duty engines.

In 1992, Miller proudly recalled this event:

> It ended up great for the industry because it converted us
> from a relatively low-technology industry to an extremely
> high-tech industry. We learned more about engines than we
> ever would have, had we not been under this pressure. We
> actually improved fuel consumption as well as reduced
> emissions, something we thought we couldn't do to start
> with.

Charles Powers, a Cummins executive in the 1970s, recalls
many a luncheon engagement at which Miller and Cummins
executives suffered through long, awkward silences after having
argued unpopular positions with business colleagues. "We were
always prepared to be pariahs on matters of real principle," says
Powers. "But one of the things that made Miller magnificent was
his ability to leave meetings gracefully without compromising
himself."

SPIRIT-LED MANAGEMENT

If there is one principle that Miller has always sought to honor
in his business management, it is to engage the whole person,

not just as a technician or specialist but as a spiritual being as well. "The good things in this world," Miller once said, "have never been the things we can hold in our hand and call ours. The good things for all of us always have been the good feelings which have risen within us, and for a moment taken possession of us. But you can no more experience good feelings, if you cannot feel, than you can lift a weight, if you have let your muscles atrophy."

But "the good things" are complicated, Miller hastens to point out, "by the ongoing dialogue between Athens and Jerusalem" that started centuries ago. "There are two schools of thought in this world, and one was first started by Aristotle. He said that ethics can be defined as the currently accepted practices in any society. There's another right alongside of it that comes from the Judeo-Christian tradition, which says there are certain principles of human behavior that are born in you. And the debate between those two has been going on for more than 3,000 years. It's a very fruitful debate. Probably will never be settled."

Because it can be quite complex to ascertain what is "ethical" business behavior, Miller suggests a ready rule of thumb: "Business ethics are really an effort to do really good long-term planning. In that sense, I'd say the fundamental reason for business ethics is to say, 'What will I wish I had done if I could be around fifty years from now?' "

There is another rich avenue for better understanding ethics, Miller advises. It is art. "The artist is one of the most important and powerful influences in ethical instruction in Western society, and always has been."

And what work of art most inspires and instructs a man of Miller's idealism and discernment?

An American primitive painting hangs unobtrusively in his private dining room, *The Peaceable Kingdom*, by self-taught painter Edward Hicks. It is a rich landscape depicting the prophecy of Isaiah, with the lion lying down with the lamb, and a reign of harmony among people and between mankind and nature.

"Edward Hicks wanted to be a Quaker preacher," Miller explains to a guest, "but he had an incurable stammer. But he discovered he had a talent for painting. So in the Pennsylvania area of the country, he would *paint* his sermons. He expressed his sermons artistically in a way that words can't match."

So it has been with J. Irwin Miller, who discovered that business offered an unexpectedly rich canvas for his highest aspirations.

22

James W. Rouse

BRINGING DIGNITY AND DELIGHT TO AMERICAN CITIES

To talk with James W. Rouse—urban visionary, master builder, social activist—was to discover the indispensability of certain words: *Community. Civilization. Delight. Yearning. Respect. Love.*

Such lofty words might seem more fitting coming from a poet or college professor than from one of the most famous real estate developers in the country. To be sure, James Rouse, who died in April 1996, knew a few things about mortgage financing and cash flow. But his success over the course of five decades, he would insist, stemmed from an intimate understanding of these delicate words.

Rouse's canny insight into the human dynamics of both the city and suburbia yielded some enduring archetypes of development: the enclosed shopping mall, urban redevelopment, the planned community of Columbia, Maryland, "festival market-places," and low-income urban housing.

Although Rouse's development concepts were usually ambitious and daring, the man himself projected a more conservative style. Sitting in his homey office in Columbia, Maryland, Rouse radiated the concern of a kindly uncle and the modesty of a church elder. Peering through his horn-rimmed glasses, he talked in slow cadences, occasionally flashing an impish grin or bursting into a passionate speech.

If there was a north star that guided Rouse's singular business odyssey, it was a recognition that the needs and aspirations of people had to be kept foremost. The "ultimate test of all design and all development," Rouse told the Harvard Graduate School of Design in 1963, is, "Will it help to grow people? Is there any other legitimate test for the success or failure of our civilization than what we do to people? Do we elevate or degrade? Do we dignify or oppress? Do we create an environment that promotes the growth of people?"

Rouse told another audience in 1965, "If we are to humanize our urban environment, we must turn the planning process upside down and start thinking about the conditions that are important to human growth—to man's heart, soul and nervous system, as well as his mind." To be sure, Rouse was not cavalier about economic realities. "Profit," he said, "is the thing that hauls dreams into focus." But what distinguished Rouse was his unwillingness to accept the prevailing marketplace norms. Idealism had to come first, he insisted: "We should always examine the optimums and forget about feasibility. It will compromise us soon enough. Let's look at what might be and be invigorated by it."

It comes as no surprise that Rouse liked the sentiments of nineteenth-century planner Daniel H. Burnham, who wrote: "Make no little plans. They have no magic to stir men's blood and probably themselves will not be realized. Make big plans. . . . Let your watchword be order and your beacon beauty."

The competitive, high-stakes world of real estate development is not a likely setting for such soaring ideals and fragile dreams. What accounted for James Rouse's remarkable success?

A Tireless Champion of City Life

From an early age, Rouse learned that the pursuit of big plans meant adversity and struggle. At age 16, in 1930, Rouse's idyllic upbringing on Maryland's Eastern Shore ended abruptly when both his parents died within nine months of each other. The youngest of six siblings, he soon fled to Baltimore to "seek his fortune," and ended up parking cars by day while attending the University of Maryland by night.

Upon earning his law degree in 1937, Rouse took his first job at the Federal Housing Administration before moving on to the mortgage department of a commercial bank. In 1939, Rouse and a partner borrowed $20,000 to found their own mortgage banking company, which would become the Rouse Co. After a stint in the Navy during World War II, he returned to his firm in Baltimore.

By the late 1940s, Rouse had become deeply involved in numerous civic crusades to rehabilitate Baltimore's slums and reconstruct its downtown. Soon, as a nationally recognized expert on urban revitalization, Rouse became chairman of President Eisenhower's 1953 task force on housing, which was the catalyst for a major overhaul of federal housing programs. The reforms began by awarding urban renewal grants to cities that had their own renewal programs, and encouraging housing rehabilitation as opposed to demolition. It was during this time that Rouse popularized a phrase coined by Miles L. Colean, a leader of the urban planning movement—"urban renewal."

"The thing that gets me about Jim Rouse," an old friend told a reporter in the early 1960s, is "the sight and sound of a leading citizen who, instead of giving out the old flapdoodle about nothing ever getting done around here, goes out and gets things done." Rouse got things done because he had a rare combination of talents: management skills, financial sophistication, civic commitment, a Christian social conscience, and a powerful can-do optimism.

As founding chairman of the American Council to Improve Our Neighborhoods, for example, Rouse gave a brash title to his 1955 redevelopment manifesto for Washington, D.C.: "No Slums in Ten Years." The same spirit infused a speech that Rouse gave in 1967: "Cities That Work for Man—Victory Ahead." Rouse had no apologies for his extravagant visions. "It is not enough to say that you're going to 'work on' a problem," he explained. "You have to dedicate yourself to solving it."

MAIN STREET COMES TO SUBURBIA

Rouse's creativity was not confined to American cities. As the postwar suburbs boomed and cities decentralized, Rouse realized that hordes of new suburbanites had a great deal of leisure time yet no convenient places in which to shop or meet. At the same time, retailers, long anchored in cities, were searching for ways to tap into the burgeoning purchasing power of suburbanites. "The automobile emancipated the consumer but not the merchant," noted *Architectural Forum* in 1949.

For Rouse, the regional shopping mall was a socioeconomic breakthrough just waiting to happen. So, in the mid-1950s, Rouse took the prosaic highway shopping strip, gave it bold new twists, and came up with one of the most influential institutions of the late twentieth century: the suburban shopping mall. The first merchants Rouse approached were "dumbfounded" by the idea and skeptical that diverse retailers could operate in one large, enclosed complex governed by a single management and detailed rules. They had no frame of reference for judging retailing innovations such as open storefronts, interior landscaping and fountains, air-conditioning, and other amenities now taken for granted.

Rouse had a strong hunch that regional shopping centers would work because he detected a void in the life of suburbanites. They did not have an *agora*, a public marketplace or Main Street, where they could transact routine business while sharing common civic and cultural concerns. Rouse's first test of his idea, in 1958, was the Harundale shopping center in Fort Meade, Maryland. It was the first privately developed, enclosed shopping center in the nation, and it was an immediate success.

Imitators quickly learned that in the virginal suburbs of the 1950s and 1960s, virtually any large group of stores with good access roads and parking facilities could succeed without much planning. Yet Rouse believed that the most successful malls would strive to become genuine community institutions that could "help dignify and uplift the families who use them."

In the ensuing stampede to build new suburban malls, the Rouse Co. was distinguished by the pains it took to ascertain and meet community needs. Virtually all Rouse malls were built with community meeting halls, and others had special sites for symphony concerts, political campaigns, and even churches. The Wilde Lake Shopping Center in Columbia, Maryland, rented space to a counseling center, which helped drug abusers, the mentally ill, and others.

To many Americans, suburban shopping malls are a dubious innovation most notable for their inhuman scale and oppressive commercialism. "The music, the fixtures, the forced air can all be dreadful," one critic wrote in *The New Republic* in 1975. "At certain times of day there is an inertness, a deadness about the centers which no city space ever quite descends to." As early as 1962, Rouse enumerated the design shortcomings of various malls, including his own, and urged architects and developers to avoid mall designs that were "ugly, cheap and disorderly."

"Quality," Rouse insisted, has a powerful multiplier effect for both the community and businesses. In the 1960s, when merchants at the Cherry Hill Mall in New Jersey found that the quality of their clerks was far higher than anything they had experienced before, they attributed it to the carefully designed character of the mall. People who would not normally seek jobs as department store clerks clamored to work for mall retailers. A superior sales force in turn spurred sales.

The Rouse Co. proceeded in the 1960s and 1970s to become one of the nation's largest mall developers and managers. It pioneered the first mall "food courts," in which various ethnic cuisines and fast-food restaurants were situated around a common eating area. The Rouse Co. also became a leader in bringing malls to many urban centers, where they often revitalized ailing downtowns.

By the time Rouse retired in 1979, the company owned more than sixty suburban and urban malls. "And doggone it," Rouse insisted, "without exception they are delightful places. They respect people. That's very important."

CREATING A GARDEN FOR PEOPLE: COLUMBIA, MARYLAND

In the 1950s, as developers transformed vast expanses of countryside into ticky-tacky suburban housing tracts, Rouse exclaimed:

> What reckless, irresponsible dissipation of nature's endowment and of man's hope for dignity, beauty and growth!

> By this totally irrational process, non-communities are born
> [which are] so huge and irrational that they are out of scale
> with people, beyond their grasp and comprehension, too
> big for people to feel a part of, responsible for, important in.

Rouse believed that suburban developments contributed to "frantic, fractured living, the loneliness amid the busyness, the rising delinquency among middle-class children, increasing neurosis, alcoholism, divorce, the destruction of nature."

"Can there be any doubt among us about the size of our opportunity and our responsibility?" he asked the National Association of Mutual Savings Banks in 1966.

James Rouse's response was to build a whole new city from scratch. Although more than a hundred "new towns" had been built in the late 1960s and early 1970s as self-conscious alternatives to urban blight and suburban sprawl, few approached the sheer size of Columbia, Maryland, which projected 100,000 residents. None attempted such comprehensive, meticulous planning.

Rouse had four goals in seeking to build "a garden for growing people": (1) to build a real city, not just a better suburb; (2) to respect the land; (3) to plan thoughtfully for the well-being of people; and (4) as a natural offshoot of these goals, to make a profit.

After convincing Connecticut General, then the nation's eighth-largest life insurance company, to provide the initial financing, Rouse secretly bought 140 parcels of land in Maryland's rural Howard County, between Washington, D.C., and Baltimore. In October 1963, Rouse told startled Howard County residents that he planned to build a new city on one-tenth of their land. Taken together, the 15,000 contiguous acres purchased for $23.5 million, or an average of $1,500 an acre, constituted an area nearly as large as Manhattan.

In planning his new city, Rouse was leery of relying on traditional developers, architects, and engineers, whose views he considered parochial. He was determined to elicit some interdisciplinary, humanistic perspectives on the nature of community and fresh ideas on how to build "a better city."

Soon he sat down with fourteen prominent thinkers in the

fields of education, health care, recreation, sociology, and other social science disciplines for a total of 200 hours of discussion. Some of the issues the group dealt with were: How can racially integrated, economically diverse neighborhoods be achieved? How can a town be designed to give residents a greater sense of community identity and responsibility? Can neighborhoods be designed to relieve homemakers of the isolation they often feel?

In the end, the Rouse planners built the town around villages of 10,000 to 12,000 people, which in turn consisted of neighborhoods of 1,200 houses apiece. Public facilities were grouped at three distinct levels of community life: town (hospitals, hotels, theaters); village (shopping, recreation); and neighborhood (playgrounds, general stores). Special attention was lavished on creating more innovative schools, parks, preventive health care centers, arts groups, and other public institutions.

Rouse took bold steps to ensure that Columbia would be a "truly open city" dedicated to integration. In a blunt 1967 memo to developers and their sales associates, he declared, "It is our hope that Columbia's policy as to race may be so clear and vivid from the beginning that it will be unmistakable to everyone." He explicitly required developers to sell or rent housing without respect to people's race—a policy not required by federal law at the time. Advertising for Columbia's developments stressed the interracial character of the city, which later marketing studies revealed to be a compelling reason that newcomers moved there.

Determined that anyone from "the company president to the janitor" could live in Columbia, Rouse made sure that there were three-bedroom row houses sold for as little as $15,000. The Rouse Co. actually hoped that 10 percent of Columbia's residents would be welfare recipients, a goal assisted by federal housing tax credits until President Nixon eliminated them in 1972. Thirty years later, Rouse himself admitted that Columbia had fallen short of this ambitious goal.

The town has had its critics. "There is little at Columbia to strike joy in the hearts of design sophisticates," wrote *Architectural Forum*. Others carped that Columbia had "an overmanicured ambience" and "a bad case of the cutes," as exemplified by playgrounds called "tot lots" and streets named "Tufted Moss." More critically, the profitability of the development sagged because it never reached its target population of 100,000. (Its population in 1995 was 70,753.)

Columbia has also had its share of social and political problems. "Rouse did not envision the social separation between Blacks and Whites that has occurred," writes anthropologist Lynne Burkhart, "nor did he predict the plethora of interest groups that would emerge along the cultural lines of race, class, religion, age, and marital status." Yet there is no doubt, she adds, that Columbia "is a heterogeneous community that comes closer each day to being a working pluralistic community."

For all its failings, Columbia does seem to embody the optimistic, community-minded ethos that Rouse himself personified and that he tried to capture in the city's logo: a silhouette of people with upstretched arms, growing from a common base.

THE BIRTH OF THE FESTIVAL MARKETPLACE

If there was a common theme uniting James Rouse's diverse development ideas, it was the desire to build genuine communities through creative architecture and design. By the late 1960s, as affluent professionals and manufacturers fled to the suburbs, a new challenge presented itself: the now desolate concrete jungles of dozens of once-flourishing American cities.

The trend greatly disturbed Benjamin Thompson, the former chairman of the architecture department at the Harvard Graduate School of Design, who became obsessed with renovating Faneuil Hall and the adjacent Quincy Market buildings near the Boston harbor. Once a noisy public square, the unsightly waterfront buildings were now shabby backdrops for vegetable vendors and aimless bands of homeless people.

After years of futilely trying to persuade developers to renovate the buildings, Thompson and his business partner and wife, Jane Thompson, approached Rouse in 1972. Rouse initially viewed the Thompsons' proposal with "considerable skepticism," but he soon saw its enormous potential. The site was at the center of a city of four million people who represented substantial purchasing power, and it was a stone's throw from the recently developed Government Center and City Hall. The location, Rouse thought, was a vacuum waiting to be filled.

Rouse shared with the Thompsons the goal of wanting to recover what he called the "spirit of the marketplace." From time immemorial, Rouse said, the marketplace has been not just a place where business is transacted but a place where people gossip, laugh, eat, drink, stroll, flirt, and take in the colorful spectacle.

But what sort of facility could rejuvenate that spirit? Rouse started with the premise that the buildings must reflect the distinctive history and architecture of Boston. They would also need to be intimate and human in scale, something that would not interest the large retailing chains. Rouse wanted to foster "the relationship between the people and the merchant, with the owner behind the counter greeting the people, coming to know the people, conversing with them and laughing. All this is very humanizing."

The plan that ultimately resulted was a marketplace of small vendors, especially food shops. At its core would be "individual proprietorship with immense, chaotic variety." This defied the iron law of retailing that any mall must have one or more "anchor" department stores. But Rouse was convinced that the "noise and color and fragrance and feeling" would make it a place of sheer human delight and that people would flock to it.

Boston's conservative banking establishment sniffed in disdain, however. "Pouring more than $40 million into fixing up some low-rise old hunks of granite in the literal center of Boston, on potentially very valuable land, and fitting them out with little shops and cafés, did not seem like anything more than a well-intentioned but inevitably disastrous idea to a lot of people," writes mall historian William Kowinski.

Although Rouse had no trouble obtaining $20.5 million in long-term financing from New York City banks, no local bankers would touch the project. Rouse was forced to spend more than a year convincing nine Boston banks and a state development corporation to sign on to a complex financing package for the final $3.75 million.

When the grand opening of Faneuil Hall finally took place near the end of the bicentennial summer, 1976, a massive throng of 100,000 jubilant Bostonians converged on the renovated buildings to celebrate their resurrection. The site has since become a mecca for businesspeople, tourists, conventioneers, suburbanites on day trips, and pedestrians passing through—a grand mix of the human race. The site attracts some twelve million people a year, and retail sales volume is a phenomenal $500 per square foot per year—more than twice the sales of the average suburban shopping mall.

The project's success spurred New England Telephone to transform a waterfront building of switching equipment into offices for white-collar workers. New retailers and restaurants sprouted up nearby. The nearby waterfront underwent a $125-million redevelopment. And the city of Boston has reaped a bonanza in real estate taxes and civic pride. The Faneuil Hall/Quincy Market restoration became "the mall heard 'round the world," as one wag declared—a transforming prototype of urban design that is compared to Rockefeller Center.

Faneuil Hall's most important legacy may be how it changed the psychology of urban redevelopment. "Our biggest single problem was to make people believe that this could succeed," Rouse recalled. For so long Americans had come to believe that the urban center must be old, worn-out, and ugly. No one dared believe that it could be anything different. Because of Faneuil Hall, wrote urban planner Craig Whitaker in *Architectural Record*, "private parties were now willing to come forward and with a minimum of political pain turn municipal liabilities into assets." The new model was not just the idea of waterfront malls, but a new form of public/private partnership.

THE RESURRECTION OF THE BALTIMORE WATERFRONT

Within five years, the Rouse Co. brought a similar transformation to 3.2 acres of Baltimore's decaying waterfront in a project known as Harborplace. Once again, the marketplace featured Rouse's artful mix of tasteful details—aromas of fresh-baked breads, street performers, pushcart vendors, and colorful banners. The Rouse Co. created a special unit to recruit African-

American-owned firms, resulting in seventeen such businesses out of the initial 134 businesses.

The American Institute of Architects would call the Inner Harbor restoration, of which Harborplace was the centerpiece, "one of the supreme achievements of large-scale urban design and development in U.S. history . . . a masterpiece of planning and execution that took a ramshackle, rat-infested, crumbling old dock and transformed it into one of the most beautiful, humane, diverse center-city places in the world."

Like Faneuil Hall, Harborplace sparked a powerful wave of economic revitalization, civic pride, and hope. The idea was later replicated in another Rouse Company marketplace, the South Street Seaport district in New York City, and in more than a dozen additional festival marketplaces developed by a subsequent Rouse-founded company, the Enterprise Development Company.

The proliferation of festival marketplaces provoked great debate in architectural circles. Was this new milieu too "prettified," self-conscious, and tourist-oriented? Was it spreading a formulaic model that stifled the search for new redevelopment alternatives? Should local governments surrender so much control to a private developer?

Rouse shrugged off most such criticism, especially the sniping about aesthetics. "I've always had this friendly battle with architects," he said. "They would be much truer to their profession and to their own soul if they were trying to find out the best that they ought to be as a servant to mankind, rather than as an artist to mankind. . . . What will be beautiful and lasting is that which really serves mankind."

HOUSING THE VERY POOR AND HOMELESS

When he retired in 1979 at age 65, Rouse faced an unexpected challenge: What should he do with his irrepressible energy and talents?

It turned out that the seeds for a new career had already been planted six years earlier when his pastor at the Church of the Savior in Washington, D.C., asked him to meet with two social crusaders who wanted to rehabilitate and rent housing for the urban poor. Rouse recalled, "I was very saddened by my advice, which was, very simply, that there's nothing you can do about housing the poor. You're too small; you don't have the resources; you need to see your congressman or your city council; it takes a big program to house the poor."

Undeterred, the two women returned to Rouse in six months to announce that they had located two fully occupied buildings they wanted to rehabilitate. "There were no doors on the front; the mailboxes were ripped out of the wall. . . . The stench was so terrible I could not go beyond the lobby," he recalled with a grimace. Yet he was so impressed by the women's determination (they had already put down a $10,000 nonrefundable deposit) that he personally bought the buildings for $625,000, arranged for a $125,000 renovation loan, and helped them form a new nonprofit group, Jubilee Housing.

Within three years, volunteers had put in 50,000 hours of work and ninety families had new homes. Jubilee later repurchased the building from Rouse at his cost, minus depreciation. With Rouse's assistance, Jubilee Housing went on to acquire and rehabilitate many other buildings that now house hundreds of families, and to offer innovative social support services such as job placement help and medical clinics.

As he contemplated his postretirement years, Rouse realized that there were thousands of community activists with similar zeal, but most did not have managerial skills or financial expertise. This led Rouse to the epiphany that he could bring his own considerable talents to bear on one of the most intractable social problems of our time.

So, in 1982, Rouse formed The Enterprise Foundation to be a catalyst among tenant activists, church groups, block associations, and other self-help nonprofit organizations. Launched in part by a $1-million stock donation by Rouse, the foundation helps these groups acquire housing, rehabilitate it at low cost, raise money at below-market interest rates, manage the properties, and develop social support services that may be needed by the low-income tenants.

Since its founding, the foundation has worked with more than 550 nonprofits in more than 150 locations around the country and raised and committed more than $1.8 billion in grants, loans, and equity investments. It has helped create more than 60,000 homes, nearly half of which serve residents with special needs, such as senior citizens and people with HIV/AIDS.

Rouse's involvement with affordable housing inspired Rouse to dream up what he called "a vision for the transformation of a neighborhood." It entails the wholesale rehabilitation of a physically and socially deteriorated urban neighborhood. In 1990, with Rouse as an adviser, the city of Baltimore and local businesses selected the crime-ridden inner-city neighborhood of Sandtown-Winchester to see if a new "model of the possible" could be devised. The average income in this 72-square-block area of 12,000 residents was $6,900 per household; 60 percent of the households were headed by single women; and 44 percent of the men were jobless.

Although progress has been slow, by 1996 fourteen developers were working on twenty-two housing projects that will result in 687 renovated houses. The $54 million needed to renovate the structures is expected to come from federal, state, and city sources, as well as from foundations, banks, and developers. Meanwhile, The Enterprise Foundation plans simultaneously to address the neighborhood's many social problems such as the need for better schools, health care, jobs, human services, and public safety.

BOLDNESS HAS GENIUS, POWER, AND MAGIC

When Rouse was once asked why, in his search for community, he deliberately undertook such large, demanding challenges, he credited his small, nondenominational church in Washington, D.C. "The church work makes me very aware of the potential of people," he said. "The power of love can be very effective."

The inner compass of Rouse's imagination invariably returns to those words: *Community. Civilization. Delight. Yearning. Respect. Love.* They where like signposts in his mind to which he returned time and again, only to set forth afresh on new adventures.

In his lifetime, James Rouse encountered skeptics who

scoffed at his extravagant ambitions and relentless idealism. He always offered a ready rebuttal:

> I don't think people understand the power of visions. That erecting a vision of what ought to be under a given circumstance, and then believing that it can be accomplished because it ought to be, generates power; generates action by people; generates energy; generates the capacity to fulfill it, because it is held up. I believe that whatever ought to be done, can be done. That's a pretty good rule of life.

The grand impresario of the American city then searched his capacious memory for a couplet by Goethe, and quoted: "Whatever you can do or dream you can, begin it. Boldness has genius, power and magic in it."

He paused, intoxicated by the majesty of the thought, and quietly exulted, "That's a wonderful banner!"

23

Frank Stanton

THE MAN WHO BUILT THE TIFFANY NETWORK

A soldier stands coolly amid chaos. His unit is ousting villagers from their homes. As the camera watches, a correspondent narrates the activity. Casually, the soldier reaches into his pocket and withdraws a silver lighter. With a gentle flick of his thumb he sets afire the thatched roof of a hut. Terrified Vietnamese civilians watch helplessly as their homes ignite, and the village of Cam Ne is soon in flames. Several thousand miles away, millions of Americans also watch. Their living rooms are suddenly less comfortable.

America was at war, and the world was witnessing it on television.

Images of a U.S. soldier in Vietnam, a cool Kennedy countering a perspiring Nixon in face-to-face debate, a scheming redheaded comedienne—television has produced icons that are etched into the national psyche.

Frank Stanton, the president of the Columbia Broadcasting System, Inc. (CBS), for twenty-six years, understood the power of television and believed it could positively serve the public. "Television can serve the public good in three ways," Stanton once said. "It can give and provide the best news service possible, in pictures and speech; it can ventilate and bring attention to public issues; and it can provide a good menu of entertainment."

A businessman and visionary, Stanton developed CBS from

an obscure chain of radio affiliates into the preeminent television network of his time. Under his leadership the CBS News division emerged as an influential, independent public resource, a vehicle of depth and immediacy that brought seminal events to the public consciousness.

Stanton was that rare creature in the executive suites of television, a Ph.D. in behavioral science. Fusing his interests in audience psychology and television, Stanton devised revolutionary methods to measure and analyze radio and television audiences, many of which are still in use today. The techniques were a critical tool in helping CBS to create successful programming and increase advertising.

But Stanton's greatest contribution to broadcasting, many observers believe, was his steadfast commitment to effective and uncensored broadcast journalism. At the dawn of a new age of journalism, he insisted upon the highest standards of integrity and recruited some of the most respected television journalists ever. Stanton was so resolute in defense of journalistic freedoms that he risked imprisonment when he defied a congressional subpoena demanding outtakes from the CBS documentary "The Selling of the Pentagon" in 1971. As a result of these and other efforts, CBS News became synonymous with quality independent journalism.

It is a measure of Stanton's refinement that his discerning taste in architecture and design, as well as his patronage of the arts, earned him respect and kudos from the artistic community. It was Stanton who painstakingly supervised the construction of CBS's famed New York City headquarters, commonly known as "Black Rock."

YOU CAN TAKE THE BOY OUT OF THE COUNTRY . . .

Born in Muskegon, Michigan, Frank Stanton grew up in Dayton, Ohio. Independent and industrious even as a child, Stanton took his first job as a newspaper delivery boy. Showing an early propensity for business, he determined his own delivery region, worked diligently to recruit nearly a hundred customers, and then sold his route for a small profit. By age 13, he was working at Dayton's largest clothing store for men, the Metropolitan, which gave him nine years of exposure to retail sales.

Stanton attended Ohio Wesleyan, a Methodist college of about 1,800 undergraduates located ninety miles from Dayton. Intending to become a physician, Stanton worked his way through school by pursuing his own innovative business ideas: restructuring the yearbook and turning a profit, and producing fraternity and sorority dances. He also originated the idea of using 16-millimeter movies to film the offensive and defensive plays of opposing football teams. He capitalized on his photographic and business skills by shooting and selling exclusive football photos. Stanton received straight A's in his two majors, zoology and psychology.

After three years of undergraduate study, Stanton had completed his premedical requirements and was eligible to begin medical school. Unable to afford the cost of a medical school education, Stanton instead accepted a position as a junior art director at the prestigious Philadelphia advertising agency A. W. Ayer in 1929. The stock market crash prevented him from assuming his duties, however, and Stanton returned to Ohio to complete his undergraduate work.

While taking some elective courses, Stanton pursued other interests, including psychology and business administration. At the time, analysis of radio advertising was a new idea, and Stanton received special permission to study it. As he analyzed how to use radio as an advertising tool, he wrote to numerous advertisers directly because there was no existing information available in the library.

In 1932, Stanton earned his master's degree in psychology, with a thesis entitled "The Influence of Surface and Tint of Paper on the Speed of Reading." While working on his Ph.D., Stanton wrote to CBS and NBC, describing his belief that people retained more of what they heard than of what they read. CBS executive Paul Kesten had become interested in Frank Stanton's work, particularly his analysis of radio's impact on audiences. He wrote a long, personal letter to Stanton, asking him to forward any relevant information. (NBC replied with a form letter.)

In the early days of radio, audiences were measured by the Crossley Report, a telephone survey in which respondents were asked about their listening habits and favorite programs. CBS consistently lost to NBC, but Kesten and others strongly believed the study, based solely on memory, was biased.

To more accurately measure audience preference, Stanton built a simple mechanism, a small black box that could be plugged into a radio to indicate which frequency the dial was set to at a given time. The device would serve as predecessor to the Nielsen audimeter, the monitoring system that later measured television viewing habits for more than forty years.

THE SCHOLAR PUTS THEORY TO PRACTICE

In 1935, at Kesten's invitation, Stanton joined the staff of the Columbia Broadcasting System's two-man research department. Drawing from his exhaustive research as a scholar, Stanton carefully examined all facets of listener habits: what they listened to, when they listened, what they did while listening, and, of special importance, how what they heard affected their purchasing decisions. Each of his analyses was supported by statistics. Although seen as a "numbers man," Stanton sought imaginative ways in which to analyze and apply the data.

Stanton's effort to provide advertisers with better service was a central reason why CBS was able to surpass NBC in procuring additional sponsors and, over time, to build the CBS empire. His extensive research drew advertisers, attracted affiliates, and determined how and which programs the network developed. Under Stanton's tutelage, the research department grew to 100 people, and in 1938, he was made its director.

He soon made the discovery that the same audiences could be reached and retained if certain programs were scheduled together. The new network strategy of "block programming," which included news broadcasts, provided advertisers with a more targeted audience and higher ratings overall. Block programming is still a popular scheduling technique used by broadcasters today.

Outside of CBS, Stanton continued his academic pursuits. He served as associate director of the Office of Radio Research at Princeton University from 1937 until 1940. In 1953 he became founding chairman of the Center for Advanced Study in the Behavioral Sciences, a center for distinguished scholars from around the world.

Although William S. Paley, the head of CBS, often found (or negotiated away from NBC) "star power," Stanton too had an eye for talent. He discovered Arthur Godfrey in 1941, signed Jackie Gleason to the fledgling CBS television network in 1951, and, that same year, arranged to carry a show about a wacky redhead called *I Love Lucy*.

Stanton's ambition, intelligence, and dedication hastened his climb up the CBS corporate ladder, and in 1942 he was named vice president and general manager. As general manager, he was responsible for research, advertising, sales promotion, public relations, building construction, and operations maintenance. He also supervised the seven CBS-owned stations.

A skilled administrator who understood how to build a corporation, Stanton was propelled by a strong work ethic and high personal standards, which he credited to his parents. Notes Sally Bedell Smith, author of *In All His Glory*, a biography of Paley, "[Stanton's] contribution was essential to the success of CBS. He is one of the great managerial talents of the century."

In the early 1940s, Stanton began to think about leaving the company to start his own business. But he soon realized he was too caught up in the excitement of building a new industry, of defining a product of the future. When Paley offered Stanton the CBS presidency in 1945, he readily accepted. A year later, at age 36, he officially took over.

To increase the company's efficiency, Stanton almost immediately set about reorganizing CBS into three divisions: radio, television, and laboratories. These divisions were set up as their own profit centers and had their own presidents and staff. For ethical and regulatory reasons, Stanton was always careful to keep the entities separate. He worried, for example, that promoting the music of CBS Records on CBS stations would constitute a serious conflict of interest that might jeopardize the license renewals of CBS stations.

The ingenious overhaul also promoted the success of individual stations. Merle Jones, then president of CBS Television Stations, credited the autonomous character of the stations with allowing each station manager to develop his own community affairs and local business outreach, thus boosting the fortunes of each station and the network as a whole.

Stanton proved himself a mastermind at organizational development, and CBS continued to prosper. By the mid-1960s, CBS was cash-rich, and Stanton decided to diversify. This led to investments in profitable Broadway shows like *My Fair Lady*, which would recover CBS's initial investment many times over. CBS also owned Columbia Records, the Fender Guitar Company, and an interest in the New York Yankees.

Although Stanton's reputation and knowledge intimidated some employees, he was generous with his time and advice, making efforts to understand all viewpoints. Co-workers saw him as ambitious, hardworking, and disciplined. Dick Jencks, former president of the CBS/Broadcast Group, says, "Frank Stanton was always careful to thank people. . . . it was one of his great leadership qualities, and it was an immense boon to employees."

Stanton does not take credit for inspiring loyalty or pulling in talented employees. "Television and communications attracted people," he says. The fact remains, though, that CBS was able to keep top people in the "revolving door" business of broadcasting. *Forbes* magazine noted in 1964, "CBS has given its top men a remarkable sense of security. This has helped assure continuity in operation. It has left talented men free to concentrate on their jobs, not their security." At the time, the heads of the seven divisions had each worked for the company an average of twenty-one years.

Paley and Stanton were seen as complementary leaders, a fact that was vastly important to the company's success and stability. Bedell Smith wrote, "Paley, in effect, provided the architectural drawings, Stanton turned them into steel and concrete." In a business infamous for its flashy excesses, Stanton brought a sense of classy understatement and respect to the entire enterprise. It is why Bill Paley always felt comfortable leaving Stanton in charge.

Donald V. West, Stanton's personal assistant in the late 1960s, recalls, "I'd give him 2,000 names—his personal mailing list—at 5:30 P.M., and the next morning, at 8 A.M., there would be the list back on my desk with corrections and notations. I'd wonder, 'When in the hell was he doing this?' " Stanton described himself as a "bore" who worked "around the clock."

CBS's Struggle to Commercialize Color Television

From the start, Stanton was strongly committed to the innovative work of CBS inventor Peter Goldmark in perfecting color television. Although the technology could not be used on existing sets, Goldmark's version of color was actually superior to that of competitor RCA, the parent company of NBC. A series of events, however, prevented CBS from commercializing its color technology in the early years of television.

"From a management standpoint, the toughest challenge was bringing television into being while keeping our head above water in radio," Stanton recalls. "We weren't in manufacturing like our competitors, so we didn't have that financial base." Goldmark introduced color images to CBS executives as early as 1940, but during World War II, the government halted much non-defense-related technological research and development. By the time Stanton got the CBS color system approved after the war, it was incompatible with most existing television sets.

Nonetheless, Stanton believed that CBS could better compete if it manufactured its own television sets. So, in 1951, CBS bought the Hytron Radio and Electronics Corporation, a substandard manufacturer of televisions and tubes that Stanton was confident could be turned around. When the government again asked manufacturers to stop producing television sets—this time because of the Korean War—black-and-white sets flooded the market. By the time the ban was lifted, twenty-three million black-and-white televisions were already in use. Faced with such overwhelming numbers, CBS scrapped further manufacturing plans. CBS would lose $50 million on Hytron over ten years.

Stanton Builds a Formidable News Tradition

While Paley focused on CBS's entertainment schedule, Stanton developed the vehicle that he believed would best enable broadcasters to fulfill their obligations to the public: the news. To Stanton, it was important to keep the news independent, accurate, and objective and to aggressively deal with public affairs. Thus he oversaw development of *See It Now*, the ground-breaking public affairs series featuring Edward R. Murrow. He also conceived of *CBS Reports*, a series of news specials scheduled for prime-time, from which came Murrow's famed "Harvest of Shame" documentary concerning the deplorable lives of farmworkers.

Stanton continued to build CBS, expecting to become CEO when Bill Paley turned sixty-five and retired in 1966. But when that time came, Paley convinced the board to waive the retirement rule so that he could remain. Stanton stayed on as president until he assumed the title of vice chairman in 1971. He retired from the board at the conclusion of his term, but continued to serve as a consultant to the company for the next fourteen years.

MR. STANTON GOES TO WASHINGTON

As a broadcaster committed to the public's right to know, Stanton stoutly opposed government efforts to influence the news or to withhold information. "I would do everything I could to open [government] up," he recalled in 1993. "Making information public is central to the long-term life of democracy." Stanton believes it is the duty of the free press to test, search, and investigate all angles of a potential story and to cover it responsibly.

Throughout the 1950s, Stanton did in fact "open it up." In his first network editorial, he asked the Senate to let broadcasters cover the censure of Senator McCarthy. When CBS aired *Face the Nation* featuring Nikita Khrushchev—despite criticism by President Eisenhower and Secretary of State John Foster Dulles—Stanton took out a full-page advertisement in *The New York Times* defending CBS's journalistic judgment. The next year Stanton encouraged development of a prime-time hour of news, *Where We Stand*, which compared U.S. and Soviet technology after the launch of the Sputnik satellite. Again there was criticism. Many in the administration took CBS to task for focusing on U.S. weaknesses.

In 1959, Stanton had a confrontation with Congress that would define him as his industry's leading statesman. In the mid-1950s, audiences had become enamored of television quiz shows like *The $64,000 Question* and *Dotto*. Viewers sat entranced as they watched participants win thousands of dollars for answering trivia questions. But when contestants began to come forward with allegations that the shows were fixed, Congress jumped into the fray.

Stanton ordered an investigation and found that independent producers were guilty of widespread rigging. He took responsibility for the oversight, acknowledging that CBS should have maintained tighter control over its shows. But he insisted that the networks be allowed to exercise responsible judgment and monitor themselves. As a result of Stanton's eloquent leadership, the networks were not brought under government control.

An ardent defender of the First Amendment, Stanton prevailed upon the Federal Communications Commission to temporarily suspend its equal time rules so that Richard Nixon and John F. Kennedy could square off in their famous face-to-face debates of 1960.

On other occasions Stanton protected the CBS News department from government intervention. When *CBS Evening News* aired images of marines burning down huts and killing civilians in the village of Cam Ne, as reported by correspondent Morley Safer on August 5, 1965, an enraged Lyndon Johnson accused Safer of being a Communist and ordered an investigation of him. Stanton refused to be pressured by the White House. He steadfastly supported the CBS News division and, in a 1966 speech to broadcasters, he vehemently defended the right of CBS News to report on stories like Camranh Bay.

Stanton faced similar government pressures for airing a 1971 documentary, "The Selling of the Pentagon," on the Pentagon's public relations efforts. It used the Pentagon's own PR statements and videotapes to illustrate the organization's waste and deceit in promoting Cold War propaganda. The House of Representatives subpoenaed CBS scripts and outtakes, but Stanton refused to comply, telling Congress that "compliance with the subpoena would have a chilling effect on the freedom of the press to cover government activities." The contempt of Congress charges were eventually dropped by a vote of 226 to 181.

Not surprisingly, broadcasters hailed Stanton as a heroic statesman. Marvin Kalb, a news correspondent who served under Stanton, said, "Whenever there was trouble with the U.S. government, and there was plenty of it, especially with the Nixon administration, he [Stanton] stood as a giant for journalistic integrity."

Stanton's relationship with the government was not always adversarial, however. Throughout World War II, Stanton acted as a consultant to the Office of Facts and Figures, the Office of War Information, and the secretary of war. Stanton also served as chairman of the Rand Corporation from 1961 to 1973, and as trustee from 1957 to 1978.

STANTON'S UNERRING SENSE OF STYLE

At CBS, Stanton was responsible for creating the corporate image. He oversaw the design of the CBS "eye," supervising its placement on everything that was connected with the network, from studio marquees and press releases to cuff links and neckties. The eye became the company's symbol and calling card. Sally Bedell Smith said of Stanton: "His speech, conduct, and look gave CBS a personal dignity quite apart from what was appearing on living room TV screens. Stanton's contribution to CBS's image was incalculable."

Further evidence of Stanton's discerning taste is evident in the CBS headquarters at 51 West 52nd Street. Stanton oversaw every detail of the design and construction of the building, hiring the renowned architect Eero Saarinen to design it. Stanton chose the art works, carpets, furniture, and typeface used throughout the building, and even traveled to Norway and Sweden to find the right granite for its exterior. Joseph Dembo, onetime head of WCBS, the CBS-owned radio affiliate in New York, said, "That building is a monument to Frank Stanton. It was his imprint and marvelous aesthetic taste . . . that molded it."

Upon his retirement from CBS, Stanton served in a series of influential foundation and nonprofit posts—as chairman of the American Red Cross, as a trustee for the Rockefeller Foundation, and as visiting "overseer" at Harvard, one of only two non-alumni asked to fill the post in this century. Stanton also led numerous organizations devoted to the arts and architecture, becoming commissioner of the National Portrait Gallery, chairman of the Presidential Design Awards, and a board member of the International Design Conference, among others.

A psychologist, business executive, broadcaster, and patron of the arts, Stanton has been hailed as a Renaissance man with an astonishing range of interests and expertise. With such talents leading a major broadcast network, it is no exaggeration to say that Stanton helped shape the past half century of American culture. And as even his rivals admit, he did so with conscience and integrity.

"A remarkable combination of character, insight, wisdom, and charm" is how Albert Carnesale, dean of Harvard's Kennedy School of Government, summarizes Stanton's singular career. "This is a man who is fully prepared to make hard decisions today, but who insists on taking into account the effects those decisions will have not only tomorrow but a decade from now and beyond. This is a man of integrity and vision."

24

The Haas Family of Levi Strauss & Co.

A VALUES-DRIVEN BUSINESS IN A GLOBAL MARKETPLACE

In 1982, a group of concerned employees approached Levi Strauss & Co. chief operating officer Robert Haas requesting permission to distribute information about a newly identified sexually transmitted disease called AIDS. Instead of trying to distance his company from this extremely controversial matter, Haas himself took turns handing out the literature in the lobby of LS&CO. headquarters.

"People needed help," he explained simply. "And there was no need for them to be stigmatized. They were trying to help other employees, so why not?" By the mid-1980s, all Levi Strauss & Co. employees in the United States were required to attend a one-hour class about AIDS, which included an informational video.

The video, which featured several gay men from San Francisco headquarters talking frankly about AIDS, was offensive to some of the company's Southern employees. LS&CO. eventually went back to the drawing board to produce a video that included more heterosexual employees and incorporated scenes with sewing machine operators, bundlers, and fabric cutters openly discussing their misconceptions about the virus. The company's efforts to educate its employees and the public enabled it to continue using the talents of those already infected with AIDS by creating a supportive work environment, and also to help limit future losses, to the company and to society at large, by slowing the spread of the disease.

Bob Haas's experience with the problem of AIDS is emblematic of his and his family's approach to the myriad events and issues they have confronted since the company's inception: They are willing to take risks and to constantly assess and improve their strategies, for the benefit of their company and the betterment of society. And through the unprecedented success of Levi Strauss & Co., they have demonstrated that private firms can be a powerful engine for positive social change.

THE BEGINNING OF A LEGACY

Integrity, humanity, and innovation have been traditions at LS& CO. since its founder arrived in San Francisco in 1853 with a load of dry goods with which to start a wholesale business.

Legend has it that Levi Strauss made the first jeans from a canvaslike material called cotton duck at the request of gold miners. But the true genesis of blue jeans dates to 1872, when Reno tailor Jacob Davis came up with the novel idea of putting metal rivets in the pocket corners of the pants he made for his customers. Davis and Levi Strauss patented this process in 1873, and the first manufacturing facility for the "copper-riveted clothing" was opened in San Francisco.

From the beginning of his career as both a dry goods merchant and a manufacturer, Levi Strauss established a reputation for high quality, fair prices, and a strong commitment to his community. He supported area orphanages and a local school for the deaf, and also endowed scholarships at the University of California at Berkeley. He was known, moreover, as an employer who treated his employees with exceptional dignity and respect. Upon his death in 1902, Strauss was hailed among the business community as "a pioneer merchant whose success was only equaled by his good deeds."

Strauss's nephews, Sigmund and Jacob Stern, took over the business after their uncle's death. They maintained the tradition of quality and fairness even after the devastating earthquake and fire of 1906 destroyed LS&CO.'s facilities. The Stern brothers placed a notice in the city's newspapers advising all LS&CO. employees that they would continue to receive their salaries while the company was rebuilding and working out of temporary quarters in Oakland. Both the business and the values that these men established were to flourish under the leadership of Sigmund Stern's son-in-law, Walter Haas—and later under *his* sons, Walter Jr. and Peter, and grandson Robert, the company's current chairman of the board and CEO.

THE HAAS FAMILY TAKES CHARGE

Fierce competition and sudden shifts in demand make the apparel industry a treacherous one, even for well-established brand names. When Walter Haas, Sr., joined the company in 1919, his product did not enjoy even that advantage. The few clothing items that LS&CO. manufactured—including lot number 501 denim waist overalls, later the flagship product—amounted to only one-third of sales. The other two-thirds of revenue came from hosiery, linens, and housewares produced largely in the East.

Because LS&CO. was not a government contractor—its work pants were used mostly by miners, lumberjacks, and cowboys in the western United States—the wartime boom had very little impact on the firm. Profits were only $45,000 on an investment of $1.6 million in 1918, according to historian Ed Cray in his book about the company, *Levi's*. Seeing their meager profits dwindle, Sigmund Stern asked Haas to stay with the firm for two years, but if business did not turn around, they would consider liquidation.

Haas decided to persevere. He invited his brother-in-law and cousin, Daniel Koshland, into the business and together they began to restructure the company around the LS&CO.'s "Two Horse" brand of clothing (whose strength was dramatized by two teams of horses futilely trying to pull the garment apart). By the late 1920s, annual revenues had increased substantially, with the patented waist overalls generating by far the greatest share of the profits.

But just as production was moving into full gear at the Valencia Street factory in San Francisco's Mission district, the market for the overalls suddenly fell flat when the stock market crashed in 1929 and the national economy deteriorated. On farms and ranches and in forests and mines, the demand for Levi's jeans all but dried up among the working people who were the main customers for the famous riveted pants.

Determined not to lay off any employees, even when the jean pants had piled up on the factory floor, Haas put workers on a shortened workweek so that they could at least continue to draw their paychecks. In 1932, with sales at half their pre-crash levels, more than 100,000 pairs of pants were piled even into the rest rooms at company headquarters. LS&CO. posted its third straight year of losses, saw a number of its indebted dealers go bankrupt, and was operating solely on the family's financial reserves. But Haas and Koshland put people to work refinishing the factory floors rather than lay them off.

JEANS FOR MUNITIONS WORKERS
—AND A NEW GENERATION

As the nation's economy began to turn around in the late 1930s, so did LS&CO.'s fortunes. Its garments soon became a symbol of the romantic, rough-and-tumble life on the range that was captivating Eastern city dwellers. Though the company adopted the fashion themes made popular in B-grade movies, even introducing lines of satin western shirts, the quality of their work pants continued to be absolutely top-of-the-line. "It just came naturally to us," Walter Haas, Sr., once explained. "We just believed in furnishing good goods, and believed in the long run quality would tell. In the long run it's just good business."

LS&CO.'s sturdy products held up as well in the workplace as they did on the range, leading the U.S. government to declare the waist-high overalls an "essential" industry good needed for wartime production. But consumer demand for LS&CO.'s premier denim product could not be contained for long. GIs came home looking for the tough shrink-to-fit blue jeans they had found in their post exchanges overseas.

Walter Haas, Jr., who had joined LS&CO. in 1939 before leaving to serve in the armed forces, rejoined his father and uncle after the war. Walter Jr. took command of the company's marketing and merchandising strategies from the corporate offices on Battery Street in San Francisco, while his younger brother Peter took on the operations end at the Valencia Street factory. This second generation of the Haas leadership team was poised to confront a rapidly changing society and business climate with the same set of values that had served their forebears so well.

"My father and uncle insisted that the company be responsible in all the communities in which we operated, in a variety of ways as the company started to grow," Walter Jr. recollected. "Peter and I consciously sought to strengthen and enhance these policies through the years."

Though Walter Haas, Sr., did not formally end his tenure as company president until 1955—a position that Walter Jr. assumed in 1958—Walter Jr., together with Peter Haas, had already begun to lead the company in earnest in the late 1940s. (Daniel Koshland served as president from 1955 to 1958.)

Their resolve to be successful, responsible corporate citizens was put to the test almost immediately. Demand for their denim pants was exploding, rapidly transforming the small, regionally scaled firm into the nation's preeminent clothing manufacturer. Between 1945 and 1947 alone, gross sales increased nearly 50 percent, from $8 million to $11.8 million.

The company was selling over four million pairs of jeans per year. That figure soared still higher over the next decade as jeans-clad rebels in films such as *The Wild One* (1954) made blue jeans the uniform of a new, and rapidly growing, generation.

A Corporate Pioneer for Racial Equality

In the late 1940s, LS&CO. began opening plants in the southern United States, and by the end of the next decade the company had a total of ten manufacturing or distribution facilities up and running.

After employing a racially diverse group of workers in California for more than a decade, the Haas brothers decided to confront the segregated hiring norms that prevailed elsewhere in the nation. It was in the small southern town of Blackstone, Virginia, that local LS&CO. officials approached the Haases with the idea of integrating the all-white facility. To capitalize on the entire labor pool, the Haases notified community leaders that the $1.5-million facility would have to be closed if the work force could not be drawn from all applicants, regardless of color.

It was 1959, several years before the fierce debates about the Civil Rights Act, and Blackstone officials tenaciously resisted the plan to integrate. They insisted that if they had no choice but to hire black workers, then the company must build a wall through the plant separating the races.

When the Haases refused, town leaders pressed for a white line to be painted down the middle of the facility, creating separate but equal production lines. When the Haas brothers rejected this idea, too, the town argued next for separate rest rooms and drinking fountains and a separate cafeteria. Peter Haas finally met with community representatives, impressing upon them his company's determination to completely integrate the plant or shut it down.

Blackstone officials eventually acquiesced, and the Virginia facility was the first among several LS&CO. plants in the South to open its hiring practices, years before federal legislation would require it.

"It may sound easy in the re-telling," cautioned Robert Haas, Peter's nephew and the current CEO of LS&CO., "but it wasn't." When his father, Walter Jr., had hired the first Filipino secretary at company headquarters in San Francisco, according to Robert Haas, "a number of employees, including the highest-ranking woman, protested that they didn't want to use the same toilet facilities." But, he added, "My father refused to agree to their demands." If many public and private institutions had eventually to be prodded into integrating, Walter Jr. and Peter Haas made a risky break from convention for the sake of doing what they knew was right.

While many other firms were still struggling to desegregate, the Haas brothers were taking new, ambitious steps toward making LS&CO. job opportunities open to both sexes and all races. In 1967, LS&CO. launched its affirmative action plan, three years before the federal Fair Employment Practices Act required any such action. The plan provided for new training and sought to increase the number of professional, sales, and management personnel from minority groups. "If we are to meet today's challenge," Walter Haas, Jr., explained to the people at LS&CO. in the late 1960s, "it is vital that we utilize every talented individual at our disposal."

THE CHALLENGE OF INSTITUTIONALIZING VALUES

Recognizing his social vision in business, President Johnson appointed Walter Haas, Jr., one of nine regional chairmen of the National Alliance of Businessmen in 1968. Johnson called on Haas to enlist business leaders throughout the West Coast to recruit and train 500,000 workers from among the "hard-core unemployed"—a goal that Haas met. Haas later credited the experience with provoking "the real change in my thinking in my life." It became, he said, "the springboard for a lot of things that we undertook in subsequent years."

One such reverberation was the LS&CO. Community Affairs Department, created by Walter Jr. in 1968. Haas was convinced that local residents knew better than anyone else what needed to be done in their communities, and how to go about it. Through the Community Affairs Department, the company helped organize workers nationwide into groups of volunteers, offering them start-up money and matching the groups' own fund-raising efforts. The first of these so-called Community Involvement Teams, or CITs, was established at the San Francisco headquarters in 1970. Neither Peter nor Walter Jr. anticipated at the outset how far-reaching and lasting the program would become.

"Whenever I visited a plant," Walter Haas, Jr., recalled in an interview in 1994, "I'd always meet with the CIT team. It was impressive because being a sewing machine operator is hard work. Yet, on their own time, they volunteer to help their neighbors. It was just a very moving experience." Groups of workers all over the country have used the organization and its funding to support dental care for the underserviced; stock the shelves of local food pantries; renovate playgrounds; and clean up beaches, among many other projects. Twenty-five years after the volunteer program was initiated, there are now more than a hundred

Community Involvement Teams operating in forty-four different countries.

SHARING THE FRUITS OF COMMERCIAL SUCCESS

Building such a robust Community Affairs Department in the early 1970s by no means detracted from the company's commercial success. With the company's growth still galloping along, CEO Walter Haas, Jr., and President Peter Haas in 1971 took the company public for the first time in its 121-year history. Ignoring the advice of underwriters, the Haases inserted a statement in the stock prospectus advising would-be shareholders of their steadfast commitment to managing a socially responsible business.

To encourage minority entrepreneurs in the San Francisco Bay Area, for example, LS&CO. provided technical assistance to six small retailers for several years during the early 1970s. They next lent their expertise to an Oakland manufacturer, Ghetto Enterprises Incorporated, with which the company contracted for some of its production.

The disappointing results of these early ventures did not discourage Walter Jr. and Peter Haas or lead them to walk away from them. Rather, like any experimentation in business, the risk taking yielded valuable lessons that were incorporated into future programs. "There are many times we stub our toe," Peter Haas admitted, "but that's not for want of trying. We hope we learn from our mistakes."

That commitment to the learning process eventually gave rise to an effective minority purchasing plan, initiated in 1972, which channeled increasingly larger percentages of LS&CO.'s purchasing power toward minority-owned firms. By the late 1970s, LS&CO. was buying nearly $3 million per year in goods and services from minority vendors.

By 1981, when Peter (having succeeded Walter Jr.), stepped down as CEO, the company was selling over $2.5 billion worth of LS&CO. products and managing operations in more than forty countries around the world. And although the Levi's name had become synonymous with quality and integrity in almost as many languages, the giant clothing maker—indeed, the entire apparel industry—was on the verge of still greater transformations.

THE THIRD HAAS GENERATION CONFRONTS THE GLOBAL MARKET

LS&CO.'s extraordinary growth in the 1970s was to give way, in the 1980s, to more dynamic competition from abroad combined with rapidly changing product demand. Consumers were asking for loose-fitting stone-washed blue jeans one day and for closely cropped jet-black denim pants the next, with tastes varying widely in different regions of the world. And retailers were expecting the right styles in the right sizes to be delivered floor-ready in a matter of days.

In the United States, demand for blue jeans in general began to fall steeply during the early 1980s. In particular, the core constituency for 501 jeans—men between the ages of 16 and 24— composed an ever smaller proportion of the population. And as baby boomers grew older, their tastes were shifting away from the shrink-to-fit denim pants of their youth. The company's international operations were hit doubly hard when sagging demand for jeans in Europe met with record high valuations of the dollar. Meanwhile apparel manufacturers around the world were offering consumers everywhere a greater selection of cheaper products.

These sudden changes were a shock to LS&CO., which had been accustomed to steady, if not phenomenal, growth. As a massive global enterprise employing 48,000 people in 1980, with more than a hundred facilities worldwide, and offering an overly diversified line of products, LS&CO. was simply not as nimble as many of its competitors. In the early 1980s, profits and revenues began to fall steeply for the first time since the Great Depression. When he became CEO of the company in 1984, Walter Haas, Jr.'s son, Robert, confessed, "I did not have an agenda for how we would turn the company around."

It was clear, however, that if LS&CO. was going to compete in the new global marketplace, it would have to reshape itself into a leaner, more agile organization. The transition would be a difficult one. From 1985 to 1990, LS&CO.'s U.S. head count decreased by over 5,000 through layoffs and attrition. For a company that had always been very personally committed to its employees and their communities, the cutbacks were especially painful and provoked a great deal of soul-searching. "It has been a time for careful reflection about who we are," Haas remarked, "about what we need to do to resume growth and about the meaning of our commitment to responsible corporate behavior."

This introspection resulted in Robert Haas taking LS&CO. private once again, in 1985. At the time, the $1.6-billion leveraged buyout was the largest such buyout deal in history. Haas then laid out his new strategy for commercial success in the Mission and Aspiration statements of 1987—two documents that seek to reconcile LS&CO.'s commitment to compete in the global marketplace with the Haas family's values and tradition of social leadership.

The statements spell out the company's determination to make even the most difficult business decisions with honesty, fairness, and integrity. And because the prospect of lifetime employment is no longer realistic, the statements codify LS&CO.'s commitment to provide all employees with a dynamic opportunity to learn, grow, contribute, and advance in an open corporate culture that respects diversity and rewards candid feedback. The Mission and Aspiration statements are not intended as an ethical or operational rule book but, rather, as a framework of values that the company seeks to actualize in decision making at every level.

Articulating a values-driven business strategy did not exempt Haas from having to make more difficult and unpopular decisions, however. "Dockers," the line of casual pants the company had introduced in 1986, had very high sewing costs, and encroaching competitors forced the company to contract more of its labor from abroad. When LS&CO. announced the closure of one of its San Antonio, Texas, facilities in 1990, a group of employees and community advocates charged the company with heartless profiteering and called for a boycott of LS&CO. products. Though the facility was closed—after numerous attempts to retool production—Haas explains: "Sometimes the only solution is to close a plant, and if we don't have the guts to face that decision, then we risk hurting a lot of people—not just those in one plant."

While LS&CO. could not avoid making the tough choice in San Antonio, its unorthodox approach to the plant closing reflects the company's acute concern for its host communities and employees. Not only did the company's paid notice period and severance package far exceed industry standards and federal requirements, LS&CO. staffed a job placement office for fifteen months after the closure; contributed nearly $2 million to employee and community assistance programs; and offered substantial rent discounts to any company that would move into the facility and create employment opportunities for the community.

Rather than simply mitigating the effects of any future cutbacks, the company is now completely revamping production in most of its facilities to improve its competitive advantage and make further dislocations unnecessary. To show their mutual commitment to each other's success, LS&CO. and the Amalgamated Clothing and Textile Workers Union (ACTWU) entered into an unprecedented partnership agreement in June 1994. The company is facilitating union organization in the nearly half of its production and distribution centers that are already unionized, while unionized workers actively help to reduce costs, increase productivity, and improve health and safety conditions.

ANOTHER LS&CO. INNOVATION: GLOBAL SOURCING GUIDELINES

Because a significant percentage of the work that goes into its products is not done by LS&CO. employees and may escape company supervision, Haas and his leadership team promulgated Global Sourcing Guidelines in 1992. The standards set forth here concern the maximum work hours per week and minimum age of workers allowed, as well as safety and environmental requirements. These requirements are applied to every contractor who manufactures LS&CO. products overseas.

Trained inspectors closely monitor contractor compliance among the company's 600 suppliers worldwide.

At the time the guidelines were first implemented, LS&CO. terminated business with 5 percent of its contractors and required improvements from another 25 percent. The standards have since become industry benchmarks, with companies like Nike, Reebok, Sears, and Wal-Mart quickly following suit.

When LS&CO. encountered unexpected ethical complexities arising from its guidelines, it did not shrink from further initiatives. For example, when company inspectors found that two of its contractors in Bangladesh were employing forty workers under the age of 14, it could have simply laid off the young workers and washed its hands of any charges of using child labor. But these children were contributing significantly to their families' incomes, and a summary layoff could have been more harmful.

After wrestling with the ethical dilemma, the company arranged to pay for the children's schooling while the contractor continued to pay their wages. The contractor also agreed to offer them employment when they come of age.

Haas's innovative, values-centered approach to problem solving has occasionally attracted criticism. He recalls some of it:

> When we developed our Global Sourcing Guidelines, we had an outcry in the company amongst our merchandisers, who said if we can't have child labor, or if we can't let our contractors work more than 60 hours, or if they have to spend a lot of money to gussy up their plants, or if they have to put in pollution controls in their finishing facilities, it's going to add cents per unit to our garments and we'll become priced out of the market.

> That was the concern we heard. And we have had a number of record years of sales and earnings ever since then, so I guess those concerns didn't come to pass.

Since 1985, LS&CO. has in fact averaged sales growth of roughly 10 percent and net income growth of nearly one-third each year.

Business as a Force for Economic Justice

Walter Haas, Jr., a board member of The Business Enterprise Trust until his death in October 1995, was not shy about sharing his convictions with other business audiences. In his closing remarks at the 1992 Business Enterprise Awards ceremony, Haas urged his fellow business executives to strive for profitability, but also to honor those values that are "too rich and complex" to be captured by any bottom line:

> Each of us has the capacity to make business not only a source of economic wealth, but also a force for economic and social justice. Each of us needs to recognize and use the power we have to define the character of our enterprises, so they nurture values important to our society.
>
> Only then will each of us know the full rewards that a career in business can yield. Only then will business achieve the true potential of its leadership. Only then will business fulfill its obligation to help build an economy worthy of a free society and a civilization worth celebrating.

25

The Xerox Corporation

THE PRAGMATIC IDEALISTS

Hollywood itself would have difficulty improving upon the basic story: Visionary leader of a small business in upstate New York sees epoch-changing promise in an obscure scientific idea. He devotes fourteen years to developing the technology, betting the entire company in the process, eventually introducing a machine that dramatically changes modern life in hundreds of ways.

Meanwhile he shows great leadership by integrating his highest social ideals into the company's business operations, and leaves behind a robust global enterprise that conscientiously strives, in his words, to "combine the forces of technology with the forces of humanism."

That, in brief, is the story of Joseph C. Wilson and the company he built, the Xerox Corporation. Now a $19-billion colossus, Xerox plays a commanding role in the growing global marketplace for "graphic communication," which includes copiers, digital publishing, computer equipment, and related technologies.

Wilson was responsible for developing Xerox's distinctive internal gyroscope: its research prowess, long-term vision, customer focus, staunch social commitment, enlightened labor relations, and organizational resilience and tenacity. But it took three remarkable successors—C. Peter McColough, David Kearns, and Paul Allaire—to sustain and enrich those fragile virtues over the course of five turbulent decades.

JOE WILSON AND THE HALOID COMPANY

After his training at Harvard Business School in the 1930s, Joe Wilson reluctantly agreed to become an assistant sales manager at his father's small manufacturing business in Rochester, New York. The Haloid Company, founded in 1906, was "a very small, very sedate and very undistinguished" maker of photographic paper, according to one historian of the company. Nonetheless, Wilson thrived, and in 1945, at age 36, succeeded his father as president of the firm.

From the start, the force of Wilson's distinctive personality radiated throughout the company. He maintained a keen interest in politics, public life, and culture, read Browning and Keats for pleasure, and routinely threw himself into various community causes. Although somewhat shy, sentimental, and quirky, Wilson was a generous man of quiet self-assurance and tenacious optimism.

Living in the shadow of Eastman Kodak, Rochester's largest employer, Wilson realized that the Haloid Company could be quickly snuffed out by a competitor, particularly if a new technology were invented. So he was intrigued when he stumbled across an obscure inventor working out of his apartment in Astoria, Queens, who had created a process to transfer images from a photoreceptor drum to paper using electrically charged particles. The amateur physicist, Chester Carlson, called the novel process "electrophotography."

Nearly two dozen major companies, including IBM, General Electric, 3M, and A. B. Dick, declined to buy Carlson's patents, believing they had no future. To keep his vision alive, Carlson entered into an agreement with the Battelle Memorial Institute of Columbus, Ohio, a private research facility, to try to develop electrophotography into a commercially viable product.

But Joe Wilson, believing that Carlson's invention would have revolutionary implications, began plowing 25 percent of Haloid's net income, or $25,000, into supporting Battelle's research. After consulting with a classics professor, Wilson also replaced the word *electrophotography* with a more euphonious one, *xerography*, taken from two Greek words for "dry" and "writing."

After numerous technical advances based on Battelle's re-search, Haloid in 1949 felt confident enough to introduce the "XeroX Copier Machine, Model A," a machine that required about a dozen manual steps in order to produce a single copy. Yet Wilson aspired to do better—to create a fast, automated, mass-market copier that would not require messy mimeograph masters, special zinc-coated paper, or photosensitive paper that sometimes faded in sunlight. Furthermore, he wanted a copier that could use any sort of plain paper (and not rolls), and could be leased or sold at competitive rates.

These were wildly ambitious goals. No one had ever tried to creatively integrate three distinct scientific realms—electricity, chemistry, and mechanical engineering—into a single product. Furthermore, each of these processes in xerography was scien-tifically obscure in itself. The magnitude of the engineering chal-lenges alone is suggested by Haloid's research director, John Dessauer, who calculated that the machine they were trying to build would have "over 1,200 parts, most of which are in them-selves assemblies of smaller parts. When I say there will be a minimum of 30,000 events leading to the final production of a desktop copier, I am underestimating."

Haloid scientists spent years trying to overcome a long list of seemingly insurmountable technical problems, including static-charged paper sticking to the photoelectric drug; me-chanical misfeeds of paper; and toner powder that produced un-sightly blobs. In solving hundreds of such problems, the com-pany accumulated more than 500 patents on xerographic proc-esses.

It is a measure of Joe Wilson's faith in the concept that the Haloid Company spent a remarkable $75 million between 1946 and 1960 in bringing xerography to the market. This was a phe-nomenal sum for a company whose revenues in 1955, for exam-ple, were only $21 million.

Peter McColough, the company's second chairman, would later recall, "For the first seven years that I was with the com-pany [1954–1960], Joe Wilson spent more on research than the total profits of the company—which means we had to borrow money for research!" In the meantime, many company employees were mortgaging their homes to buy Haloid stock, in order to keep the xerography project alive.

Beyond the engineering challenges, it was not clear how the new invention could be priced. Who would spend $10,000 for a copier when other machines were selling for several hundred dollars? Yet leasing the new Xerox copier at a flat monthly rate would be impractical because small offices might make only a few dozen copies while large companies would make tens of thousands of copies. Yet a complex set of pricing tiers would be equally impractical.

Xerox's inspired solution: metered pricing of copies. By charging $95 for the first 2,000 copies, then 4 cents for each additional copy, any business, big or small, could lease the new copier. It was simple, flexible, and equitable. Although a familiar concept today, per-copy pricing was a breakthrough at the time, and the foundation for the company's stupefying financial success in the 1960s.

Still another challenge was how to manufacture the machine; Haloid had no manufacturing facilities whatsoever. Wilson approached IBM to propose a joint venture, but IBM rejected the idea after Arthur D. Little, the management consulting firm, concluded that the nation's current and future demand for the envisioned copier would never exceed 5,000 machines. "Here was the mightiest office equipment company in the world saying, 'You have just gone down the wrong road,' " recalled Peter McColough in 1994. "And if they were right, of course, it was absolute bankruptcy."

A STAR IS BORN: XEROX IN THE 1960S

At once anxious and giddy at the prospect of going forward alone, Haloid Xerox took the plunge in 1959 and began production. As if to recognize its imminent rebirth, Haloid Xerox changed its name the next year to the Xerox Corporation, and began a new era.

Its new machine was a 600-pound giant that could barely squeeze through office doors. It was dubbed the 914, a number that referred to the dimensions of copies that could be made, 9 inches by 14 inches. Since the 914 was obviously too big for on-site demonstrations, a bold decision was made to buy advertising on the fledgling medium of television.

The ads were a huge success, and soon thousands of businesses and government offices were clamoring to lease 914 copiers. The United States government alone, by 1966, had installed some 55,000 Xerox machines, according to the General Services Administration. Eventually, a total of about 200,000 914's were installed throughout the nation.

"None of us had the slightest idea that there would be this outpouring of demand with which Xerox could not cope," recalled Sol Linowitz, chairman of the Xerox Executive Committee and of the board of directors through 1966. What everyone failed to realize was that people would use the 914 not only to make file copies (as existing copiers had been used), but also to share much more information with each other in more spontaneous ways. In other words, the 914 functioned not just as a copier but as a new communications medium. It changed literally thousands of contexts of social and business practices, particularly in commerce, law, education, and government.

In words eerily prophetic of the coming computer and telecommunications revolution, Xerox's top scientist, John Dessauer, told shareholders in the early 1960s:

> It is becoming abundantly evident that we are in a new stage, one substantially different from earlier stages such as oral culture, alphabetic civilization, or book-oriented society. The combination of the electronics revolution and revolutionary imaging methods, along with satellite telecommunications, will permit contemporary man finally to be able to master time and space in an unprecedented way.

Xerox's willingness to be a pioneer was soon yielding phenomenal results. The company's annual operating revenues soared from $33 million in 1958 to $176 million in 1963 to more than $500 million in 1966. Income before taxes, which stood at $3.7 million in 1958, skyrocketed to more than $100 million by 1966.

The company joined the New York Stock Exchange in 1961,

and within ten years the number of its shareholders went from 9,000 to more than 145,000. By the end of the 1960s, Xerox stock had split 180 times. A $10,000 investment in Haloid Xerox in 1960 was worth a million dollars twelve years later. At least forty of the original Haloid executives became millionaires as a result of their stock holdings. Six years after the introduction of the 914, Xerox stock was valued at $4.5 billion, making it the twelfth-largest company in the nation in terms of the market value of its stock.

Much of this value was fueled by a concerted global expansion through partnerships with The Rank Organisation in Great Britain and Fuji Photo in Japan. Sol Linowitz played a leading role in these new ventures, as well as in Xerox's expansion into Latin American countries. Joe Wilson continued as Xerox's guiding visionary and CEO until 1968, and as chairman from 1966 until his death in 1971.

With the 914, Xerox had almost literally created a new industry. Previously, sales in the copier/duplicating business were tens of millions of dollars a year. By 1994, the black-and-white copier industry worldwide was estimated to be a $40-billion business, and electronic printers based on xerography represented an additional $35 billion.

XEROX'S EXPANSIVE SOCIAL VISION

The same sense of optimism, determination, and enthusiasm that fueled development of the 914 also animated Xerox's commitment to social issues. Xerox had long been actively involved in the life of Rochester, New York, generously supporting its schools, the university, educational television, and cultural activities. When racial unrest suddenly hit Rochester in the 1960s, the company collaborated with its union to devise a job training program for inner-city residents. The company also sponsored a women's job corps training program and helped to found and offer technical assistance and purchasing contracts to FIGHTON, Inc., an inner-city, minority-owned manufacturing firm.

Another refreshing precedent that Wilson established was

that of progressive labor relations. A firm believer in labor unions, Wilson developed a relationship of trust with the Amalgamated Clothing and Textile Workers Union (ACTWU). Unlike other major corporations, which were crippled by strikes and other labor unrest, Xerox sought to work collaboratively with union leadership, sharing information and cultivating trust. This cooperation proved particularly important in the 1980s when Xerox's future was threatened by Japanese competition. "I think we were able to go through many hard changes with the cooperation of the union," said David Kearns, who led Xerox from 1982 to 1990. "The union helped us change the business and put things in place that helped make us competitive around the world and not go out of business."

One of the most controversial instances of Xerox's social engagement was its 1964 sponsorship of a series of network television programs showcasing the work of the United Nations, a less established, more controversial institution than it is today. The John Birch Society denounced the commercial-free series as anti-American and Communistic and flooded Xerox with more than 15,000 letters.

It is fair to say that Wilson dwelt in a world of visionary hope tempered by pragmatism. He shrewdly realized that high, noble ambitions are critical to the vitality and effectiveness of a business organization. Wilson challenged Xerox executives to "set high goals, to have almost unattainable aspirations, to imbue people with the belief that they can be achieved," because he believed these intangibles are as important as the bottom line or familiar quantifiable factors—perhaps more so."

But could the organization sustain this spirit over time? "It's an everlasting battle, which we may or may not win," Wilson fretted in 1966.

PETER MCCOLOUGH AND THE PROBLEMS OF GROWTH

If anyone could follow in Joe Wilson's footsteps, it was C. Peter McColough, a broad thinker and intuitive manager who was willing to strike out in bold new directions. First hired by Wilson in 1954, McColough had become general manager of sales, building a national sales force of more than 7,800 people. A brilliant marketer, McColough had also been responsible for the seminal idea of metered pricing for copies. McColough's ascension to the posts of president in 1966 and CEO in 1968 was widely applauded.

McColough's most urgent priority was to manage Xerox's breakaway growth. Profits had zoomed from $2.5 million to $138 million between 1961 and 1968. People were being hired so fast that it was difficult to properly screen and integrate them into the company. From 1959 to 1969, the number of employees grew from only 1,800 to 55,000. A new corps of professional managers had to be recruited and built into a new team. Sales and service, too, needed to be more tightly organized as tens of thousands of Xerox copiers proliferated across the nation. Strategic planning, basic research and development, new manufacturing controls and efficiencies—all had taken a backseat to the heady imperatives of growth. By the late 1960s, a consolidation and restructuring was long overdue.

While investors remained impressed with Xerox's startling growth, they also began to worry that Xerox was still a one-product company. Anticipating that an entirely new "architecture of information" would evolve in the 1970s—a world of copiers, computers, and advanced telecommunications—McColough set out to reposition Xerox to compete with IBM and other computer giants.

His first step was to buy a major computer maker, Scientific Data Systems of El Segundo, California, for a hefty $908 million. This was followed in 1970 by his creation of the Xerox Palo Alto Research Center, known as PARC.

The center quickly became a hothouse for some of the most creative computer breakthroughs of the time. Dazzling young minds such as Butler Lampson, Chuck Thacker, and Alan Kay helped invent some of the basic components of personal computers: graphic software icons, laser printers, the fax machine, local communications networking (Ethernet), object-oriented programming language, and a "wysiwyg" ("what you see is what you get") word-processing program for nonexpert computer users. PARC researchers, in fact, built the first personal computer, the Alto, introduced in 1973.

To help expand Xerox beyond the copying business and attract a more worldly breed of executive, McColough in the early 1970s moved the company's headquarters from Rochester, New York, to Stamford, Connecticut. Instead of having all decision making centralized at the top, as it had been under Joe Wilson, McColough decentralized authority.

McColough brought that same kind of muscular activism to Xerox's social commitments. One of his most unusual innovations was creating a social service "sabbatical" program, which gives employees full-paid leaves for up to a year to apply their business skills to innovative community projects. Since the program's inception in 1971, more than 400 Xerox employees have participated, working as legal advocates for mine safety, counselors at rape crisis centers, and job placement advisers to released prisoners, and in many other roles as well.

A complementary initiative has been the Xerox Community Involvement Program, a company-sponsored effort to help employees volunteer in their communities. Since 1974, with the company's administrative and financial support, over 200,000 employees have worked on an estimated 8,470 community projects: counseling young people on probation, working with preschool children, helping in women's shelters, and more. Each year the company enlists more than 20,000 employee volunteers.

McColough also continued Xerox's staunch commitment to racial equality by setting minority recruitment goals in accordance with, or exceeding, federal guidelines in the 1970s. McColough held group managers accountable for achieving the goals by making them a key criterion in performance appraisals and the granting of monetary bonuses. In the 1970s the company also identified "pivotal jobs" that lead to top management posts, so that women and minorities could more readily rise through the ranks.

Xerox's strategies have paid off handsomely. Nationwide, African-Americans compose about 13.5 percent of all employees and 10 percent of managers. But at Xerox, in 1991, minorities made up one-fourth of all employees, 21 percent of professional employees, 19 percent of officers and managers, and 21 percent of senior executives. Women represented 32 percent of all employees and 23 percent of all managers.

DAVID KEARNS REINVENTS XEROX IN THE 1980s

As the 1970s wore on, Xerox found that many of the grand ambitions it had set for itself were simply not materializing. Some of its attempts to diversify into other fields, such as computing, yielded disappointing results. The company consistently had trouble commercializing many of the basic computer components invented at PARC, while upstarts like Apple Computer transformed the same technologies into the most explosive new product in a generation, the personal computer. Some Xerox acquisitions, such as Scientific Data Systems, real estate ventures, and financial services firms, also proved to be disappointments.

The more serious problem was burgeoning competition. At the high end of the market, IBM and Kodak were introducing faster, more sophisticated copiers, taking market share from Xerox. And at the low end, Japanese companies such as Savin, Canon, and Ricoh began selling reliable copiers for several hundred dollars. These copiers soon found a huge market among small businesses, which found it much more attractive to buy the machines outright, and make unlimited copies, than to lease them from Xerox.

Xerox was slow to recognize and respond to these shifts in the market. In fact, between 1970 and 1980, Xerox's share of U.S. copier revenues dropped from about 95 percent to about 45 percent, according to the high-tech market research firm Dataquest. In 1977, Peter McColough acknowledged the pending crisis in a speech to Xerox insiders: "I see a company, which began with a culture of survival, now more than a little encrusted with the culture of success. As we have grown, we have become an unwieldy bureaucracy, with a bureaucracy's tendency to bloat."

David Kearns would later ask, "How bad off were we? To put it bluntly, if nothing were done to correct things, we were destined to have a fire sale and close down by 1990. And the final humiliation for me was that it would be on my watch."

Kearns, an IBM salesman for seventeen years, had joined Xerox in 1971 and became president in 1977. He succeeded Peter McColough as CEO in 1982. From his work with Fuji Xerox, the company's Asian partner, Kearns saw firsthand how the Japanese, who had targeted Xerox as the company to beat, were transforming the playing fields of competition.

In response, Kearns began an ambitious organization-wide effort to reinvent Xerox, which he dubbed the "Leadership Through Quality" program. Between 1983 and 1987, Kearns forcefully pushed decision making down to managers closer to the market; cut the number of vendors doing business with Xerox from 5,000 to 400; and, with regrets but resolve, cut 15,000 employees from the payroll.

Kearns also fostered closer collaboration between Xerox headquarters and Xerox PARC, so that research and development would cater to actual market demands. Xerox divisions were required to identify the best companies in their respective fields (marketing, manufacturing, etc.) and then to use their performance as benchmark goals. A new set of hiring and promotion criteria was developed to reward quality-related attitudes and skills over all else.

The improvements made a demonstrable difference. As *Fortune* magazine observed, "When the customer pushes the button on a 50 Series copier today [1990], he has about a 98 percent chance of getting good copies. In 1982 when he pushed the button on a 10 Series machine, he had only a 90 percent success rate."

It was this kind of dramatic change that helped the company win the prestigious Malcolm Baldrige Quality Award in 1989. Xerox also became the only company to win, in addition, Japan's Deming Award and the European Quality Award. It was not surprising to see the return on assets, which stood at 8 percent in the early 1980s, increase to 14 percent by the early 1990s.

Throughout the 1980s, Xerox maintained its many socially oriented programs and commitments, particularly its minority hiring. Kearns told his managers that regardless of the Reagan administration's relaxed government guidelines, they would continue to be judged by how well they achieved work force diversity. While "national trends may fluctuate," wrote Kearns, "this company's stance is unwavering." By 1989, Xerox had a dozen African-American vice presidents, more than any other major U.S. manufacturer.

Kearns also spent the 1980s as an outspoken advocate for

educational reform. He called on business to help radically change the public schools, elaborating his ideas in a book, *Winning the Brain Race: A Bold Plan to Make Our Schools Competitive*, written with Dennis P. Doyle. After raising more than $40 million from business to directly help "invent" innovative schools, Kearns retired from Xerox in 1990, at the age of 60, to promote his reform ideas as President Bush's deputy secretary of education. Today Kearns continues his advocacy through affiliations with The Harvard Project on Schooling and Children and the New American Schools Development Corporation.

PAUL ALLAIRE STRIKES OUT IN NEW DIRECTIONS

The president of Xerox since 1986, Paul Allaire, a former financial analyst and senior manager, became chairman and CEO in 1990. Realizing that Xerox needed a more focused mission and cash to achieve its objectives, Allaire shed some of the major acquisitions Xerox had made in the 1980s. To help bring the company's mission back into focus, Allaire dubbed Xerox "The Document Company," a term that offered both a precise and expansive framework for organizing the company's diverse businesses.

In the high-end market, Xerox in 1990 came out with the pioneering DocuTech machine, a high-speed digital electronic copier and printer that can scan, copy, and print documents, as transmitted from within an electronic network. The highly versatile machine is designed to automate corporate print shops and replace traditional low-end offset printing presses.

Meanwhile Xerox began marching into burgeoning market segments that it had previously ignored, such as color copiers and copiers for home offices and small businesses. By 1994, Dataquest concluded that Xerox was the market leader in two of seven market segments, and a competitive second in three other segments.

Xerox PARC has brought forth a plethora of new products such as a computerized blackboard that can store and transmit text, graphics, video, and audio; a machine that can scan large quantities of documents into computers; and a device that can turn printed words into digitized speech. Since many promising ideas generated by Xerox's $500-million annual research budget simply do not fit within the company's overall plans, Allaire set up Xerox Technology Ventures, an in-house venture capital firm that has invested some $30 million in business start-ups dedicated to technologies developed at Xerox.

"Xerox Is Hot Again," proclaimed *Forbes* in June 1994, publicizing a widely held conviction in the industry and on Wall Street. Allaire credits the company's revival to his long-term project to revamp Xerox's "organizational architecture," by which he means the management structure and ethos that affect all aspects of the company. "We intend to create a company that combines the best of both worlds—the speed, flexibility, accountability and creativity that come from being part of a small, highly focused organization, and the economies of scale, the access to resources, and the strategic vision that a large corporation can provide," Allaire told the *Harvard Business Review* in 1994.

Rather than let managers become passive, rigid, and risk-averse while market conditions change and new technologies emerge, Allaire has sought to make Xerox a "learning organization" that can "evolve and modify itself as technology, skills, competitors and the entire business change." To foster this sensibility, the company established a new grid of twenty-three ideal characteristics for managers—the basis for executive recruitment and promotion—which stresses the capacity for teamwork, strategic thinking and implementation, personal confidence, and integrity.

Work force diversity continues to be a cornerstone of the Xerox culture, as a matter of competitive necessity. Says Allaire:

> We have created an environment where people of all backgrounds want to join Xerox. That gives us an opportunity to select the best people from every group. Secondly, we feel very strongly that we benefit by having a diverse population working. They bring different ideas, different backgrounds, different approaches, and that stimulates a great amount of activity in the organization.

The hardest stuff is the soft stuff: values, personal style, ways of interacting. We are trying to change the total culture of the company.

THE PRAGMATIC IDEALISM OF THE XEROX CORPORATION

Bold technologies, strong management, grand ideals, social commitment, business success: These have been Xerox's goals. While some critics see sharp dichotomies, and even contradictions, among these various goals, Xerox's chief executive officers have generally seen them as different parts of a seamless web. The real achievement comes in not pushing one or another goal to an extreme but in honoring the constructive synergies that exist among them. Just as Joe Wilson aspired "to be a whole man," it could be said that Xerox's leaders have aspired to lead a holistic company.

Joe Wilson always stood firm against critics who argued that corporations have no responsibilities but to obey the law and maximize shareholder value. "Our society needs businessmen who can articulate lofty goals and demonstrate high dedication to those goals while they simultaneously profit from the services they offer." It is a spirit of doing business that has given the Xerox Corporation a special vigor and resiliency over the course of two generations.

ACKNOWLEDGMENTS

One of the happier responsibilities of writing a book is publicly thanking those who shared in the burdens.

My foremost debt is to Norman Lear, a man of uncommon grace. His steadfast vision and sheer bravado have given life to The Business Enterprise Trust, animated the stories in this collection, and immeasurably fortified me. Norman *always* aims higher, and it rubs off on anyone who comes within ten feet of him. I am blessed.

I am grateful as well to Kathy Meyer, executive director of the Trust, whose suggestions have greatly improved this book over the five years of its preparation. I cannot count how many times she has rooted out errors and offered invaluable ideas. She has also been a glorious partner in the ongoing adventures of The Business Enterprise Trust.

The board of the Trust has been an indispensable resource in the development of the stories in this book. For that, and especially for the contributions of executive committee members James E. Burke, Sol Linowitz, Henry B. Schacht, and Norman Lear, I am most appreciative.

A book of this magnitude could not be completed without considerable research assistance. For this I owe a great debt to several people who did primary research or authored monographs that became the basis for some chapters. I am pleased to recognize Laura Wattenberg, for her work on the chapters featuring Mario Antoci, Rachel Hubka, Hal Rosenbluth, Inland Steel, and Fel-Pro, Incorporated; Stephanie Weiss, for the chapters on Gun Denhart, GE Plastics, and Inland Steel; Jonathan Eisenberg, for the chapters on Finast and Julia Stasch; Nicole Pearce, for the chapters on Frank Stanton and Howard Schultz; and Lisa Taber, for the chapter on the Haas family.

For her meticulous research on other chapters I am grateful to Suzanne Allen, who energetically obtained the permissions needed for the quotations excerpted. Joan Clay not only helped with permissions but facilitated my travels and expenses in ways I have shamelessly taken for granted. Marilyn Turner, too, has been a ready troubleshooter and friend.

Blanche Brann is a literary agent of vigor and insight, talents that were vital in finding the right publisher. That publisher, AMACOM, the publishing arm of the American Management Association, has shown a gratifying commitment to the book, its values, and The Business Enterprise Trust. The enthusiasm of editor Adrienne Hickey has been especially welcome.

While the staff members of the Trust, located on a different coast, are only my *virtual* office mates, their presence is no less vividly felt and appreciated. Yet here on my own coast, there is no substitute for sharing my days with Ellen and our sons, Sam and Thomas, whose sublime humor and spirits nourish all my endeavors, including this book.

David Bollier
Amherst, Massachusetts

The author is grateful to the following for allowing him to reproduce excerpts from their works.

Chapter 1: Comments about the SRB Fund from "Reducing Risk and Maintaining Profitability in Affordable Housing Lending: Lessons from the SRB Fund of Vermont National Bank," *Tools for Housing,* Issue No. 2 (Winter 1993), Federal Home Loan Bank of Boston. Reprinted with permission.

Chapter 3: Comments concerning Leonard Graff reprinted with permission of Knight-Ridder. John E. Fisher's comments reprinted with permission from *Best's Review,* Life/Health Edition (June 1990). Fred Bush's comments reprinted with permission from *Life Association News,* the official publication of the National Association of Life Underwriters.

Chapter 11: Scott Allmendinger's comments, which first appeared in *Restaurant Business,* reprinted with permission of *Restaurant Business.* Corporate Cashflow's conclusions excerpted from *Corporate Cashflow* (July 1994), copyright © 1994 by Argus Inc., a division of Intertec Pub Corp., Atlanta, GA, reprinted with permission.

Chapter 12: Jack Stack, *The Great Game of Business* (New York: Doubleday, 1991), pp. 78–79. Reprinted with permission of Doubleday, a division of Bantam Doubleday Dell Publishing Group, Inc.

Chapter 13: Interview with Kathy Perez, 1992, printed with permission.

Chapter 17: Ray Oldenburg, *The Great Good Place,* reprinted with permission from Paragon House (1989).

Chapter 18: Kim Hubbard and Toby Kahn, "For New Age Ice Cream Moguls Ben & Jerry, Making 'Cherry Garcia' and 'Chunky Monkey' Is a Labor of Love," reprinted with permission from *People* Magazine (September 10, 1990). Excerpt from *1994 Annual Report,* Audit of Ben and Jerry's, and excerpt from Ben & Jerry's Mission Statement reprinted with permission of Ben & Jerry's Homemade, Inc. Andrea Asch's comments from "What's the Scoop?" that appeared in *Grassroots Magazine,* V2/2, reprinted with permission.

Chapter 19: Arthur W. Curry's comments in Chapter 19 that appeared in Kris Hachadourian, "GE Mixed Altruism, Teamwork," *Union News,* Springfield, MA, reprinted with permission.

Chapter 21: Comments by T. George Harris about Irwin J. Miller that appeared in *Fortune* Magazine are reprinted with permission from *Fortune* Magazine, copyright © 1957 Time Inc., all rights reserved. Also, courtesy of *House & Garden Magazine,* Michael Sorkin, "Tastemasters: J. Irwin Miller," *House & Garden* (April 1983).

Chapter 22: Lynne C. Burkhart, *Old Values in a New Town* (New York: Praeger, 1981), reprinted with permission of Greenwood Publishing Group, Inc., Westport, CT. © 1981. Neil Harris, "American Space: Spaced Out at the Shopping Center," *The New Republic* (December 13, 1975). Reprinted with permission of *The New Republic,* copyright © 1975, The New Republic, Inc., for nonprofit, educational purposes only.

Chapter 25: John Dessauer, *My Years With Xerox: The Billions Nobody Wanted* (New York: Doubleday, 1971), pp. 157, 200, reprinted with permission of Doubleday, a division of Bantam Doubleday Dell Publishing Group, Inc. Jeremy Main, "How to Win the Baldrige Award," *Fortune* (April 23, 1990), copyright © 1990, Time Inc., all rights reserved. Robert Howard, "The CEO as Organizational Architect: An Interview With Xerox's Paul Allaire," *Harvard Business Review* (September-October 1992), p. 111. David Kearns and David Nadler, *Prophets in the Dark: How Xerox Reinvented Itself and Beat Back the Japanese* (HarperCollins Publishers, Inc., 1992), p. xiv.

INDEX

ABOUT THE BUSINESS ENTERPRISE TRUST

The Business Enterprise Trust is a national nonprofit organization that seeks to shine a spotlight on exemplary acts of courage, integrity, and social vision in business.

Founded in 1989 by eighteen prominent leaders in American business, academia, labor, and the media, the Trust identifies bold, creative leadership that combines sound management with social conscience. It focuses on the *stories* of these socially minded business innovations as sources of instruction and inspiration.

To honor exemplary companies and businesspeople, the Trust each year hosts a major awards ceremony held in New York City; produces short video documentaries narrated by journalist Bill Moyers; and prepares business school cases and teaching notes that are distributed by Harvard Business School Publishing. These materials are currently being used in more than 450 business schools, universities, and corporate management training programs throughout the country.

For general information on The Business Enterprise Trust, its teaching materials and videos, or to nominate an individual or company for a Business Enterprise Award, contact:

The Business Enterprise Trust
204 Junipero Serra Blvd.
Stanford, CA 94305

Phone: 415-321-5100
Fax: 415-321-5774
www.betrust.org